"The way to keep any child from getting unhealthy attitudes about himself is to give him the feeling that he's enjoyed for himself and the feeling that he can make progress."

Here is a dependable reference to which the parents of the handicapped child may turn at all stages in his growth.

An invaluable section of the book is devoted to the mastery of the tools and techniques—braces, crutches, wheelchairs, artificial limbs, hearing aids—that the disabled child employs to develop his capacity to the fullest.

This is also a book that will be welcomed by physicians, therapists, social workers, ministers, and everyone concerned with the treatment and rehabilitation of the disabled youngster. It is packed with information and wisdom about the many aspects of disability that influence or determine the happiness of hundreds of thousands of children.

Caring For Your Disabled Child

BENJAMIN SPOCK, M.D.
MARION O. LERRIGO, PH.D.

A FAWCETT CREST BOOK

Fawcett Publications, Inc., Greenwich, Conn.
Member of American Book Publishers Council, Inc.

PRINTING HISTORY
The Macmillan Company edition published April 28, 1965
Two printings

First Fawcett Crest Printing, January 1967

Published by Fawcett World Library
67 West 44th Street, New York, N. Y. 10036
Printed in the United States of America

ACKNOWLEDGMENTS

The authors wish to express their appreciation to the Association for the Aid of Crippled Children for several kinds of encouragement and support. The basic theme of the book and the proposal for its writing originated with the Association. Throughout the course of manuscript preparation staff members of the Association offered valuable assistance at every level of the editorial task without restricting in the slightest the freedom of the authors with respect to viewpoint and content. Ultimate responsibility for the text thus rests entirely with the authors. Thanks are also extended to the many people in hospitals, clinics, schools, and numerous rehabilitation agencies who cooperated by supplying information and making useful suggestions.

Benjamin Spock, M.D.
Marion O. Lerrigo, PH.D.

CONTENTS

Caring For Your
Disabled Child

INTRODUCTION:
YOUR HOPES FOR YOUR CHILD

As the parent of a child with a handicap you face all kinds of problems, at times more than you can bear. Some have to do with his medical care. Others have to do with his upbringing. His basic needs are no different from those of all children and this means that he has to have the affection and guidance and control you'd give any child. But he also needs a lot of help with the unusual problems that are caused by his handicap. It will often seem to you that there is a conflict between these two aims.

You've probably suffered heartaches while watching your child struggle with his handicap and you've probably been depressed. At other times you may have become too optimistic. Then, if disappointment follows, it is doubly bitter. There's no doubt that the hardest job is to learn to be realistic without losing the optimism that's justified.

There have been tremendous advances in recent decades in the care of persons who have disabilities. Much more can be done now to help them live a real life, one that includes independence in getting about, looking after themselves, going to school, finding a job, developing interests, enjoying social life and community activities, perhaps even making a marriage and a home. Not all these aspects of life will be possible for all handicapped persons, they aren't even possible for all the nondisabled. But the New York Institute for the Crippled and Disabled has estimated that 97 per cent of all handicapped persons can be rehabilitated to the degree that they can lead productive lives. That's a lot. And the earlier rehabilitation begins, the more effective it is likely to be.

The meaning of realistic optimism is illustrated by the

story of victory over paraplegia. Not so many years ago so little could be done for the spinal paraplegics that their life was scarcely worth living. When the spinal cord is severed or severely injured the body is paralyzed from the site of the injury downward. It's without voluntary movement, without sensation, without control of bladder, bowel, or sexual functions.

Paraplegic patients used to be kept flat on their backs, immobilized by plaster casts. The best they could hope for was to be kept alive. They developed bedsores that became infected and grew worse; as a result of the bladder paralysis their kidneys were also infected. These complications usually brought death—often quickly, sometimes after two or three years.

Just before World War II a great neurologist and neurosurgeon, Ludwig Guttmann, escaped from Nazi Germany to England. In 1944, the British Government asked him to open a Spinal Injuries Center at the Stoke Mandeville Hospital in the hope that something better could be done for the war casualties with spinal injuries.

Experience had already shown that rehabilitation was possible for persons with many other severe disabilities, and Dr. Guttmann believed that the paraplegic, too, could live a satisfying, productive life. He knew that people ordinarily use only a very small part of their real capacities—perhaps 20 per cent, and that they can draw on their great reserves of mind and body to adjust to new conditions and to surmount extraordinary difficulties. Dr. Guttmann wanted his paraplegic patients to be able to leave their hospital beds and to go out into their communities to live much like other people, to enjoy their own homes and the companionship of family and friends, to hold a job.

The Stoke Mandeville staff knew it was realistic to take a hopeful view of the possible accomplishments of the paraplegic patients. At the same time they knew that their patients' spinal injuries would continue to make a big difference but that this difference could be handled best when it was frankly acknowledged.

Dr. Guttmann taught his staff that bedsores and urinary infection are not inevitable. The old treatment, which required immobilization, meant that even unparalyzed muscles became flabby from lack of use, so the patients were given exercises to make the healthy parts of their bodies strong and skillful enough to compensate for useless muscles. They learned to take care of their own daily needs: to dress themselves, to pick things up from the floor while in a wheelchair, to attend to their personal grooming and toilet, to get from bed to wheelchair and back again, to stand in parallel bars, to walk with crutches.

While the patients were still in bed they were given regular work to do, because the goal they were given from the beginning was to return to work. Many of the young soldiers were in wheelchairs within eight weeks of their injury and, as early as five weeks later, were working at a bench in the Center's precision instrument shop.

Many sports—archery, javelin-throwing, table tennis, wheelchair polo, and basketball—proved to be adaptable. The first sports competition between teams from different spinal injury centers took place in 1948. The numbers of competitors and sports events have increased since then and have become international in scope. In 1955 the Stoke Mandeville Games were attended by competitors from 18 countries.

On the tenth anniversary of the Stoke Mandeville Center a study was made of the first 1000 patients.[1] Most of them were living at home and had regular jobs. Some had married and had children of their own; others had adopted children. Less than 9 per cent had died.

This story will give you an idea of the major guidelines you can use yourself:

Be realistic about the extent of your child's disability. Help him come to terms with it.

Find good medical care.

Help your child work hard to make the most of the abilities he has and those he can develop. That will give you both enough to do without straining after the impossible.

Enjoy your child for what he is. It's unfair to yourself and him to keep thinking of what he might have been.

REFERENCE

1. Ludwig Guttmann, "Victory Over Paraplegia," in *Conquest of Disability*, Sir Ian Fraser, ed. New York, St. Martin's Press, 1956.

PART I

Living with Disability

UNDERSTANDING YOUR OWN PROBLEMS

The mother of a fifteen-year-old boy who had been born without an arm was talking with a social worker. She suddenly said, "You know, this is the first time since he was born that I've felt I could let go and talk about myself." Parents very much need to talk about their own feelings so that they can get them sorted out and understood. This isn't only for their comfort. This is how they can be of greater help to their child. For the way parents feel about their child's disability will be the chief factor affecting his own attitude toward it.

You may have known someone with a severe disability who seemed to pay little attention to it, who had great zest for living, enjoyed his friends, made a good life for himself. Although the disability was serious, his own healthy attitude kept him from being severely handicapped. You may also have known someone who became so preoccupied with some minor flaw in his appearance that he became really handicapped in his personality and in his social life.

How did two people develop so differently? To a degree each one's attitude was probably a reflection of the attitude his parents took toward him and toward his disability. If you want your child to develop positive feelings about himself and his future, you'll need to outgrow some of your own anguished feelings.

The importance of parents' attitudes is illustrated by the contrast of two small boys who attended the same prosthetic clinic. Tom was a five-year-old who had been born without a lower right arm. His mother had always been able to encourage him to play with the other children in the neighborhood, taking it for granted that he should mingle freely with people. When other children had questions about Tom's prosthesis, his mother helped him with the answers—if he needed help—and she encouraged him to show his friends how it worked. She was proud of his accomplishments in using the artificial arm and the two-pronged hook that substituted very well for the missing hand. As a result, Tom too felt comfortable about it.

The mother of the other child couldn't help feeling so embarrassed and so sorry for her child when people stared that she let him use the artificial hand only when he was at home. He took over her embarrassment and shame. He wore the prosthesis less and less, and never became proficient in its use. He withdrew from his playmates and became a lonely child.

The Problems Are Real, the Feelings Run Deep. It is easy enough for others to describe how parents ought to feel. You'll probably get very irritated by all the hints you'll receive from your professional advisors about what your attitude should be. But these supposedly ideal attitudes don't come on command. Parents of disabled children suffer deeply. Their feelings are turbulent, full of conflicts, hard for them to understand. Most parents at first have great difficulty in establishing a comfortable relationship with their handicapped child. This can be seen in reports that come from a number of sources.

The Bureau of Educational Research of the New York City Board of Education[1] interviewed 64 parents of disabled children of the fifth and eighth grades. The great majority of them revealed that, mixed in with their love for their children, were strong feelings of irritation and resentment. These are normal, but hard to face at first. Of the 123 families of children who were at the Institute of Physical Medicine and Rehabilitation in New York as inpatients in 1957,[2] more than 80 experienced difficulties in parent–child relationships. Some of the parents felt unable to let their children develop any independence from them. Others reacted in the opposite direction and pushed their children too hard. Many felt resentful of the great demands on them resulting from the child's disability. In more than 50 families, the parents were clinging to quite unrealistic goals for their child. In 40 cases, parents were still unable to accept the fact that the child would have a residual disability when his treatment was completed. You can see how difficult it is to acquire a sensible outlook.

A group of parents of cerebral-palsied children, who came together regularly for counseling,[3] emphasized their own intense suffering and the terrible emotional costs incurred by the disability. Some believed that their marriages had suffered, some feared that they had neglected their other children. Many resented the failure of relatives, friends, or neighbors to understand and accept their child. To still others, the worst despair came from the loss of hope that their child would continue to grow, mentally and physically. Several spoke of their resentment toward the professional people who advised them to place their child in an institution, or toward their counselors who failed to understand them. They were scornful of the doctors who didn't seem to know enough about cerebral palsy. They blamed teachers for not helping their child and the school officials for being insensitive.

The worst of it was that these parents felt alone. They felt isolated from the parents of nonhandicapped children, particularly when such parents would not let their children play with the cerebral-palsied child. They thought that no one except other parents of handicapped children could understand them. Everyone else seemed to be an "outsider," including those professional people to whom they had to turn for help. They even felt isolated from one another. One mother complained that even the group treated her as if she did not belong with them because her child was retarded as well as cerebral palsied.

The parents in this group came to recognize how similar their concerns were, and this dissolved some of the bitter feelings of isolation. Each of them gained something from the others. Then they were able to spend a little more time talking about experiences in which they and their children had been accepted and what they might do to foster still greater acceptance in their neighborhoods and in the schools.

These parents discovered that talking together about their experiences and feelings gave them more understanding, relieved some of their tensions, and made for happier relationships with their children. They began to realize also that some "outsiders" would give them sincere understanding, provided they themselves were able to go half way.

Parents Are People.   Some husbands and wives are able to share their anxieties and their misfortunes in a way that draws them closer together. Some parents can inspire their other children to share gladly part of the responsibility for caring for the handicapped one; then the healthy children, far from being hurt, are made more mature, understanding, and generous. But if a marriage is strained anyhow, the unexpected problems arising from a child's handicap may create greater tensions between the parents. Or these problems may strain the relationship between parents and the other children of the family.

Like all people, parents need the satisfaction that comes from achieving their ambitions. They usually feel that their children are their most worthwhile contributions and look to them to reach the goals that they themselves had hoped for. In a sense, their children are still a part of themselves. When a handicap affects a child, the parents' sense of adequacy is bound to suffer. For example, a mother may feel that her in-laws look down on her if her child has a birth defect. A father who is a teacher perhaps feels that his own status is somehow lowered because his child is mentally retarded. A couple may have had great hopes that their son would be a surgeon, or carry on his father's business, or take over the farm. Or that their daughter would be a dancer, or marry well and have a fine family. When a handicap makes such goals impossible, it may hurt the parents' pride even more than it disappoints the child.

Under the burden of excessive responsibilities it is easy for parents to forget that they, too, need a chance to play. They are apt to feel that it is something they can't afford, either in time or money. Yet they, more than most people, need the pleasure that comes from doing what they like to do just because they like it. It will give them renewal of strength.

When parents first learn that their child is disabled, their faith may well be shaken. In their anguish they ask searching questions: Why did this have to happen to me? What kind of world is it in which such pain can be inflicted on people? Is there any meaning in our suffering? Any meaning in life? Are my child and I not worth-while people? Am I being punished for something I've done? Most parents need to discuss such questions again and again—with each other and with a professional counselor or minister.

Mixed Feelings and Guilty Feelings. Parents are not saints or martyrs. If they set impossible goals for themselves, they are sure to fail and then feel guilty.

Even the most loving parents have mixed feelings toward their *unhandicapped* children. The young mother, struggling with formulas, diapers, and a fretful baby, wonders why she ever thought it would be fun to have a child. A father, discovering that his son has ruined a piece of equipment that he has been forbidden to use, blows up in a rage. Generally, parents can manage such angry feelings without difficulty and can smile about them later, secure in the knowledge that their love for their child is unshakable, that their irritation is only temporary.

But parents are more apt to set an impossible ideal of perfection for themselves if their child has a handicap. They feel that they should never scold, never lose their tempers, always be ready to make more sacrifices. Yet underneath they cannot help resenting the child at times because they have to forfeit so many of their own pleasures and ambitions, so much of their energy—in fact, so much of their lives—to help them. When they sense this resentment toward the child they feel guilty, for they love him too.

Almost all parents of a noticeably handicapped child will feel sensitive about his appearance to some degree, whether it's that his gait is awkward, or he can't control facial grimaces, or his mental comprehension is clearly retarded. For some parents the sense of shame about these visible defects is agonizing, and interferes with every satisfaction in their lives.

Parents are especially likely to feel guilty if they think that the child's defect is hereditary. Usually there is no logical reason for them to feel this way. Many so-called "hereditary" birth defects are not strongly hereditary; they are not passed along regularly as family traits. They are the accidental results of unlikely combinations of genes. Biologists believe that all of us carry some imperfect genes and that if two normal parents could have a large enough number of children—say 100—there would surely be at least one child born defective.[4] Only chance determines whether the defective child might be the first, fifth, twentieth, or last born. (If there is reason to believe that a defect is strongly hereditary, it is wise to consult a specialist about the chance of its occurring again in another child. See Chapter 4 on genetic counseling.)

Sometimes the child's handicap is the result of accident or illness. Then the parents are particularly apt to feel responsible or to blame each other for not having been careful. But of course if a child were so well protected that he never had an accident or serious illness, he would have to be completely isolated from all human contact and he would never develop properly.

Serving Yourself or Your Child? Guilt often drives parents to do too much for their child. Feeling that they must make up to him for his handicap, or for their own hidden resentment or disappointment, or for their inability to love him wholeheartedly, they feel they must do everything for him. In some cases this compels them even to undo the good that has been accomplished by his therapy. He may then become increasingly dependent and lose the chance to develop his own abilities.

Or they don't feel right unless they spend extravagantly of themselves and their resources, even when they know that he can't really profit by this, even when they know that it is depriving the other members of the family. The trouble is that the child will either feel guilty and uncomfortable about the excessive sacrifices made in his behalf or he may lose all his ambition and self-respect, feeling that the world will have to do everything for him.

Ignoring the Handicap. Some hard-striving parents try unconsciously to solve their child's problem by thinking and acting as if the handicap simply doesn't exist. They urge the child to perform tasks which they don't realize are beyond his capabilities. They may reproach him for being slow and lazy, when laziness isn't his trouble at all.

Of course the person with the handicap yearns at times to forget all about it, too. One veteran whose arm had been amputated said, in reply to a question of how one is to adjust to misfortune, "If he doesn't think about it, it won't bother him." But the impossibility of such a "solution" is at once apparent in another veteran's reply to the same question: "More or less forgetting about it is the best thing, but how are you going to forget when everybody keeps reminding you of it?"

When a mother and father pretend to each other that there is no real handicap, it also sets up a wall between them. They are afraid to relax the pretense. It becomes harder and harder to talk about the family's real problems, and their relationship is apt to grow distant. The effect of the pretense on the child may be that he thinks his parents don't understand him, and he grows increasingly reluctant to voice his real feelings to them.

You help your child by accepting his handicap and admitting that he has a problem. Then you can begin to concentrate on his abilities.

Accepting Help. Most parents need help both in easing their conflicted feelings about their child's handicap and in making the best plans for his care. Such help is available. Above all, you need competent medical advice, usually over a long period of time. But in addition you want advice on perplexing matters affecting your entire family's welfare: your disabled child's schooling and vocational guidance, the amount of cooperation you should demand of him, the management of the strains that show in your other children at times, your own depression or irritation.

Sometimes joining a group of parents of handicapped children is a good way to get some insights into your problems and those of your child. Hearing about how other people solve various kinds of difficulties gives you a fresh point of view. Some groups have been formed as chapters of national organizations, and some hospitals and clinics specializing in the treatment of handicapped children arrange parent study groups.

You should be able to get another kind of help by consulting regularly a professionally trained social worker who is familiar with community resources. Such a person can help you examine the advantages or disadvantages of alternate courses of action for your child and also straighten out your own feelings. It usually takes a long time to work out these difficulties.

Teachers of handicapped children are prepared by education and experience to understand the problems of such children. If your child is attending a special school or special classes, you should become acquainted with his teachers.

More and more religious leaders are receiving special training in psychological counseling. Some of them also make it a point to know the community facilities. Many parents have gained their greatest solace, in the crises of their child's disability, through their religious beliefs and the support of their minister, rabbi, or priest.

REFERENCES

1. *The Child with Orthopedic Limitations*. New York City Board of Education, Bureau of Educational Research. Publication No. 33, June 1954.

2. *Annual Report, 1957*. The Institute of Physical Medicine and Rehabilitation, Children's Division, New York University-Bellevue Medical Center, New York.

3. Alvin E. Winder. "A Program of Group Counseling for the Parents of Cerebral Palsied Children." *Cerebral Palsy Review, 19:* No. 3, May-June 1958.

4. Joan Gould. *Will My Baby Be Born Normal?* Public Affairs Pamphlet No. 272, 1958.

3

UNDERSTANDING YOUR CHILD
AND HIS PROBLEMS

Each child's personality is shaped by the interaction between his particular heredity and all his life experiences. So when a disability is part of those experiences, you certainly have to take it into account. But you can't do the best job for him if you think of his disability as the main thing in his life. Good parents know this but it's so hard for them to act on it hour by hour and day by day because the disability keeps getting in the way of their view of the child as a person.

Some Mistaken Ideas.   Perhaps the most common mistake people make in thinking about the handicapped child is that they all develop the same kind of personality. Your child won't necessarily be like any other child with the same disability. He won't necessarily be more selfish or unselfish, kind or mean, patient or impatient than any other child simply because of his handicap.

A person with a disability won't necessarily have any maladjustment of his personality. Some do, but their behavior is not peculiar to their disability. They have all the various kinds of maladjustments that you can see among nondisabled people; a few become timid, withdrawn, self-conscious, or satisfied with daydreams; a few become aggressive, demanding, or unrealistically ambitious.

Some Common Problems and Reactions of Handicapped Children.   Considering all the special difficulties a child encounters because of his handicap, it wouldn't be surprising if he had a tendency to be moody and irritable. Such simple things as getting up in the morning and eating breakfast may be tiring. If his social experiences are limited, he may feel lonely and unwanted at times. He will be strongly tempted to be more dependent because of the physical disability itself and because it is difficult for his family and friends not to be protective. He meets more frustrations than the average, so he'll be tempted to place the blame for his failure on others. He may be tempted to slip into a passive, daydreaming kind of existence.

It's hard for the teenager with a disability to know how to relate to the other sex if he hasn't been able to take part in the usual activities through which younger boys and girls learn how to get along together. His fear that no one will want to marry him may increase his feelings of dejection and isolation.

But none of these ways of reacting to frustration are peculiar to handicapped children. Children without disability react in just the same ways if they are unnoticed, or shut out of their group, or made to feel inferior, or when they have no opportunity to achieve goals that seem important to them. So the way to keep any child from getting unhealthy attitudes about himself is to give him the feeling that he's enjoyed for himself and the feeling that he can make progress.

YOUR CHILD'S BASIC NEEDS

Knowing That You Are Fond of Him. Any child's first need is a sense of security and trust. This begins to develop in earliest infancy when he learns through repeated experiences that he'll be fed when he is hungry, made comfortable when he is wet or cold, cuddled when he is unhappy. His parents begin showing him, by their doting behavior, before he knows any words, that they think he's wonderful and he understands this. He grins and squirms with pleasure. As he grows older, sits up, stands, and walks, he needs to be independent enough to seek new, exciting adventures. Yet he still keeps coming back to his mother every few minutes to get a new charge of security. In this way he learns to trust his mother, the world, and himself.

All children ask from time to time, when they feel disapproved of, "Do my parents love me?" The handicapped child who gradually realizes that he is different and that he disappoints his parents at times has more reason to ask that question. When his parents can show him that they enjoy him and approve of him most of the time, it reassures him and comforts him.

One way you show any child that you are fond of him is by taking an interest in his accomplishments. When an infant begins to smile, his parents delightedly coo and smile back at him. When he can grasp, they show him how to shake his rattle. They celebrate when he takes his first steps.

All this may sound obvious, but what about the baby who is born with a disability? The blind baby can't see his mother's affectionate expression. He doesn't have the incentive of seeing the bright red ball that would make him reach for it. The child who is born with cerebral palsy is likely to be very slow in his motor development. Perhaps he is a half a year later than most children in grasping his bottle or his toys, a year or more later in learning to stand alone or walk.[1] He may be slower in learning to talk. But late or early, he needs his parents' approval of his accomplishments just the same. It may be harder for them to show it, because of their sadness at the delay.

Carrying out a program of physical or occupational therapy is bound to be tedious, even frustrating for you. But if you can show your child that you've got your heart in it most of the time, if you can make some of the hours with him companionable, he senses that you are doing it because you love him. It is hard to remember, when you have a child you worry about, that he needs time with you that is just for fun.

All children notice how their parents treat them as compared with their brothers and sisters. In some families, parents act as if the child with a disability must always be given the best and most of everything. Then the handicapped child may conclude that he is the favorite or that his parents feel sorry for him. Neither conclusion is healthy, either for the handicapped child or for his brothers and sisters.

The important thing is for each child to know that his parents try to provide fairly for him. The fact that each child's needs differ, and that what is given to one may therefore differ from what is given to another, doesn't mean that parents love one child more or less than the other. If parents are clear about this in their own minds, children will accept it. In this sense, brothers and sisters can accept the special treatment given to the child with a disability—if it is fair. And if the handicapped child understands the limits of the special treatment given him, he will feel no deep jealousy of his brothers and sisters.

Children sense how their parents feel about them in the presence of outsiders. By taking a child out, introducing him to visitors as a matter of course, as you do his brothers and sisters, by encouraging him to mingle with guests on appropriate occasions, and by making him a natural part of the group, you show him that you think well of him and expect him to please other people.

The Need for Friends and Social Acceptance. A child with a disability needs help particularly in learning how to be socially appealing. The heart of this matter lies in his feelings about others and about himself. If he's always thinking about his limitations, he will be insecure with others. But even if he is comfortable about himself he won't be able to make friends until he has learned to share interests with others. A child doesn't get this practice in a family if he is too much the center of attention; he becomes accustomed to receiving without ever having to give.

Until about three, children are predominantly self-centered. They don't think often about pleasing other people. If they are forced to share their toys before they are ready, they may even become more possessive, in self-defense. But by three or four, happy children come to feel generous impulses toward others. Parents should foster these feelings by helping children to share toys, to play cooperatively, to make gifts for others, and to be helpful within the family.

Parents may need considerable ingenuity to find ways in which a handicapped child may be useful, but even a bedfast child can do some things. Maybe it's polishing the apples for a bowl of fruit or drying the tableware. Perhaps the child who uses his hands awkwardly can still shake the scouring powder into the bathtub and scrub it.

If his disability limits his social contacts, you may have to find subtle ways of helping your child make friends. You can set the example by being friendly and hospitable when other boys and girls come to your home. You make them want to come by providing attractive play equipment and simple treats. You invite other children to meals and serve dishes that are their favorites. If you can take your child on excursions or picnics, you can bring another child his age along.

Is it better for your child to associate with other handicapped children or to find his friends among children without disabilities? This has always been a controversial question. It will come up in a particularly serious way if you must decide whether to send your child to a special school or to a regular school, or a special camp or Scout troop. There are advantages and disadvantages both ways.

If your handicapped child can share happily in at least some of the activities of nonhandicapped children, his childhood will be richer and it will be good preparation for the experiences he will have with all kinds of people when he is grown. In order to have a happy companionship with nonhandicapped boys and girls, however, a child has to be able to accept his limitations comfortably and cheerfully, not be depressed by the comparison of his achievements with theirs.

Especially in the early stages of learning sociability, some handicapped children find themselves more at ease when they are part of a group with disabilities and problems similar to their own. They can feel that their difficulties are understood. After they gain confidence, it will be easier for them to enter into social activities with nonhandicapped children.

An example of the development of social ease was shown in a small arts-and-crafts group for teenagers with cerebral palsy, organized by the United Cerebral Palsy Associations of New York.[2] After a number of months a few nonhandicapped young people were added to the group. For a while the original members of the group kept pretty much to themselves, concentrating on the work. Then friendly relations began to develop between the handicapped and the nonhandicapped. The group expanded its social program to include group singing, publishing a newspaper, and taking trips. Later the cerebral palsied members of the group were introduced to another organization where they could take part in already established groups of nonhandicapped young people. At first they made slow progress in social relations, but gradually they fitted in.

The Need for Play and Recreation.   Play is an essential part of a child's way of growing up. When he is riding a tricycle he is having fun, but he is also improving his coordination. The youngster pulling or pushing his toy truck is learning something about the grown-up world of transportation. The child playing store is finding out about arithmetic and about the way people act when they buy and sell. The boy who comes home dirty, breathless, and jubilant from playing ball has learned about obeying the rules of the game, being a good sport, and getting along with the other fellows.

Handicapped youngsters have a great need of the pleasures and rewards of recreation but they have fewer opportunities than the average. Sometimes parents are unduly cautious about letting them participate. And the neighborhood children may just assume that the orthopedically handicapped or blind or deaf child is unable to take part in games and social events. Actually, many handicapped persons have become proficient in games and sports. Many more can enjoy physical activities when these are adapted to the limitations of the disability.

Every child needs a fair amount of unorganized, undirected free time when he isn't being "managed." Play and hobbies provide freedom of choice and freedom from obligation. A hobby can be put aside temporarily—or abandoned altogether. In fact, a certain amount of changing from one interest to another can be very useful to youngsters in the serious business of discovering their abilities and talents.

Because of the importance of play and recreation for the child with a disability, all of Part V is devoted to this subject.

The Need for Guidance, Control, and Discipline. Lots of parents shrink from the very thought of disciplining their handicapped child, especially if they think of discipline only as denying the child what he wants or inflicting physical punishment. Their own mixed feelings—especially their guilt about the disability—make this unusually difficult for them.

The purpose of discipline, in the broad sense, is education in conduct and control. Every child needs this kind of guidance. It develops his own standards of behavior so that as he grows older he can depend less on external authority. Punishment and denial may be necessary at times, but they are only a small part of the education in right and wrong that every child needs.

Conscientious parents wouldn't dream of leaving it to an unhandicapped child to learn all by himself which kinds of behavior are good and which will get him into trouble. They'd say it was bad for him. Yet that is what they often do to the one who is disabled, as if he didn't have all the same human temptations! Every general rule about discipline applies equally well to him.

A child will be better liked and therefore happier if he has learned how to get along with others. The handicapped child must learn how to satisfy his own legitimate needs in ways that are acceptable to other people. He needs help in recognizing the wishes of others. He must learn to behave agreeably when he can't have what he wants, or when he must wait a while before his wishes can be satisfied, or when he fails in what he tries to do.

There has been plenty of argument in recent years about the merits of permissiveness and strictness. The truth is that some loving, warm-hearted parents can be moderately strict and others moderately permissive with equally good results. What parents actually do depends partly on their philosophy but most of all on how they were brought up themselves. Those who were brought up strictly tend to be strict and this works well if they are fond of their children, too. Those brought up leniently get good results with the same attitude as long as they are clear and confident about what they expect. But severity without love never works. And parents who are permissive because they are afraid their children won't like them if they are strict are apt to have ill-behaved offspring. Parents should stick to what they think is right.

If you believe in being fairly strict about good manners and prompt obedience, for instance, by all means let your child know it. If you are easy-going about such things as children being noisy and interrupting at meals, you can still bring up children who are cooperative and reliable, as long as they respect you and respect the rules you do make.

When a child is young he needs to have you set limits and make those decisions which he is still too inexperienced to make. As he grows older he will still respect your authority, as long as you are confident about it yourself and use it reasonably, though he may complain and balk at times. He senses even in adolescence that your concern about his behavior is one aspect of your love. Naturally, at each stage of growing up he needs wider limits and an increasing share in making decisions.

With any child the routines of the day—dressing, eating, going to bed—can become occasions for friction. In the case of the child with a disability, when the routine may be part of a prescription that has been carefully worked out by doctors and therapists, problems of discipline are even more likely to arise. Parents have to stick to their guns when they are helping to carry out the doctor's instructions. If they show that they are uncertain or anxious, or that they disagree with the doctor, the child will become more resistant. But they can still be tactful and pleasant. Sometimes a simple explanation will increase a child's willingness to cooperate. It also helps if you let your child know that you understand his objections, even though you insist on compliance with the doctor's instructions.

Children react to frustration in different ways. Some accept defeat rather apathetically; others fight for what they want. Still others react with anger. A young child may cry or throw himself on the floor in a furious tantrum. An older child may take out his anger on other people, perhaps behaving rudely to his parents or blaming his failure on someone else.

The heat of anger is not a good time for discussion, especially if you feel angry too. One young child may calm down more readily if he is left to himself; another may need an affectionate gesture from one of his parents in order to forget his resentment. It helps if parents occasionally remind a child who has been angry that they know he feels cross with them sometimes, as all children do. But this doesn't mean that they permit rudeness.

The handicapped child may be particularly subject to frustration if what he was trying to do is too hard for him. A thoughtful parent may be able to help him set his sights a little lower. If what he wants to do is quite beyond his abilities, he needs help in finding something interesting that he *can* do. If he can't play baseball, perhaps he can keep score. If he can't skate, perhaps he can learn to swim. Even though he perhaps can't hear, he may become a very well-informed stamp collector or learn a great deal about astronomy.

Often the parents of a child with convulsions are afraid to discipline him for fear of bringing on a spell. A child quickly senses such a state of affairs and takes advantage of it. This is apt to lead to more scenes and perhaps more convulsions. It's much better to get it clear from the start that there will be no nonsense about behavior.

Parents may become confused about disciplining a mentally retarded child. In their eagerness to have him mature they may expect him to do things that he doesn't understand, and they may penalize him when he falls short of their expectations. Mental retardation affects not only the child's school work but also his ability to carry many simple kinds of responsibilities and to develop social relationships. This is a situation in which most parents need regular counseling.

The Need for Independence. Although a baby is almost totally dependent upon other people at birth, he soon learns to grab, sit, stand and walk. Before long he wants to put his own clothes on. When he is able to take care of himself in these rudimentary ways, his sense of security no longer depends so much on the knowledge that his mother or father is just around the corner. Going to school exposes him to a whole new world of independent ventures; he learns things his parents don't know. He makes more and more decisions for himself.

Children work hard at learning to do things for themselves. They often attempt things that are still too hard for them. They may feel dependent one day and scorn assistance the next. But in the long run, well adjusted children want to move toward adulthood and independence. Although a disabled child may have to take a longer way around to reach this goal, and although some children can never go all the way, each child should be encouraged to become just as independent as he can. He needs encouragement in acquiring the physical skills that enable him to do things for himself, he needs opportunities to make decisions and to carry suitable responsibilities, he needs a sense of personal worth to build his self-esteem. Like other children, he needs an education that will develop his capacities and give him the opportunity to be self-supporting, if that is possible.

Certain disabilities mean permanent dependency—at least physical and financial dependency. Occasionally this has a deeply depressing effect on a child. He may become morbidly afraid of what would happen if the people on whom he depends should cut him off from their help. Then, for fear of displeasing them, he may become completely inactive. Such a frame of mind is unlikely to develop when the child is sure of his parents' love, and when those who look after him encourage him to do all he can. When a depressed mood persists, however, a child needs psychiatric help. A local chapter of the National Association for Retarded Children, a family service agency, or some of the other agencies discussed in Chapter 5 may help you find it. Books such as those listed in the Suggested Reading are also useful.

Many disabled boys and girls require training in activities

of daily living, in order to master the practical matters of everyday life. A detailed program is usually prescribed by the child's physician and is worked out by him and the therapists in accordance with the child's needs and capacities. The therapists who carry out the program are professionally trained. Not every child with a disability can become completely independent in self-care, but each thing that he can do for himself is a great gain: it saves parents' time and energy; more important, it boosts the child's morale. Food tastes better when he can feed himself. He feels more of a person when he can dress himself. Friends are more fun when he can go to their houses to return the visits paid to him.

Children whose disabilities don't confine them may need special help too. The deaf child, particularly if he has been deaf since babyhood, needs encouragement in ways which his parents may not realize. His world is quite different. When his mother enters the room, her footsteps and the sound of the opening door do not warn him; her entrance is a surprise. When she leaves, although she smiles encouragingly, he hears no word to tell him that she will be back in a moment. In his silent world there are no explanations or descriptions. It is harder to reassure him when he fails, and it takes more effort to encourage him to try again.

It is inevitable that the parents of a child who has been blind from infancy should at first feel that they must protect him from all harm, but it is easy to shelter him so much that he has little incentive to do things for himself. If toys are placed in his hand why should he ever try to reach them? Mother will feed him; why should he bother with the struggle to fill his spoon and get it to his mouth? Mother will dress him; why should he explore the baffling mystery of sleeves and buttons?

Overprotection can discourage the blind child so much that he may even seem mentally retarded. Quite a few overprotected blind children at three years of age do not walk or talk, are still bottle fed, are not toilet trained, and are very reluctant to leave their mother's side.

A blind child's abilities to take care of his personal needs can be surprisingly well developed by the time he is three or four. Learning to move about confidently is the first essential. In a short time, with encouragement, he can learn to move freely in familiar surroundings and avoid obstacles. He can learn to run up and down stairs, use a tricycle, jungle gym and swings, splash in a wading pool, or dance to music. In strange surroundings, and in walking along the street, he will still need guidance. But he will also need continued encouragement as he grows older, to overcome the fear of open spaces.

No matter what his disability, a child should have some responsibility for duties around his home. This gives him the feeling that he, too, is a useful appreciated member of the family. He also needs increasing opportunity to make decisions as he grows older. Learning to make decisions begins in a small way when the child is very young. It may be an occasional choice of a bedtime story or, a little later, a choice between two sweaters or what to put into a lunch box. (There is no sense in offering a small child many decisions that really belong to his mother.) With gradually increasing experience, children will learn to make sensible decisions about more important matters. This sort of growth is as possible for the handicapped child as for the nonhandicapped.

The Need for Varied Experiences.   The boy or girl with a disability is often deprived—unnecessarily—of a great many experiences through which children learn about their neighborhood, about nature, and about the way people work and play. It is easy to see why this happens when children have to spend long months or years in a hospital, but it is also true of some children who are confined to wheelchairs or who can't get around easily for some reason.

An interesting study was made of 100 preschool children with physical disabilities and an equal number of nonhandicapped children in the same area in order to compare the variety of their experiences inside and outside the home: trips to neighborhood stores, to special points of interest, to vacation or recreation spots; attendance at movies and ball games, social activities at parties or church; spending money, taking care of pets, using tools, helping with household chores; using public transportation and the telephone; operating a radio or record player, etc.

In most instances the handicapped children had had many fewer experiences, even of types with which their disabilities would not interfere. For instance, although 95 per cent of the normal children knew the story of *Goldilocks and the Three Bears,* only about half of the handicapped children were familiar with it. Most of these particular experiences could easily have been provided for the handicapped children if parents had realized their importance. For the fact is that every child matures by his experiences. If he has substantially fewer than other children his age, he will not be able to keep up with them socially and scholastically.

The limitation of the experiences of the handicapped child often continues into his school years to an unnecessary degree. Half of the parents of fifth- and eighth-grade children with orthopedic handicaps who went to certain New York schools reported[4] that the children spent all their time at home in passive, noncreative activities much below their age level—listening to the radio, watching television, or reading comic books. Only about one-fifth of the children had creative interests and hobbies. A few said their children had no home activities at all. Over half of these boys and girls engaged in no activities outside the home. Only a few of them took part in games requiring any skill or physical exertion, and the only excursions made by many of them were to the clinic or doctor's office.

The most probable reasons why parents like these give their handicapped child so little encouragement may be that they are still depressed by his problem; or they are so preoccupied with the disability that they forget the person. When parents fully realize the importance to their child of a rich breadth of experience, they can usually find oportunities for him in spite of his limitations. A parent's job is to help any child of his to maximum development of his capacities, whatever they may be.

COMING TO TERMS WITH A DISABILITY

If you can treat your child naturally and accept his handicap in a fairly casual way, you will ease some of his own tensions and free him from the pressure of trying to do the impossible. Your manner also serves as a cue to others—particularly children. They will reflect your attitude.

Perhaps your child is a diabetic, and the occasion is a picnic. The cake with rich icing is not for him, so you prepare a special dessert for him. Your matter-of-fact manner in serving it shows that this is hardly important enough to make a big fuss about, or to try to hide, either.

If your child is an amputee who uses a prosthetic hook for a hand, taking it for granted that he will wear his prosthesis in public as well as at home, whether the occasion is school, church, or a party, makes it easier for him to be un-self-conscious about it. If your daughter uses crutches, you must look for some special features—such as roominess in the sleeves and the back—when you shop with her for a dress. If you explain your requirements to the clerk, directly and simply as you would on any shopping errand, it helps both the clerk and your daughter to be at ease.

Talking with Your Child about His Disability... A close, warm feeling between parent and any child depends on easy communication, freedom to share feelings. This closeness is difficult to achieve when there is something they don't talk about. When you talk with your child about his disability as naturally as you do about any other phase of his life, this tells him that you accept him as he is. If you are silent about it, he won't feel free to bring any of his worries out into the open. Most children, we've learned, at first regard their disability as punishment for being "bad." Unless they gain their parents' reassurance they may go on feeling that there is something very sinful about themselves.

A child may conclude from his parents' silence that his condition is more serious than it really is. This makes him unnecessarily fearful or depressed. Depending on his age and his ability to comprehend, he needs to have reasonable and reassuring explanations about his disability and about what medical care will do for him.

Remember that anyone is likely to become uneasy when he is involved in new experiences. At a time of change, such as when you move to a new neighborhood, or bring a new baby home, or when your child has to go to the hospital, it is particularly important to be alert to his need to ask questions and talk about things that worry him.

Teen-aged children are often reluctant to tell their parents anything or to ask for advice even when they would really like to. This is part of their striving for independence. If you can talk with your teenager in a way that recognizes his growing maturity—discussing an issue instead of saying, "Do this"—he will probably be more inclined to come to you. But you have to accept the fact that most youngsters of high school age will talk more freely with adults outside the family, such as a favorite teacher.

There are problems sometimes when you have to talk about your child's disability with other people in his presence. Try not to say anything that you haven't said or wouldn't say to the child himself. Remarks beyond his comprehension will stir up worries just because he doesn't understand. When this has happened, as when you have taken him to his doctor for an examination, remember to give him a reassuring explanation as soon as you can.

When your child seems unable to make his own explanations to other people, it will be better if you can explain to them in a matter-of-fact way why he is restricted, or why he must follow a certain routine. If the child wants to add to your remarks, so much the better. At times you may need to engineer a change of subject. When some misguided visitor exclaims in front of your child, "Poor dear! How terrible that he can't walk!" you can counter the effect with some such remark as "The physical therapist says he's doing very well with his exercises, and he'll soon be walking with crutches." Your child doesn't want pity; he wants intelligent understanding.

Your Child's Insight into His Abilities and His Limitations.
The ordinary child is able to size up his abilities with a fair amount of realism through his everyday experiences. Johnny knows that two or three other boys in the block run faster than he does, but he's a better pitcher. Mary paints some of the best posters in her class but admits she's poor at algebra. Yet even nonhandicapped children sometimes make mistakes in their estimates of what they can do.

A handicapped child with limited experience and a strong desire to be normal may have a very hard time estimating his own capacities. He may have no realization that the girl who plays the violin in the school orchestra practices long hours each day or that the Eagle Scout had to work for years to earn all his merit badges. His idea of what he can expect to achieve in overcoming his handicap may be fantastically optimistic or pessimistic. To avoid these misconceptions he needs constant education from his therapists, doctors and you. Even more, he needs a wholesome feeling about himself.

Children are easily defeated by what seems too difficult or too long-range. One way of helping your child sustain interest and ambition is by encouraging him to tackle small projects that offer a reasonable chance of success soon. When he has mastered the simpler steps, he can go on to what is a little more difficult. Success lures him on. Failure can be very discouraging.

There is a strong temptation to be overly enthusiastic toward a child about his accomplishments, especially one with a disability. This doesn't do him any good. Naturally he needs appreciation and encouragement. But there's a difference between commending him for making a good try and pretending that what he has done is better than it really is. A handicapped child needs an honest appraisal of his work even more than other children do, since he himself may sometimes feel that excessive allowances should be made for him just because of his disability. But if his disability will allow him to compete in study and work with nonhandicapped people, he will need to be quite objective about his real capacities.

No handicapped person can tell what his potentialities are until he has been trained in the activities of daily living (known among rehabilitation workers as ADL) or until he can use whatever aids are available for him. The child who is without an arm or a leg has no way of knowing how much he can accomplish until he has been fitted with an artificial limb and has had training and practice in its use. The blind child can gauge his capacities more accurately after he has learned to read Braille and can go to school. The deaf child cannot know the possibilities for communicating with others until he has learned to read lips.

As your child grows older, he should progressively understand the medical side of his disability. This helps him know what is and what is not possible for him. The young child who has frequent medical examinations will be interested in the doctor's equipment and want to know what it is. He'll be satisfied with simple answers. The high school student should be told how the results of the examination figure in the doctor's decision about his activities, preferably by the doctor himself. After all, when he is grown he will have to be able to carry out his own health program and he will need the facts to guide him in his choices of activity, relaxation, food, sleep, and so on.

Emotional Acceptance of a Disability. Some people think that "accepting" a disability means passive resignation. Not Anne H. Carlsen, who was born without arms and feet, completed college, became a school principal, and then a child guidance director. This is what she has to say about acceptance:

"Ever since I can remember, I regarded my handicap as being just one of those things that happen, that it was no one's fault, no one wanted it, but it was there and it had to be worked around.

"I was in a gang of youngsters from the time I was three years old, in a small Wisconsin town. It was a neighborhood gang. Our house was headquarters. They used to come there before I got up in the morning. My brother would kid me about calling the roll at breakfast time to be sure they were all there.

"I did everything with them. They never put any limitations on what I could do; consequently I didn't either. They didn't adjust their games particularly except to revise a few rules in baseball. At that time I couldn't walk at all, but I could crawl, and they found out by timing me that I could crawl about as fast as they could walk, and so the rule was they were supposed to walk when they batted the ball. However, I did all the running games and never thought anything of it. I went sliding, I went skating. I didn't skate, but they pulled me around on the sled—and I think if you have those experiences as a child, when you get to be an adult, you just naturally expect people to accept you for what you are, and you figure that after they get over the first shock of seeing you minus a couple of things, they will realize that, after all, those aren't essential."[5]

Stories of what other handicapped people have done sometimes help a child accept a disability with better feelings. A realization that others have overcome, or at least minimized, their disabilities may inspire him to work harder in his therapy program. On the other hand you certainly want to avoid giving him the impression that you expect him to try for anything more than his doctor and therapists have good reason to think he can accomplish. And it would not be wise to use another person's success story as an object lesson to prove that people who are worse off than your child are making better use of their opportunities than he is.

At some point a big snag in your child's acceptance of his disability will be his objection to being "different." This is a very special problem for teenagers. They are so uneasy about being different that they force themselves to fit the exact mold of their particular gang. Yet, paradoxically, the teen-ager admires those who stand out above the crowd. Competence is highly regarded. It's easier to say than to do, but if your son or daughter can develop some skill which will give him recognition he will feel proud of himself and it will matter less to him that he is different.

Good grooming and dressing becomingly in popular teen-age styles help overcome to some extent the disadvantage of looking different. Girls get an extra boost from cosmetics and a new hair-do. Both boys and girls can learn to select clothing that emphasizes their good points. Attractive, reasonably priced clothing is now manufactured for handicapped people who must use wheelchairs, braces, or crutches.

Knowing how to cope with other people's reactions toward him is another element in a child's acceptance of his disability. He wants to be treated just like other people, to be appreciated as a person, on his own merits. When friends come to visit him, he wants them to come because they enjoy it, not because they consider it a duty. When they admire some of his handiwork, perhaps an airplane model, he wants to feel that their admiration is in recognition of a skillful job, not a patronizing pat on the back because he has a handicap. His desire to be treated like everyone else, from this point of view, is wholesome.

Children also need some help in learning how to take it when people pity them. A self-respecting child resents pity, because it makes him feel inferior. You can point out to your child that people who have had no experience with handicapped boys and girls are often embarrassed and really don't know what to say or how to act. If your child can learn to put the other person at ease with a courteous remark or explanation, he'll be doing someone else a favor, and aiding his own adjustment.

A handicapped boy or girl has to reach some kind of an understanding of his own feelings about the help that people offer him. In one sense he never wants help because it spells inability. But he is more willing to accept it when it is absolutely necessary. However, his definition of "necessary" may differ from that of the average person. Take a teen-aged boy, for example, partially paralyzed following polio, who is learning to use crutches. With good intentions, his parent opens a door for him. Instead of being grateful, he acts disagreeably. In this case the truth is that he needs to open the door himself because he can do it and because he must always be working toward independence.

There are many situations in which it is quite natural to offer help, whether to a disabled or to a normal person. If your child can learn to respond with a casual remark, such as, "I think I can do it myself, thank you," he explains his wish for independence in a way that helps his friends understand his real needs. On the other hand, your child has to learn to ask for help without embarrassment when he wants it. He has to learn—and to accept the fact graciously— that everyone needs help at times.

REFERENCES

1. Viola E. Cardwell. *Cerebral Palsy: Advances in Understanding and Care.* Association for the Aid of Crippled Children, New York, 1956.

2. Ernest Weinrich. "Group Work with the Handicapped in a Community Center Setting." *The Group,* Vol. 17, April 1955, pp. 15-18, 22.

3. LeRoy Larson. "Preschool Experiences of Physically Handicapped Children." *Exceptional Children,* Vol. 24: No. 7, March 1958.

4. *The Child with Orthopedic Limitations.* New York City Board of Education, Bureau of Educational Research. Publication No. 33, June 1954.

5. *Achieving Goals for the Handicapped.* Proceedings 1949 Convention, National Society for Crippled Children, Chicago, pp. 26-27.

4

FAMILY LIVING

The Effects of Disability on Family Life.   Probably no one needs to tell you that the family problems raised by disability are numerous. They are illustrated by a study made in New York City of the families of children with rheumatoid arthritis.[1]

Almost all these families were so heavily burdened financially, particularly during the first year, that more than one-fourth of them went into debt. Others reduced their standard of living drastically, cutting out every possible expenditure for such things as clothing, furniture, recreation, or vacations. Some fathers took extra jobs, and some mothers had to work. About two-thirds obtained help in meeting the costs of the illness by means of reduced fees in clinics, camps, visiting nurse services, or care in convalescent homes. Assistance was given by the state agency for aid to dependent children, the Red Cross, fraternal organizations, employees' benevolent organizations, or the Arthritis and Rheumatism Foundation.

In the hope of aiding their child's recovery, some families moved to more expensive quarters, some to a warmer climate, and others to a location nearer to medical facilities. In several instances, grandparents moved nearer to the child's home in order to relieve the parents of some part of the child's care. About one-third of the mothers suffered serious physical and emotional strain as a result of their anxiety and extra duties. Some of them became sick enough to require medical care.

Transportation to the doctor or clinic was a serious problem. If the child was wearing a cast, a taxi was necessary, and there was rarely any outside assistance with this ex-

43

pense. The amount of time consumed in medical visits added to the mother's problems. If there was no one to sit with the younger children, the mother had to take them along.

Many of the children were depressed, anxious, irritable, socially withdrawn or overdependent at some time during the illness. Some of the families had difficulties with the brothers and sisters, either because of actual neglect of the well children or because of jealousy. However, many other parents observed that brothers and sisters were sympathetic and understanding with the sick child.

A group of families of children with muscular dystrophy also emphasized the problem of the relationship of the handicapped child to his brothers and sisters.[2] These parents complained about their own fatigue from lifting, feeding, dressing, bathing, and toileting their child. The great amount of time required in such care almost always overburdens mothers. The curiosity of neighbors was another problem. Many parents pointed out how much more difficult the various relationships with a family are made by the presence of a handicapped child. Parents commonly felt anxiety about the child's future when they themselves would no longer be living and he would be dependent upon others for financial support or personal care.

Families solve their problems in different ways—but solve them they must. There is usually more help available than people know about. Some parents are slow to take advantage of community resources, because of timidity or pride as well as because of lack of information. Certainly parents should find out exactly what and where the community services are before they try to decide whether or not to use them. Some resources are suggested in this chapter, and further detailed discussions will be found throughout the book.

Parents themselves have taken the initiative in different parts of the country to form groups to secure community help where it did not previously exist. A number of the large national organizations for helping handicapped children grew from just such beginnings.

FAMILY AND NEIGHBORHOOD RELATIONS

A family can't maintain a really happy and unified spirit unless the needs of all the members are met. When the handicapped child receives only his fair share of consideration— not the lion's share—the results are far better for everyone, including him. If his needs are always put first, the child is apt to become self-centered, overly dependent, even tyrannical. The other children almost inevitably feel resentment toward the favored child.

There should be sensible apportioning of the family resources of money and time. If all the children have a chance to join in discussions about how to meet the family problems, they will be more likely to regard the needs of the handicapped child for special care and equipment as a family responsibility rather than as evidence of parental favoritism.

Including the Handicapped Child in Family Activities. As far as he is able, the handicapped child should be included in family activities. But what is taken for granted with other children may require special consideration in his case. His schedule should be planned thoughtfully so that he isn't busy with therapy or rest, for instance, just when the others want to be on the go.

Sometimes the difficulty is that the parents, in their apprehension, form an inflexible picture of the extent of the child's disability. He may return from the hospital or rehabilitation center with newly acquired abilities but be treated by his family as if he were still quite helpless.

The child who is limited in his speech, hearing, or vision may be present physically but not really included in a group unless other members of the family are thoughtful enough to communicate with him by whatever methods he can use. If he is dependent upon lip reading, for example, you have to be sure that your face is turned toward him. If he can't speak easily, listen carefully and wait for him to finish. Then ask him to repeat what you haven't understood. If the child is blind, he doesn't need to sit curled up in a chair while his brothers and sisters enjoy outdoor activities. Once he has learned the essentials that give him confidence of movement, he can often join them.

Being with the rest of the family at meals or as they listen to radio or television, being with the other children for the good-night ceremonies or bedtime stories, sharing the morning goodbyes as Father goes off to work, playing in the kitchen while Mother is busy there, helping brothers and sisters or being helped by them with homework, receiving guests—these are only a few of the normal home-life situations in which a child with a disability can participate.

No child is too young to be included. One young couple had been invited to a big family reunion just after they had learned that their baby suffered from a progressive muscular disease. They planned to leave the baby at home with a nurse, but their doctor advised them to take him along. "It will do him no harm. And if you start isolating him now it will be that much harder for both of you to feel comfortable with people later on." Following that principle, the parents made it a point to include him whenever possible. Now in his teens he spends his life in a wheelchair, but he is poised, friendly and able to hold his own with others.

Naturally there are family activities in which your handicapped child cannot suitably take part. The important thing is to be conscious of his need so that he is not excluded unnecessarily.

Parents' Responsibilities to Brothers and Sisters. Parents themselves worry, of course, that all their attention to their handicapped child's special problems may cause them to neglect their other children. They meet this problem in different ways. They may share the care of the handicapped child, the father dressing him and giving him breakfast, for instance, while the mother breakfasts with the other children and sees them off to school. In some families all the children can be included in a bedtime story hour, or the mother may put the handicapped child to bed while the father spends time with the others. Don't overlook the value of the companionship you give to any child when you and he are working together—maybe just washing the dishes. In fact, lots of people are more able to enjoy each other's company and share confidences on a job than when at leisure. Of course companionship is not a temporary state that can be turned on and off like a faucet. It's a fundamental relationship which is cultivated gradually by the parents' genuine interest and pleasure in their children.

Sharing Home Duties. It's good for all the children in any family to share in home duties. The amount of work isn't the important thing. In one family an adolescent girl may be sharing the housework equally with a mother who has an outside job. In another, the girl who has a great deal of homework may only be expected to take care of her own room. What's important is that each child feel that he is contributing his reasonable share to the family's welfare. It may take ingenuity to figure what a seriously handicapped child can do, but he's certainly entitled to participate somehow.

Parents should realize that the brothers and sisters of a disabled child, however much they love him, will have other conflicting feelings about him. They will feel guilty underneath that he, not they, was smitten. At the same time they may resent, consciously or unconsciously, all the attention he's receiving. One of the ways these troubled feelings may break out is in resentment over the jobs that have been assigned to them. We've learned from child guidance work that it helps a child with guilty or angry feelings to be able to talk about them with someone who understands and is not too shocked. A sensitive parent who can read his child's upset feelings may be able to help him to get them out in the open. "I think that you have been feeling cross about your brother lately. It's natural, I can understand it."

The Handicapped Child and His Brothers and Sisters. A handicapped child is apt to be disturbing to his brothers and sisters to some degree, even when they accept him affectionately. They may fear to bring other children home to play because of the remarks their friends make. ("Your brother's dumb. He can't walk or talk or anything.") Or a thoughtless young neighbor mimics the awkward gait of a cerebral-palsied child or the imperfect speech of the child with a cleft palate. Some children say they don't want any more baby brothers or sisters out of fear that another child would also be disabled. Some adolescent children, particularly daughters, feel at times that the handicapped child is interfering with their social life, that they have fewer dates and are invited to fewer parties because of him. (But then, adolescents often worry about their popularity anyway, and try to pin the blame on something.)

If the parents' attitude is one of comfortableness toward all the children, it will be easier for brothers and sisters to feel less embarrassment, to enjoy the handicapped child and to include him at times in their activities.

If brothers and sisters are to take the handicapped child's disability in their stride, they need to understand something about it. For one thing, children and adults outside the family often ask them questions. If the disability has been talked about quite naturally in the family, the children are less likely to be upset by questions. They are able to explain the disabled child's situation to their friends and to help their friends accept him too. When the handicap is accepted openly by family and friends, it is easier for the child to be included naturally in some of the unplanned activities of the gang—watching TV, scuffling, raiding the refrigerator, and making big plans for Saturday. Naturally, he can't expect to be included in everything. In fact, it's normal for each child in the family to have his own group of friends of similar age and interests, and no child in the family should expect to be included in all the activities of the other children. Certainly brothers and sisters shouldn't be expected to deprive themselves of certain kinds of fun just because the handicapped child is unable to take part.

It's right, if a child is seriously handicapped, that his brothers and sisters have definite obligations to help him in certain activities, to keep him company, and to carry out these duties in a generous spirit. This eases their guilt about being completely sound themselves. If both parents hold jobs to meet the financial pressures, the older children of the family may have unusual responsibilities for the handicapped child. But they should not be expected to give him so much time and attention that their own education and social life are jeopardized. When both parents are working, they may have to use a sitter regularly so that brothers and sisters have enough time for their own development.

Grandparents, In-laws, and Family Friends. Grandparents, other relatives, and family friends who are concerned for the welfare of the handicapped child may still have no real understanding of his disability or his treatment. They can be quite a trial to the parents, with their persistent errors and suggestions. Sometimes they mistakenly assume that a physical handicap is accompanied by mental defects, as when the child can't speak clearly because of a cleft palate. They may stick to some of the common misconceptions about even common disabilities, such as the belief that the child who is subject to seizures should not engage in active games, or that the mentally retarded child is more active sexually, or that it's better to wait until a child is old enough to know his own mind before fitting him with a prosthesis.

Sometimes relatives are critical of "the other side of the family" when they think that a congenital defect is the result of heredity. Or they bluntly urge the parents to "put the child away"; on the other hand, they may express their horrified criticism if the parents have decided that institutional care is best. They are apt to keep insisting that the parents consult some expert or use some treatment that has produced a miraculous cure, according to a friend of a friend.

The best you can do about this situation is to set the facts before them and show that you are very firm about adhering to the course of treatment that has been carefully worked out with the child's physicians.

Relationships with Neighbors and Community. The family of a handicapped child always has to help him win an accepted place in the community. A child with epilepsy, or cerebral palsy, or mental retardation, or a cleft palate, for example, is often misunderstood by the neighbors. Neighbor children are apt to tease him cruelly. They may refuse to play with him, often because the parents have prohibited it. It's better not to wait for trouble and then complain to the parents of the other children. It's more sensible to take the initiative by becoming acquainted with some of the other parents and explaining your child's condition. Tell them about the treatment he is receiving, and make casual suggestions about ways in which the other children can help him.

When the family of John, a teenager who was mentally retarded, moved into a new neighborhood, his parents noticed that neighbors called their young children inside when he went outdoors. John's parents, who did not feel up to the job of explaining his condition, asked the president of the local association for retarded children to come to their home for afternoon tea with the neighbors. He explained the meaning of mental retardation to the group, told them about the training John had received, and assured them that they need not worry about their small children. The neighbors had a chance to ask questions and to get acquainted with John. Soon afterward some of them invited him to their homes and, when they saw that he cut the grass at his own home, offered him a chance to earn money by mowing their yards. Before long, both the parents and the children of the neighborhood were John's friends. John's parents explained to the neighbors some of the things it was helpful to know about him, and that it would be polite to tell John when it was time to go home since he wouldn't realize it himself.

It is too much to expect that the handicapped child or his family will altogether escape tactless or cruel remarks. It's better to learn not to give them undue importance. If the child himself and his brothers and sisters feel secure in their family life, if the parents keep their own perspective, and if the thoughtlessness of people is occasionally discussed matter-of-factly, the children are not likely to be greatly disturbed. This is not a perfect solution, but it is better than when families withdraw from community contacts because they are hurt by indifference or prejudice. We all need to be refreshed by new faces and new ideas. It's better for the children, too, to see that their parents are accepted in the community. Many parents of handicapped children have found also that by working with a group of other parents with the same problem they have improved community understanding of their children and secured needed facilities.

Some Special Considerations about Spending. Parents certainly can't forget their financial obligations to others in the family. If the cost of a certain course of treatment for the handicapped child threatens the security of the whole family, the parents may well decide that he himself will be better off with less physical improvement but a happier family. It is often a matter of degree. Doctor and therapists may conclude that the small amount of physical improvement to be gained by continued therapy is not worth the expense, the dislocation of family life, and the strain on the child involved in frequent trips to a distant clinic. On the other hand, some families can maintain emotional balance despite severe financial deprivations.

It's natural that your hopes will tempt you to spend money unwisely. It sometimes helps to ask the advice of your doctor, after you've explained the financial situation. He may have to tell you that a further search for new kinds of treatment or medical care would be fruitless, or that there is nothing that medical science can do to correct a defect. He can advise whether the purchase of expensive equipment would be of sufficient value. In one case, the parents of a child who had had polio considered building a swimming pool for him, even though he was confined in an iron lung, because a slight improvement in his condition had led them to think that he would soon be able to benefit by swimming. The doctor explained that such a possibility could not even be guessed at for many months.

All but the richest parents will have to explore all possible ways of meeting the expenses the doctor considers essential, especially if there may be months or years of medical care ahead. Certainly most parents will have to supplement their own resources by calling on the special community agencies that provide assistance for handicapped children. (See Chapter 5.)

THE PARTNERSHIP OF HUSBAND AND WIFE

It's easy for husband and wife to become so absorbed in the practical everyday details that they forget to pay attention to each other's needs for understanding and companionship. But they must support each other's morale if they are to be successful in meeting the problems growing out of their child's disability.

When their child's disability first becomes known to them, parents usually pass through several stages of reaction. Husband and wife don't necessarily react in the same way or at the same time. In fact they usually do not. Each one's personality produces quite different attitudes toward the child and his problems. These differences may even threaten the stability of the marriage. However, the parents can preserve and even strengthen their relationship if they will make generous efforts to keep in step with each other.

The first reaction to a handicap is usually shock and grief, when the parents have no idea what they should do. Soon after may come a period of resentment, when they ask, "Why did this have to happen to us?" It's only later, sometimes months later, that parents begin to accept the facts and to focus their attention on what can be done. If one parent has begun to concentrate on plans for helping the child while the other is still preoccupied with his own hurt, it is difficult for them to work as a team.

Acceptance of the reality that a child is handicapped is difficult in any case, but it presents different problems to each individual. One parent, for instance, can accept the child and love him but can't face his disability realistically. Another deals with practical problems efficiently but can't feel comfortable with the child himself. A mother of a cerebral-palsied child will notice that her husband seems unable to understand the value of a strict therapy program. When left in charge of the child, he often removes his braces or omits the exercises to please the child. Another mother overprotects the child and does for him what he could do for himself. The father, on the other hand, is convinced that only a stubborn unwillingness to learn prevents the child from doing everything his brothers and sisters do.

Some physicians feel that the mother is usually more able than the father to accept the child and the problems of his disability. It may partly be that she just understands better because she talks with the child's doctor more frequently, meets with parents' groups, and carries the daily responsibilities for the child's care. In short, she knows him better. But also most men have been brought up to be ashamed to ask for help, and this makes some of them uncomfortable when their child needs a lot of assistance from others. They try to close their minds to the problem. Or they act impatient with the child or with the mother.

The father's help, both physical and psychological, is vital to his wife. He can listen patiently while she unloads her troubles. He can stand up for her when the relatives have been critical. He can see to it that she has time off for a little fun. An occasional mother may feel a definite resentment because her husband doesn't spend an amount of time equal to hers in caring for the child. She knows that he really can't, because his work keeps him away from home the greater part of the day; yet her tension and anxiety make her so irritable that she accuses him of being indifferent. If he understands that her complaints are not really directed at him but at the world, or at the child for being so difficult to care for, he can accept her outbursts with better humor.

A husband and wife will accept their special responsibilities more gracefully when they have been able to work out a division of labor that fits their particular family situation. One family may find that the mother is more patient in helping the child with his prolonged exercises and that the father can most efficiently do the marketing and some housecleaning at this time. Such an arrangement requires that parents be willing to overlook the traditional distinctions between "woman's work" and "man's work."

Even when the father and mother are basically of one mind toward their child and his disability, there may still be marital problems. The care of the child often requires physical exertion and emotional strain which, added to ordinary duties, leave wife or husband, or both, too exhausted for the enjoyment of companionship and sexual response.

A couple who have already established their marriage on a secure foundation can usually find ways to help each other with new problems, but even then they may want advice on some questions. When they haven't been married long enough to know how to give each other moral support, or when the marriage is strained anyway, outside guidance may be especially valuable in preserving the family. There are several possible sources.

The Child's Doctor.   Husband and wife can more easily work together in the care of their child if both can hear the doctor explain the diagnosis, the treatment, the progress, of the child's handicap. We all know how frustrating it can be to try to report on a meeting to someone who then asks questions we never thought to raise. When both parents talk with the doctor together, each may raise his particular questions, objections, fears. Usually the father can't always be present when the doctor sees his child, but it is particularly helpful if he can be there when the doctor makes his first diagnosis and discusses the outlook for the child's future and when new steps in treatment are recommended.

There is added reason for both parents to talk with the doctor when experience shows that they are unable to talk with each other about the child's handicap. A wise physician can sometimes help them understand each other's feelings as well as the nature of the child's defect. If one parent tends to blame the other for the child's condition, the doctor can straighten them out. If they disagree fundamentally over the best way of caring for the child, the doctor can make sure that they have all the medical facts on which to base a decision.

Parents' Groups and Organizations for the Handicapped. Talking with other parents who have been through the same difficulties and found solutions may clarify points of disagreement between husband and wife. A number of parents' groups provide for group counseling under professional leadership and sometimes make available trained social workers, psychologists, and psychiatrists for individual work.

Mental Health Counseling. In a majority of families with a handicapped child, there are more than enough extra strains and tensions to warrant regular parental counseling from an understanding social worker. This may be at the clinic at which the child receives care or at a family agency. A similar kind of guidance can be gained from a psychiatrist or a mental health center.

Marriage Counseling Services. Where the strains are showing up mainly between the parents, consultation with a skilled marriage counselor is another alternative. Or you may want to see a minister, priest, or rabbi in your community who is known for his wisdom in counseling. If he recognizes the need of husband and wife for the skill of another kind of specialist, he can refer them to such sources. If you don't know where to turn in your community, you should first inquire at your Red Feather or Community Chest offices. You can get the name of the marriage counseling clinic nearest you by writing to the American Association of Marriage Counselors, 27 Woodcliff Drive, Madison, New Jersey.

Genetic Counseling and Heredity Clinics. A serious cause of rupture between husband and wife may be one parent's conviction that the other side of the family is to blame for the child's disability, especially when it was present at birth. For parents frequently assume that any congenital defect is inherited.

Much of what people believe about the inheritance of defects is not true. As a result of increased knowledge of the principles of heredity, specialists have also learned that environmental factors and physical disease account for many birth defects that were once considered hereditary. For example, it was formerly believed that up to 80 per cent of severe mental retardation was hereditary. Today it is thought that most of it is due to brain damage caused by disease during pregnancy or difficulties of birth.

Some parents assume that because they have had one child with a congenital defect, all their children will be affected in the same way. Other parents assume, without knowing the facts, that "lightning doesn't strike twice." The fact is that chances of repetition are fairly high in some types of hereditary defects and inconsequential in others.

The subject is very complex, and parents should seek expert information before deciding whether to have more children. Fortunately, there are excellent sources in the growing number of heredity clinics staffed by genetic counselors. Most of them are located in universities. A list of the more prominent clinics (Amram Scheinfeld, *Basic Facts of Human Heredity*. New York: Washington Square Press, 1961) is given in the next paragraph.

WHERE TO GET ADVICE

Human Heredity Clinics

Authoritative information and advice on problems of human heredity may be obtained at the following institutions. In most cases, however, if the person applying is a layman, it is advisable that contact be made first through one's physician, particularly if the problem is a medical one. *Where not otherwise specified, address inquiries to "Dept. of Human Genetics," at any of these institutions:*

Bowman Gray School of Medicine, Winston-Salem, N.C.
Children's Memorial Hospital, Chicago, Ill.
Dight Institute, University of Minnesota, Minneapolis, Minn.
Johns Hopkins University Medical School, Baltimore, Md.
Medical College of Virginia, Richmond, Va.
Minnesota Dept. of Health, University of Minnesota Campus, Minneapolis, Minn.
New York State Psychiatric Institute, New York 32, N.Y.

The health department of your state may be able to direct you to other, possibly newer, clinics in a more convenient location if you can't get to one of these. Heredity clinics operate on the theory that they can help parents by explaining what is known about the genetic and environmental factors so that the parents have the facts on which to make their own decisions. The clinics rarely make recommendations about what parents should or should not do about having more children; that is left to husband and wife.

Parents sometimes feel that they are neglecting their handicapped child if they take time and money to seek personal guidance. The fact is, however, that you will be better equipped to manage the problems of your handicapped child and the rest of the family when you have resolved any problems of your own. When people have unburdened themselves by conferring with a sympathetic counselor—whether doctor, psychiatrist, minister, social worker—or with other parents, they gain deeper knowledge of themselves and their feelings toward their child. In the long run, the results may be as beneficial to the child as some of the more direct efforts on his behalf.

REFERENCES

1. Frances Krell. *Children with Juvenile Rheumatoid Arthritis.* New York State Chapter, Arthritis and Rheumatism Foundation, New York.

2. Arthur S. Abramson, M.D. *An Approach to the Rehabilitation of Children with Muscular Dystrophy.* The Muscular Dystrophy Associations of America, New York.

PART II

Medical Care and Rehabilitation

You are the key person in your child's treatment. His doctors are going to have to count heavily on your help. So you need to understand something about the physicians' aims, not only in treatment but in rehabilitation.

What is rehabilitation? The National Council on Rehabilitation gives a formal definition: "The restoration of the handicapped to the fullest physical, mental, social, vocational, and economic usefulness of which they are capable." Such a broad aim requires a host of specialists: physicians, psychiatrists, surgeons of many kinds, nurses, physical occupation and speech therapists, together with social workers, psychologists, special teachers, chaplains, vocational counselors, and recreation directors. No single child needs all these services, but one with a serious disability usually requires a great deal more than one doctor alone can provide.

In rehabilitation the emphasis is on the individual's abilities rather than his disabilities. The famous Dr. Howard A. Rusk, world authority on rehabilitation and Director of the Institute of Physical Medicine and Rehabilitation in New York, said that the goal is to help the individual "to live within the limits of his disabilities but to the hilt of his capabilities." This new point of view has changed the whole approach of medical experts. There is almost always something more that can be done to improve the child's ability to live a personally satisfying life. *Although your child's disability may be plain for anyone to see, it may take expert diagnostic evaluation to discover his hidden abilities. Then come the planning and the treatment.*

The next five chapters describe the steps that will lead you to medical experts. They discuss diagnostic evaluation, certain aspects of medical management, your relationships with doctors, problems of hospitalization and its effects on children. Some of the most common types of therapy are also described.

5

YOUR SEARCH
FOR MEDICAL CARE

You can expect to meet problems of one kind or another in your search for medical care. If plenty of specialists and facilities are available, you may not know which ones are best for your child. Or you may find that the experts your child needs are not readily accessible. He may require a complex program involving both medical and nonmedical specialists and a variety of hospitals, clinics, or rehabilitation centers. In some areas such services are simply not to be found. If you encounter a maze of problems, how can you find your way?

A Doctor as Your Guide. Before medicine became so specialized, the family doctor traditionally gave patients all their medical guidance and treatment. But this situation has changed, especially in large cities. Specialization has great advantages: there is a lot to know about each disease and its treatment, and no one doctor can do justice to all of them. Nowadays any doctor guides his patients to appropriate specialists when he sees the need. But still, a child (or adult) needs one doctor who is responsible for providing over-all supervision. For the handicapped child he may be a general practitioner, a pediatrician, or a specialist in the area of the child's disability. If you find such a doctor and stick with him, your child's care will have continuity, year after year. This doctor carries the *central* responsibility for the care, acting in a sense as a medical manager. He helps you select other specialists or the clinic, hospital, or rehabilitation center. He can often help make arrangements for your child's admission.

In sharing responsibility with the other specialists, he usually gives them a medical history and confers with them about the diagnosis and about a long-range plan of health care tailored to your child's needs. He receives reports of your child's progress from the others and discusses them with you. The child knows that this physician is "his" doctor. This feeling is very reassuring to a child who has brief contacts with a succession of unfamiliar specialists.

Some of the Medical Specialists. The *pediatrician* is a specialist in the general health care of children. He is especially well informed about child growth and development. He is aware of the changing problems that the disability may cause as the child grows up.

The *orthopedic surgeon* specializes in correcting deformities or injuries to bones, joints, or muscles, by means of surgery or splints or physical therapy. He often calls on the prosthetist, who makes and fits artificial limbs, hands, feet, or other replacements for parts of the body.

Physical medicine and rehabilitation is one of the newer specialties. A physician in this field is called a *physiatrist*. His special skills include massage, heat, light, exercise, bracing, and some other nonsurgical methods of treatment.

The *neurologist* specializes in physical diseases of the brain and nerves. He is often called on to diagnose and treat such conditions as cerebral palsy, epilepsy, and muscular dystrophy.

Because many children with crippling disabilities have urinary problems, the *urologist* may be called upon. Paraplegic children, for example, require special treatment to prevent urinary infections and to work out the control of the bladder and bowels.

The *psychiatrist* is a physician who helps out with emotional problems. Many handicapped children need this assistance, and so do many parents.

The *otolaryngologist,* who treats diseases of the ear, throat, and larynx, often works with the *audiologist,* who specializes in the study of hearing impairment, and with the *speech therapist.*

The *ophthalmologist,* or *oculist,* is a physician whose concern is with the eyes. (The optometrist, or optician, is not a physician. He is trained to fill the ophthalmologist's prescription for glasses.)

Still other specialists may be called upon, such as the

cardiologist, who specializes in disorders of the heart and circulatory system, or the *plastic surgeon,* who is skilled in correcting such impairments as cleft palate.

"Paramedical" Personnel. The nonmedical experts often render as important a service to the handicapped child as does the doctor. They are sometimes called "paramedical" because they work beside the doctor. Like physicians, they qualify for their work through specific professional education. Included in this broad category are orthopedic nurses, pediatric nurses, public health nurses; physical, occupational, speech, and play therapists; psychologists, social workers, recreation leaders, vocational counselors, special teachers. In some hospitals and rehabilitation centers ministers trained in pastoral counseling have a significant role in the rehabilitation program.

Getting Acquainted with the Social Worker. There are social workers on the staffs of most hospitals, clinics, organizations for the handicapped, as well as family social agencies. (A majority of these are women.) The social worker is able to help you work out various problems in the fields of family relations, community resources, finances, etc. Because she is specially trained to understand people's feelings, it may be easier to talk with her than with other professional people about the tensions that arise around the care of a disabled child.

Also, if you can give the social worker a realistic picture of the family and home situation, this will enable the other rehabilitation specialists working with your child to take full account of the advantages and limitations that exist at home. Because the social worker knows the community's facilities, she can help you make contacts with clinics, locate sources of nursing care or recreation, or find out about vocational training or special education. She may help you sort out the facts on which to base your decision about placing your child in an institution, or suggest new arrangements for meeting mounting medical costs. She won't make decisions for you, but will help you see the factors in your situation more objectively so that you can make the best decisions.

Some people think that a social worker is involved only in "welfare" or "charity" cases. The fact is that the social worker's special knowledge is useful to all people who have problems, including the well-organized and the well-to-do.

Selecting the Specialists. If a person looks for a specialist on his own, he takes certain risks. In effect he is making his own diagnosis. He is saying, "I think this is what is the matter with my child, and so I am taking him to Doctor So-and-so, who is a specialist in that field." If he is wrong, he may have wasted money and he may have delayed his child's proper treatment. It's hard to believe, but many people turn for advice to relatives, friends, neighbors, the corner druggist, or even a friendly store clerk rather than to a doctor. A recent nationwide survey disclosed that more than four out of ten persons chose their medical specialists on the recommendations of such nonmedical advisers.[1]

The person usually in the best position to select the right specialist is the family doctor, whether he is a general practitioner, an internist, or a pediatrician. But if you don't have a family doctor you can turn to other reliable medical sources. Many departments of health run child health centers (or "child health conferences") which provide general health supervision. After they have examined your child, the physicians there can guide you to suitable specialists or treatment centers. By inquiring at the local board of health or medical society, you can find out whether there are clinics for handicapped children in your community. If your child's handicap has already been diagnosed, you can inquire for a clinic that treats his particular type of disability. If you prefer specialists in private practice, the local medical society will give you the names of several.

You can look up certain facts about a physician in the *American Medical Directory,* published by the American Medical Association. (Your public library probably has it.) It lists all the licensed physicians in the United States and Canada by geographical area, giving each doctor's age, school, and date of graduation, whether he specializes, whether he has been certified as a specialist by one of the specialty boards, his membership in medical societies, his affiliations with hospitals.

Various Patterns of Medical Care. If the family can afford private care in all respects, the family doctor or the pediatrician refers the child to the specialist or specialists, and all the physicians continue to play their particular parts in caring for the child. Sometimes the child is referred by his own doctor to a special clinic or rehabilitation center where he receives the attention of all the staff people who are appropriate for his case.

Sometimes the specialists are consulted only for diagnosis and recommendations and the child's regular doctor has the responsibility for seeing that the treatment is carried out, with periodic consultations with the specialist to evaluate the child's progress.

Children from families who have no regular doctor may be referred to a special clinic by the school nurse, a public health nurse, or some health or family agency. In this case, the specialists in the clinic may be the sole source of the child's medical care. And if the child has several disabilities he may have to go to separate specialty clinics. In such cases it is particularly important for him to have one general doctor who is familiar with the whole picture, who has the confidence of the child, and who can advise the parents with the total situation in mind. If your child is dependent entirely on specialty clinic care and you feel that there are gaps in his health supervision, consult with someone on the clinic staff for ways to remedy this.

The importance of teamwork in rehabilitation has been receiving more and more attention. Teamwork is highly developed in some centers; all the specialists on one case meet together in regular staff conferences to compare notes on progress and to plan the next steps in treatment.

INVESTIGATING THE RESOURCES OF YOUR COMMUNITY

Your regular doctor has the job of recommending appropriate facilities or institutions as well as specialists, but the final decision in each instance remains yours. You can discuss the pros and cons with him more intelligently if you yourself also know about what is available.

Using Local Sources of Information. Where do you find a brace maker? Where can a blind child enjoy recreation? Where is speech therapy given? Who makes specially adapted eating utensils for a child with cerebral palsy? Do any community organizations provide camp scholarships for handicapped children?

Most likely the specialists who are taking care of your

child will guide you. But if not, your local or state health department, a family social agency, or an organization working with a specific handicap may be the best source of information. Some areas have a "council of social agencies" which is acquainted with all the services available in the community. Or you can call the headquarters of your Red Feather organization. A children's aid society or the child welfare division of the Public Welfare Department or the visiting nurse association may have the information you want.

Can Your Child Be Treated in Your Home Community?
You will naturally want to canvass the possibility of getting care in your home area before you think about going far away. But in this age of good roads and automobiles, parents can often use treatment facilities that are moderately distant from home without great inconvenience. The advantages and disadvantages of different solutions should be discussed between parents and doctor. In some cases the child may benefit by being placed in a hospital, a convalescent home, or a foster home for a while so that he is spared the fatigue of frequent trips. Occasionally the best solution is for the family to make a permanent move.

Should your child need to go away from home for part of his treatment, your doctor will help you make the necessary advance arrangements. Don't dash off without notice to some famous clinic or medical center. You will meet heartbreaking disappointment if the waiting list is long or if the clinic doesn't treat the type of disability that affects your child.

Clinics. Clinics are the most widely used special facilities for handicapped children. They are most often part of a general hospital or a specialty hospital. But clinics are also run by health departments and by organizations established especially to care for people with one certain disease or another. In some rural areas, itinerant (visiting) clinics are held periodically under the direction of a central agency such as the state department of health. Some clinics are limited to diagnostic services; others provide both diagnosis and treatment. Some treat only one type of disability; others treat a wide variety of handicaps.

It's a mistake to assume that clinics limit service to families who are unable to pay. Some do, but this is by no means true of all clinics. Many have a schedule of fees based on the ability to pay. If you find that a certain clinic has the specialists you need and can give your child excellent care, there is no reason for you to assume that you will not be welcome there just because you can afford private treatment.

Hospitals. Most disabled children who need hospital care can find it in their communities or near by. A few who require highly specialized attention may be forced to go some distance. For example, not every hospital is equipped with staff or facilities to do heart surgery, and certain centers are known to be outstanding in that work.

Rehabilitation Centers. Rehabilitation centers vary widely. Some provide inpatient care, others only outpatient service. Some are connected with medical centers or local hospitals; others are independent community projects. The program may provide both diagnostic evaluation and treatment. Treatment often includes physical, occupational, or speech therapy, play therapy, nursing care, fitting of prostheses, and training in their use. There may also be social service, psychological testing, psychiatric counseling, and educational counseling. Some have special programs such as adult education, nursery schools for preschool handicapped children, lip-reading instruction for deaf children. Recreation may be part of the program. Vocational evaluation and counseling are often found, but vocational training and sheltered workshop employment are less common.

You can find out from your department of health, or from other sources mentioned earlier, whether there is a rehabilitation center near enough for your child to use and what services it offers.

Convalescent Homes. Convalescent homes serve the children who still need rest, nursing care, and medical supervision but do not require full-scale hospital care any longer, most commonly those with orthopedic, cardiac, and rheumatic conditions. There are relatively few of them, but they fill a great need for the child who cannot be cared for at home. In addition to physical care, they should provide education, recreation, and vocational services for children who can profit by them.

Institutional Care. Several kinds of institutions other than hospitals offer residential care to seriously handicapped children, such as the retarded, the blind, the hard-of-hearing. If you have decided to place your child in a residential institution, finding the right one is an urgent matter. The best sources of information have already been mentioned, and further suggestions are made in Chapter 12. One useful directory, revised frequently, is prepared by Porter Sargent, Publisher, of Boston. It is called the *Directory for Exceptional Children.*

Community Resources for Home Care. A small but growing number of hospitals are providing organized home care programs for patients who don't really need full-scale hospital services but who need more medical care than they can ordinarily be given at home. A doctor from the hospital staff is usually in charge, and a nurse from the hospital goes into the patient's home regularly to give nursing care. Some form of rehabilitation therapy or even housekeeping may be provided. It is worth asking your doctor whether there is such a program in your area.

If your child should need temporary placement in a foster home in another community to be nearer to medical facilities, make your arrangements through a recognized family or children's social agency, set up to supervise foster home placements. There may be such an agency in your area or in your state department of child welfare.

Federal-State Programs for Handicapped Children. Every state now has an official agency to provide medical services for handicapped children. They served 339,000 children in 1959.[2] (Many of them are still called by the old-fashioned name of state crippled children's agency.) They are usually part of the state department of health.

These programs are financed by state and local funds, supplemented by federal appropriations that are administered by the Children's Bureau. Each state decides which handicapping conditions will be cared for in its program and which services will be supplied. But each program must meet certain standards to receive federal funds. For one thing, the federal standards require the agency to provide free diagnostic services for any child who is brought to the state clinics for handicapped children.

When staff members have studied a child they advise the parents about treatment. If the parents wish it, the agency helps them find the treatment facilities. In some areas where facilities are not otherwise available, the state agency operates a treatment clinic or convalescent home. If a child has to remain near a clinic or treatment center for continued treatment, the state agency may make arrangements for placing him in a convalescent or foster home for that period of time. If the parents cannot afford the recommended treatment, the state agency may bear the expense of it.

All states serve children under 21 whose handicap calls for orthopedic care or plastic surgery. This includes children with cleft lip or palate, club foot, deformed bones, and children who have been so seriously burned that plastic surgery is needed. Almost all state agencies serve children with polio and children with bone and joint tuberculosis. All the states give help to children with cerebral palsy. Over half of the states treat children with rheumatic fever and heart trouble. Some offer services to children with epilepsy, some to those with serious eye or ear impairments. The tendency now is to broaden the kinds of disability to be treated, though there are still some diseases that very few state programs include.

Federal-state clinics vary a great deal in the extent of their services. Some are run with only one doctor and one nurse. Clinics offering comprehensive diagnosis and treatment programs may have a very large professional staff. Some clinics travel from place to place and may come to your area at least infrequently. Others are permanently located and hold frequent sessions. You can find out from your state headquarters how your locality is served. If it depends on a traveling clinic, the dates are usually well advertised in local newspapers.

The state agencies work closely with state departments of education and divisions of vocational rehabilitation to coordinate plans for the child's schooling so that he can keep up with his educational program and prepare for his future.

Through special grants, the Children's Bureau of the federal government has made it possible for children who require heart surgery but live in places remote from qualified specialists to travel to regional centers serving a number of states where such specialists are available. In some circumstances, expenses are paid by the state program for handicapped children. Through other special grants the Children's Bureau has financed a special center for child amputees where medical care, appliances, and training in their use are given to children who are unable to obtain these services in their own states.

Voluntary Agency Programs. More than 100,000 national and local "voluntary" (nongovernmental) health and welfare agencies now solicit contributions totaling a billion and a half dollars annually from the general public. Many of these agencies aid the handicapped. Some, particularly the national organizations, concentrate on research or on education of the public or on education of the parents of handicapped children, to help them understand their own and their children's problems. Others, particularly the local agencies, support clinics or provide individual or group therapy. They may arrange transportation, day care, recreational programs, or camping opportunities, or support vocational programs. Some provide financial aid to families who cannot meet the costs of treatment or equipment or medications. Others establish special schools or educational programs for the handicapped. This list is far from complete, but it suggests the kinds of help you will find.

Transportation. Transportation to and from the treatment center often presents a problem. In some areas volunteer organizations, such as the American Red Cross or the Cerebral Palsy Association, arrange transportation. Inquiries through the local sources mentioned earlier may lead you to this service. If not, you might try to interest some volunteer group in organizing it.

REFERENCES

1. Jacob J. Feldman, Paul Sheatsley, and Odin W. Anderson. *What the Public Knows, Thinks, and Does about Health and Medical Care.* Health Information Foundation, Research Series No. 23. Chicago, University of Chicago Press, 1963.

2. *Annual Report, 1961,* U.S. Department of Health, Education, and Welfare. Washington, U.S. Government Printing Office.

6

MEDICAL MANAGEMENT IN YOUR CHILD'S LIFE

A reliable diagnosis is the very foundation of any medical care program. The earlier it is made, and the sooner treatment is begun, the greater are the child's chances for improvement. Club foot can usually be corrected if treatment is begun in the earliest weeks of the baby's life. A child born with a dislocated hip has good prospects for its correction if he is treated before he has begun to stand or walk. Early recognition of congenital deafness is necessary not only to start teaching lip reading but also to avoid creating emotional problems.

This does not mean, of course, that it is ever too late to start treatment. With modern methods of rehabilitation many people who for years have been considered "helpless cripples" have shown improvement.

Sometimes parents put off going to a doctor because they keep hoping that the condition they have noticed does not mean anything serious. At the same time, they may fear that the doctor might confirm their worst suspicions. In other cases they are worried about the dangers of the anticipated treatment, such as surgery for congenital heart disease. Or they can't face the prospect of prolonged hospitalization for a very young and dependent child. They may be so ashamed of the disability that they can't bear to have even professional attention directed to it. Some parents delay because they have convinced themselves that their child "will grow out of it." A few children do outgrow early disabilities, but you won't know whether this is possible for your child unless you consult a doctor.

Another quite common obstacle to early treatment is the

tendency of some parents to go from one doctor to the next, looking for one whose opinion coincides with what they hope to hear. If one doctor makes a discouraging diagnosis, they may accuse him of being careless or incompetent. Perhaps their child is mentally retarded but they want to believe he is merely "developing slowly." Or the diagnosis of epilepsy has been made but they feel sure that their child has nothing more serious than fainting spells.

When parents have finally accepted a diagnosis they may lose more valuable time looking for anyone who will promise a complete cure, when no such result is possible. Then they readily fall into the hands of quacks and charlatans. The temptation to "shop around" is particularly strong in those types of disability about which even the most enthusiastic kinds of doctors have little encouragement to offer. There are parents who feel so deeply to blame for their child's handicap that it actually gives them relief to go to the great expense of consulting one doctor after another.

Another reason parents go shopping for a new doctor is because the previous one hasn't given them adequate information. Some doctors just don't realize how much parents need full explanations. When parents fail to understand what the doctor is planning and doing for their child, they easily become dissatisfied and go elsewhere. If you feel that "doctors never tell you anything," you should insist on fuller explanations. Your doctor may be so used to his technical shop talk that he doesn't realize that he has failed to translate it for you.

Of course some doctors make mistakes, and no one doctor has a personality that suits all patients. If you are dissatisfied with the diagnosis or the treatment, you can always ask for a consultation. If you can't hit it off with your doctor after several attempts, you can change doctors entirely. But if you have been on a prolonged medical shopping tour, you ought to examine the causes. It may be that you are dodging the truth about your child's condition. When responsible physicians have examined your child thoroughly, outlined a plan of treatment and discussed it with you, medical shopping is a terrible waste of time and money and effort.

Diagnostic Evaluation in Rehabilitation. You ask your doctor, "What can be done to help my child? Will he get better? What is the outlook for his future?" The doctor may feel that your child needs to be examined by several specialists before he can know the answers. The examining experts consider the extent of the involvement, the degree of handicap, and the effect of the disability on the child's physical, mental, social, and emotional life. At the same time, they appraise the child's assets and potentialities. The complete "work-up" of the child's case, bringing together the observations and opinions of all the specialists, becomes the basis for a plan for medical care and rehabilitation.

Diagnostic evaluation should put the emphasis on what the child *can* do instead of what he *cannot* do. It helps the medical specialists to maintain perspective, too. A doctor without much training in the philosophy of rehabilitation may be so keen to discover exactly what is wrong that he overlooks the importance of helping parents appreciate what is right with their child. But if he is working as one of a team of specialists, he must also take part in making a plan for development of the child's capacities.

One evaluation isn't always enough, because the child is growing and changing. Successive evaluations have to take account of changes in the disability and in the child's ability to cope with it.

THE GENERAL SCOPE OF DIAGNOSTIC EVALUATION

Many questions have to be included in the evaluation—medical, psychological, familial, financial. For example, a child with a paralyzed leg may have braces prescribed; but the doctor must also be concerned with the reasons for his overweight, if that is of any consequence. The child's inner strengths and weaknesses determine how he copes with his disability, and so the physician may call on the psychologist to observe and test the child. Information about parent-child relationships, home environment, community background, and the financial resources of the family may also be important in the evaluation.

General Health Appraisal. Usually a complete general health examination is needed, including the history of previous illnesses, infection or accidents, the reasons for earlier medical or surgical care, the mother's health during pregnancy, and delivery.

Medical Appraisal of the Disability. Orthopedic examination is needed if the child's muscles, bones, or joints are affected, in such disorders, for instance, as cerebral palsy, polio, muscular dystrophy, club foot, dislocation of the hip, arthritis. An inventory is made of the child's abilities in the activities of daily living and self-care to find out just how extensively the illness has handicapped him and what special training he needs.

Neurological examination is called for when conditions causing impairment of the brain or nervous system are suspected. Included are cerebral palsy and polio again, epilepsy, mental retardation, and a variety of much rarer diseases. The neurologist painstakingly checks the sensation, the motor power, the reflexes of every part of the body, and he may also utilize the encephalogram to test the normality of the "brain waves."

Diagnosis of speech impairment often requires examination by several specialists, since it may arise from such varied causes as cleft palate, deafness, mental retardation, or emotional disturbance. The ears of the child who is hard of hearing must be examined by the otologist (who is a physician), and his hearing is tested in great detail by the audiologist. The child with imperfect vision needs to be examined by the ophthalmologist.

Psychiatric examination is often very useful in the evaluation of the child's assets and liabilities. To include it doesn't mean that a child is mentally ill; it helps determine the causes of the emotional and behavior problems that interfere so often with the rehabilitation of handicapped children and how they can be alleviated.

Psychological Evaluation. Knowledge of your child's level of mental ability is a key to selecting the proper school, deciding whether he should go to college, and choosing a vocation. An elaborate process of psychological testing isn't always necessary. The doctors and you may know enough about the child through your observations of his behavior combined with school records and reports from his teachers. This is usually so for a well-adjusted, intelligent child.

In many cases, however, it is impossible to determine the child's personality and intelligence by commonsense observation. For example, a normally intelligent child with cleft palate may be considered mentally backward because of his speech problems. Or a retarded child with pleasing manners may be thought so much brighter than he is that too much is expected of him. Psychological testing usually gives an accurate estimate of the child's capacities. (See Chapter 11.)

Some Examples of Diagnostic Evaluation. One or two examples will show how diagnostic evaluation may be carried out and used as the basis for setting up a plan of treatment.

At the suggestion of the family doctor who had delivered the child, a mother brought her very young baby who had club feet to an orthopedic clinic in a rural area. There they were seen by the pediatrician, the orthopedic surgeon, his nurse, and the social worker. The pediatrician's examination showed that the baby was in good health except for his feet. The orthopedic surgeon applied splints and bandages to the baby's feet and told the mother how to take care of him between clinic visits. She seemed confident that she could do it and readily agreed to the schedule of return trips to the clinic. The diagnosis of a simple disability and the plan of treatment were quickly made by a small medical team working with an adaptable mother.

Bill's case was more complicated. He was a ten-year-old whose legs were paralyzed during an illness. After he recovered he had a severe lumbar lordosis, or "hollow back," with hip contractures, and could stand erect only by bending his knees and walking on his toes. He had another problem in bed-wetting. When his mother finally took him to an orthopedic clinic in a large hospital, a pediatrician examined Bill and a social worker talked with his mother. Bill and his mother attended a conference with the clinic staff where the pediatrician, an orthopedic surgeon, a psychologist, a psychiatrist, a physical therapist, and a social worker were present. Before Bill and his mother came, the pediatrician summarized Bill's physical condition.

During the conference, Bill showed the group how he walked, and the orthopedic surgeon examined him. The mother had a chance to ask questions and to mention her anxiety over the fact that Bill was not in school. After mother and son left, the staff group discussed Bill's problems. The orthopedic surgeon recommended six to eight weeks of intensive physical therapy at once, to be followed immediately by surgery if Bill's posture failed to improve. The pediatrician proposed that Bill be examined by a urologist to find out whether there were any physical causes of the bed-wetting, and that he be checked at the psychiatric clinic to see whether the bed-wetting was a symptom of emotional problems for which he needed psychiatric help.

It was agreed that the pediatrician and the social worker could discuss these recommendations with Bill's mother and that they would be her regular advisers so that Bill and she would not feel lost in the long-term, complex medical program that lay ahead. The full clinic staff would continue to pool their ideas about treatment and would periodically appraise his progress. Fortunately, all the needed treatment facilities were at hand in this one large medical center.

Regularly scheduled talks with the doctor in charge of their child's treatment are usually the keystone of the plan to help the family adjust to the problems they face and thus to help the child. Often a social worker or a nurse is available to answer questions, clear up points of confusion, and help in such practical matters as referrals to another clinic. There may be a social worker or other member of the team specially appointed for counseling with parents on their problems in parent-child relationships or on decisions about their child's schooling. In some centers, parents are invited to meet in groups to discuss such questions under the leadership of a specially trained person.

The Long-term View of Treatment. When the diagnostic studies of your child have been completed, your doctor will discuss with you the immediate treatment he proposes and perhaps some aspects of the long-range medical care. The timing of treatment is sometimes of great importance; that is to say, a particular type of treatment, in order to be most beneficial, may need to be given at a certain stage of the child's growth. An operation early in the first year usually brings the best results in correcting a cleft lip, whereas the best time to operate for the same child's cleft palate may be anywhere between eighteen months and six years.

In some cases the doctor can tell parents what to anticipate and help them plan ahead quite definitely. For example a child who has been fitted with a brace and special shoes will surely outgrow the shoes at fairly frequent intervals and the braces will go out of adjustment eventually. A baby born without a hand will require changes in his prosthesis periodically as he grows older. But another child's treatment can be planned only step by step, for the doctor must await the outcome of one phase before deciding about the next. Moreover, the child's needs may change radically and unpredictably from time to time. Continuous medical supervision is obviously necessary to maintain improvement.

The child's *total* health needs must be cared for, too. He should have the benefit of periodic medical and dental check-ups, protection through immunization, regular supervision of his diet and general health habits, and medical care for any illnesses or accidents.

SOME WIDELY USED TREATMENTS

Special Therapies. Physical therapy, speech therapy, and occupational therapy are so widely used that an entire chapter will be devoted to them at the end of this section.

Surgery. Surgery is used to treat such birth defects as club foot, dislocated hip, spina bifida, cleft lip, and cleft palate. New methods of heart surgery help more and more children: it is estimated that about 80 per cent of children with serious congenital heart defects can be helped by operations.[1] Some children with cerebral palsy benefit by orthopedic surgery. Plastic surgery can improve a child's appearance or improve his use of a part of the body, as when scar tissue from a burn interferes with the use of a joint. Some eye defects and some hearing impairments are helped by surgery.

The risks of surgery have been tremendously reduced at the same time as new skills and techniques have rapidly developed. Nevertheless, surgery is a big step. The decision to operate is made only after careful consultation. If you have any doubts you should discuss them freely and frankly with the doctor before you agree to the operation. Parents of children with all sorts of handicaps would like a miraculous cure through surgery, but of course there are many more conditions that can't be helped by surgery than can.

Drugs, Medication, and Antibiotics. Though most handicaps can't be cured by drugs, medication plays an important part in the care and treatment of some diseases. The diabetic is saved by insulin. The seizures of the child with epilepsy and the child with cerebral palsy can usually be prevented or greatly reduced by means of correctly prescribed drugs. The

child with rheumatic fever will need medication to control
infection and prevent reinfection; this also applies to children whose disabilities make respiratory infections particularly hazardous, such as cystic fibrosis. Some arthritic
children are helped by medication, and new drugs are increasingly successful in the treatment of tuberculosis.

Dental Care. Regular dental care is more than ordinarily
important for certain children. Those who have heart disease
need regular preventive dental care to reduce the need for
tooth extractions. If dental surgery does become necessary,
the dentist should of course be told that the child has heart
trouble so that he can take precautions.

Children with cleft lip or cleft palate often have dental
problems. Some have teeth missing, others have extra teeth
or poor position of teeth. Dental specialists can correct mal-
positions. They also prepare dental plates when a cleft palate
has not been corrected by surgery.

Dental care for the cerebral-palsied child may be especially urgent. If for one reason or another the development of
his teeth is delayed or faulty, and if his tongue makes a great
many abnormal motions, the shape of the roof and the position of the teeth may be affected so that the teeth don't meet
in a good bite. Involuntary movements of the chewing muscles may result in tooth grinding that wears down the biting
surfaces. A child who falls down often runs the additional
risk of breaking his teeth. Furthermore, it may be hard for
him to clean his teeth if he can't use his hands efficiently. Taking the child to the dentist regularly from his early years
helps, but many of these children require the attention of a
specially trained dentist.

In some cities, the local cerebral palsy association lists
dentists and dental clinics prepared to serve children with
cerebral palsy. Some dentists are very skillful in helping
the child relax, but for some children a sedative, or even a
general anesthetic, is necessary. This is also true for children with certain other disabilities. The important thing is
to find a dentist who has had experience with handicapped
children and wants to help them.

Hopes for Improvement. When your child's doctor proposes a plan of treatment, you will want to know just what
improvement he expects. He may be aiming for a more
limited goal than you had hoped for. He may be expecting
that perhaps the child can learn to walk with crutches,

whereas you had hoped that he could walk without them. But improvements that seem limited to you may open new vistas in your child's life. A youngster using braces and crutches learns to go up and down a curb and two steps—a small thing—but it opens the way for him to use the city's buses and to travel independently to school or to work.

It's fine to hope for a little more improvement than the doctor promises—after all, some doctors are very cautious in their expectations—so long as you carry out the treatment and protect yourself and your child against disappointments. Concentrate your efforts first on the things your child can learn to do, so that he has the satisfaction of succeeding. Cultivate the habit of taking pleasure in each small step, even such little ones as learning to lace shoes or drink through a straw. When your child sees your pleasure and your confidence in him, he will be encouraged to keep trying.

Some courageous children have succeeded in mastering disability to a far greater extent than ever seemed possible, so a thoughtful doctor hesitates to say with finality, "Your child's accomplishments will never go beyond this limit." But he generally does you a kindness when he keeps your expectations within realistic bounds.

"He'll Grow Out of It." A doctor may say to parents, "Don't worry, he'll grow out of it." Sometimes a child does outgrow a disability or a delay in development. But in other cases he does not. Then parents may be understandably resentful.

When a doctor sees a baby whose development is slow, or is different from that of other children, he will examine him as carefully as seems necessary. If the results show no disease to explain the delay or the difference, he points out that wide variations in the rate of development are perfectly normal. He usually advises the parents to bring the child back for continued medical observation as long as there is the least doubt.

Of course there are occasions when a doctor is mistaken in believing that a child's delay in development is within the normal range. On the other hand he may be mistaken in concluding that there is an abnormality. If a doctor is more reassuring or, for that matter, more pessimistic about a child's development than seems justified to the parents, they can always ask for a consultation. They can even change doctors.

Dependence and Independence toward Treatment. A child is expected to work actively in his program of treatment. Self-help is basic to rehabilitation. He'll need to learn new skills, and learning takes place only when he makes the effort himself. The specialists and parents are only teachers. So there is great emphasis on independent effort. At the same time, the child has to adjust to dependence—for example, to learn to accept help without losing self-respect.

Sometimes a child and his family are kept so busy carrying out the doctor's orders that his daily life is completely dominated by his care. Or the parents become so wrapped up in it that they treat all their conversation with the child as a drill in speech therapy, or think that all his toys and play activities should be used only for the purposes of occupational therapy. The child may be so overwhelmed by the earnestness of doctors and parents that he becomes too docile and compliant instead of self-confident and independent.

A child whose life is full of medical regulations and supervision still needs opportunities to use his initiative. There are scores of decisions that you can encourage him to make for himself: selecting his clothes, his hobbies, his books, gifts for his friends. Include him in family councils and let him know that you listen to his opinions.

Initiative can play an important role in medical treatment, too. In studying the life histories of more than a thousand persons with cerebral palsy, Dr. Bronson Crothers and Dr. Richmond S. Paine found a number of cases in which, although the *conventional* methods of physical treatment failed, children had gained great competence by working out their own solutions.[2] One boy learned to turn the pages of a book with his mouth while he confined his arms beneath the table in order to limit their involuntary thrashing movements. Others learned to write by holding a pencil in the mouth. The doctor who has seen a child through a comprehensive program of diagnosis and treatment is usually able to appraise the child's abilities pretty well, but now and then a child has such determination that he confounds the predictions.

Parents expect children to show some resistance to adult authority, especially during adolescence. But what if the child rebels against the doctor's instructions? Generally there can be little argument—the treatment is absolutely necessary. But sometimes a child's resistance may be justified. Certainly a frank discussion with the professional people is worthwhile.

If a child refuses to do some of the things the doctor has recommended and parents feel sympathetic with him, they will be tempted to not tell the doctor. This misleads the doctor and may confuse the whole treatment program. It's much better to discuss the objections with him honestly so that everyone concerned can re-examine the situation and reach agreement about what should be done.

Sometimes parents worry that their child will be spoiled by the extra attention his medical care requires. Giving him the help he truly needs is not spoiling him. In fact, sure knowledge that he can count on his parents for the help he really needs will enable the child to meet life with greater confidence. On the other hand if parents continually give the child help he does *not* need they may well be spoiling him. He learns to expect special favors and, at the same time, he is deprived of the pleasure and growth that come of doing things for himself. Admittedly, it isn't always easy to know the difference. This is an area in which parents usually need regular counseling.

We have to admit that sometimes the success of therapy and medical treatment is very limited. If this should happen in your family, it would of course be disappointing both to you and to your child. You would have to be careful not to blame the child or show disapproval. He would need your confidence and support more than ever. If and when the time comes to discontinue treatment, you should redouble your other productive efforts: education, vocational training, cultural pursuits—in the long run, these will make the big difference.

REFERENCES

1. Arthur J. Lesser. "Health Services—Accomplishments and Outlook." *Children,* Vol. 7: No. 4, July-August 1960.

2. Bronson Crothers and Richmond S. Paine. *The Natural History of Cerebral Palsy.* Cambridge, Harvard University Press, 1959.

7

YOU, YOUR CHILD,
AND THE DOCTORS

You'll be having a prolonged relationship with medical people and so there may well be times when you will disagree with some of their advice. After all, who knows the child best? Who knows what's good for him? You feel that your opinions should at least be carefully considered; yet you wonder whether you have the right to question the medical people's judgment—or whether they think you have the right.

If the expertness of the experts begins to overwhelm you, remember that they are dependent upon you for success, just as you and your child are dependent upon them. Teamwork in rehabilitation can't operate to full advantage unless parents are on the team too. You belong because you have the most intimate knowledge of your child and because no one else can do as much for him.

Professional people don't all have the same attitude, any more than lay people do. You may be dealing with one who seems to discount the value of parents' opinions, explains very little to them, expects them merely to follow directions. Some doctors have had unfortunate experiences with parents who have made mistakes with their handicapped child, and so they throw up their hands and exclaim, "The trouble with children is their parents!" However, some such doctors may be highly skillful and helpful despite this attitude. The smart patient or parent may have to learn how to get along with the difficult doctor, just as the smart doctor has to learn to get along with the difficult patient.

THE PARENTS' ROLE

Following Through. One of the most important practical things a parent can do to facilitate a child's medical care is to keep appointments and follow instructions. This usually requires unremitting perseverance through many years.

If the child is a patient in a large busy clinic, parents may have to keep a sharp eye out to see that he doesn't get lost in red tape or accidentally dropped from a waiting list. You must know who is in charge of his case and keep track of the schedule of his examinations or treatments.

Asking Questions. A study of the clinic experience of a large number of parents of disabled children showed that communication between professionals and parents is often shockingly inadequate. The blame for communication failure can't be placed clearly on either side. Some professionals are so accustomed to using technical language that they forget that parents don't understand it. And some parents "listen" to a clear explanation but don't "hear" it—either because they are too anxious or because the conclusions are unwelcome.

Sometimes parents' awe of the experts leaves them tongue-tied. Yet the information they want may be essential to the proper carrying out of their responsibilities. So don't be afraid to ask questions. The doctor may not be at all aware of what you know and don't know.

If your child has been referred to the clinic by a doctor, reports on the diagnosis and results of treatment should be sent by the clinic to him, and he should then discuss them with you. However, reports may not always be sent to him. Then either you or he should keep after the clinic. If your child was not referred to the clinic by a doctor, reports of his progress should be discussed with you by someone on the clinic staff. You should find out who has this responsibility for communication.

Accepting Parental Responsibility. As your child's parents you have the final responsibility for him. You take a large part of this responsibility first of all when you choose the doctor; you are making a basic decision to rely on his medical judgment.

Yet there are many aspects of care in which the parents' knowledge of their child is as crucial as the doctor's knowledge of medical science. Parents have many decisions to make—whether to send their child to a special school for the handicapped or to a regular school; whether to place him in an institution or to care for him at home; whether to risk surgery. They must make the decisions in the light of the total family picture.

When two medical experts disagree about medical procedures for a child, parents carry an especially difficult responsibility. Some parents find it easy to follow the advice of the doctor in whom they have most confidence. Others may want another, third opinion. (They should realize ahead of time that this sometimes complicates rather than clarifies the issues.) One solution is to take your child to a group of medical experts who are accustomed to working as a team, at a large medical or rehabilitation center.

Becoming Informed about the Disability. Some parents find it helpful to read about their child's disability. A lot of reliable books and pamphlets are available from government bureaus and from the health organizations concerned with specific disabilities. There are also popular magazine articles and books. It should be remembered, though, that much of it has to be oversimplified to serve the greatest number of people, so don't take it too literally. No matter how reliable the literature is, it doesn't apply equally to all cases. What may be true for your neighbor's child may not be so for yours. If you read something that seems to conflict with your child's treatment, don't jump to conclusions. Ask your doctor.

Newspapers often announce new discoveries in medicine and science, and you may well read about something that seems to promise great help for your child. But it's all too easy for a parent searching for a miracle to jump to the conclusion that a new discovery applies to his child when it really does not at all. Discuss such news stories with your doctor. But don't be surprised if his attitude is skeptical.

In some localities there are parents' groups that discuss and study a particular type of disability. Such a group may be an excellent source of information.

Keeping a Record. Even though your child's doctor—or

clinic or hospital—will keep medical records of his care, you should keep your own notebook for emergencies and for when you travel with your child. It should contain the names, addresses, and telephone numbers of his regular doctor and of any specialists who have been treating him, or of the hospital, clinic, or rehabilitation center in which he has been treated. A record of each date on which your child received medical attention, and the nature of the treatment, will be a great help sooner or later.

Ask the doctor whether it is important for you to have a written statement of the diagnosis of the child's disability, his medications, and any special precautions that are necessary. This information is of vital importance in such conditions as diabetes, epilepsy, some kinds of heart trouble, or hemophilia, for example. In the case of hemophilia, the child himself should always wear an identification tag giving his name and address, the type of deficiency, and his blood group type. Tags may be had from the National Hemophilia Foundation, 175 Fifth Avenue, New York City, or its local chapters. Your doctor can tell you whether your child should carry identifying information if he has any other condition that calls for emergency care.

If your child is dependent upon any mechanical aid, you should have available for ready reference whatever information is necessary for prompt replacement or repair—for example, the prescription for his glasses or information about places where hearing-aid batteries can be bought. A brace kit for minor emergency repairs may save your child discomfort and inconvenience if his brace should require slight adjustment. In any case, the address of the brace maker should be in your records.

If you are moving to another community, ask the doctor or clinic to prepare a report of your child's health history, with recommendations that have been made for his medical care in the future. The original records, such as x-ray photographs or electrocardiograms, probably will not be transferred, but the report should contain information about them for the benefit of the doctors who will care for the child in the new locality. Some doctors will give such a report only to another doctor; others will entrust it to the parents to pass along to the new doctor.

GETTING ALONG WITH THE DOCTORS

Your own confidence in the doctor and your child's trust in him are essential, of course. You lay the foundation for confidence when you select a doctor because you've been told that he (or the clinic in which he works) is well qualified. Then you will probably want to have a personal talk with him before any treatment begins, to be sure you understand and feel comfortable with him.

Some people place a blind belief in any doctor's ability to perform miracles, regardless of what he tells them. Doctors queried in a recent nationwide survey[1] said that this had often been their experience. Such parents, because they want so hard to believe in a complete cure, close their ears to any pessimistic word. They stretch the slightest word of hope to a promise. Then, if the miracle doesn't happen, they may blame the doctor for failure.

What the doctor actually accomplishes may result in one case in vast improvement for the child. In another it may fall short of what the parents hoped for. A child born with spina bifida, for example, may be able to establish effective toilet routines and thus be able to attend school. But if parents have set their hearts on the goal of his walking, even though they are told that it's impossible, their disappointment will prevent them from appreciating the real improvements.

Doctors appreciate confidence and trust. (In fact, they find it very uncomfortable to work with a dissatisfied family.) But no doctor wants to be considered a miracle worker when this imposes expectations beyond what is possible. A doctor knows that his patient's confidence in him is more solid when it is based on the recognition that doctors have limitations and that most medical procedures have elements of uncertainty.

Reaching an Understanding with the Doctor. Your relationship with your child's doctor is likely to be intimate and prolonged, so it's important to try to avoid misunderstandings—or to clear them up promptly. Frankness is sometimes difficult but it's essential.

You have a right to expect the doctor to be frank with you about the diagnosis of your child's disability and about the probabilities for improvement or recovery. On the basis of his experience, he will give you his carefully considered opinion. He may point out the uncertainties of his forecast. You should understand what treatment he proposes, what he thinks it may accomplish, and what risks it may involve. Tell him honestly what you hope for and ask him whether your hopes are reasonable. He can tell you whether you are expecting too much or too little, and you can adapt your attitude accordingly. If at any point you don't understand what the doctor has told you, speak up right away and ask for further explanation.

You and the doctor should discuss frankly the probable costs of the child's medical care and your ability to meet them. This is not a good time to let embarrassment stand in the way of a clear understanding. Most physicians feel responsible for helping parents work out a plan of medical care that is within their financial resources, perhaps with the help of community programs for handicapped children.

Sharing Responsibilities with the Doctor. You can help create the conditions that make it easy or difficult for the doctor to do his best for your child. Calling him just as soon as you have detected any trouble shows him that you are ready to cooperate. The average family doctor puts in about a sixty-hour work week; when you show you are considerate of his time and convenience, it helps establish a good relationship with him.

You also help the doctor when you give him full information. People withhold important information for a variety of reasons. They may be ashamed to tell the truth, perhaps about a family background of illness. They may be ashamed to admit that the school nurse warned them a year ago to take the child to a doctor. But the doctor isn't interested in placing blame. He wants the facts because this is the only way he can understand the whole picture.

You can also help the doctor by following his instructions strictly, whether they have to do with giving medicine at definite times, keeping appointments reliably, seeing that the child follows a diet, or supervising his use of appliances. Doctors differ widely in the extent to which they wish parents to use their own initiative. One may feel that if he gives clear instructions, parents should use common sense in following them and in knowing when to call on him for help. Another doctor may be very distrustful of a layman's judgment and tell the parents to call him no matter how trifling their questions. Naturally your actions will be guided by your own feelings as well as the preference of the doctor. If you need guidance, you should call him even if you think this may make him impatient.

You may find that with time you want to discuss with the doctor many decisions which ordinarily are strictly family matters. What school should your child attend? Can he go to school at all? Should he go to Sunday School, or is it too much effort for him? Should he go to camp? May your teenager try for a summer job? The doctor's familiarity with your child's condition can play a decisive role in many of these questions. It isn't always easy to know whether the medical or the nonmedical aspects are more important.

The Doctor and the Specialists. Ordinarily when a patient's doctor refers him to a specialist, the two physicians keep in touch with each other so that the regular doctor can be kept informed of his progress. There may be circumstances, however, when communication between them breaks down. This is more likely to happen when a child has been sent away from home for extended treatment.

Since it often works out that a child's regular doctor will become responsible for supervising his medical program at some future time, it is a courtesy for the parents to let the specialists know that they want the family doctor to be kept informed. Failure of the rehabilitation people to keep in touch with the patient's regular doctor is sometimes a cause of antagonism on the part of doctors toward rehabilitation.

Asking for a Consultation or Referral. The family doctor or pediatrician is usually the first person to suggest consultation with a specialist. Sometimes, however, parents want the reassurance of another opinion before the doctor has suggested it. It's much better to discuss the matter frankly with the doctor than to go on feeling uneasy and dissatisfied. Your doctor, as a rule, would prefer to know what is on your mind and to bring in a consultant when the situation warrants it, for he works under a handicap when you aren't satisfied.

Usually it is better to try to resolve your doubts through consultation than to quit one doctor for another. Sometimes a consultation clears up your doubts and results in greater confidence in the original doctor. This is an advantage, because steady medical care has positive values for the child.

A needless change means the loss of the first doctor's experience and observations and loss of time: the new doctor has to start from the beginning.

Changing Doctors.   If you should decide that the physician who has been treating your child is not the right one, be straightforward about it and tell him that you feel it is best to make a change. He may even agree with you. You should dismiss one doctor properly before coming to an agreement with another. Some physicians ask for a written release from the parents when the child is taken out of their care (to be sure they are not held responsible later for any neglect of treatment). Some doctors, observing strict medical ethics, will not accept a case until a previous doctor has been properly dismissed.

Children and Doctors.   A child greatly needs to have trust and confidence in his doctors. This feeling is not always easy to establish. The child's treatments often are disagreeable or painful, as when he must lie in traction or wear heavy braces, and when the activities he enjoys are restricted.

The doctor, on his part, wants the child to trust him. He wants the child to feel confident that the doctor tells him the truth; that when he says it will hurt some but not for long, that's the way it will be. Parents carry great responsibility for their child's belief in the doctor's truthfulness. A mother may tell her child that they are going to the doctor's office "just so he can look you over," although she knows that the child is due for an injection. When he sees the hypodermic needle, he feels betrayed by both his mother and his doctor. He has to know that he can count on what his parents tell him about the doctor.

It's hard for children to understand that a doctor's actions are meant to make him feel better and are friendly in their intent. A young child has to grow up a bit before he can realize that the doctor who hurts him is trying to help him. He may want to feel friendly toward the doctor and yet be angry when treatment is painful. Preschool children who have been hospitalized are especially apt to be hostile.

A doctor who understands children can usually overcome the child's resentment by being patient, by explaining the treatment on a level that the child can understand, by being very careful to cause the least possible pain. He is gentle with the child. He doesn't use his superior size and physical strength to force treatment on the child. Bodily restraint is as frightening as pain to some young children.

It is difficult for the doctor to build a child's trust in him when the parents use him as a law-enforcement officer. "If you don't behave, I'll take you to the doctor and he'll give you a shot!" Threats are bad for any child, but they are particularly harmful to the disabled child whose welfare depends so much on a good relationship with his doctor, over many months and years. Doctors feel strongly about this.

As a child grows older, he needs opportunity to go in to the doctor by himself, a chance to talk with him alone now and then. It is part of growing up for any youngster to want to form his own ties with other adults, and his doctor is certainly one of the really significant adults in his life. What's more, a perceptive doctor may learn important things about the child and about the illness when the child is speaking for himself. If a child has a chance to talk with his doctor without being "interrupted" by grown people, it helps him feel that the doctor is "his" doctor. This sense of having a close, personal tie with at least one of the many doctors, nurses, and other specialists who may be treating him is very comforting.

A child in his teens can sometimes make his own appointments or go alone to see the doctor. He pays more attention. He develops a growing sense of responsibility for his own medical care and for following instructions. This will be important for the rest of his life. Moreover, a direct, authoritative explanation from the doctor may impress him more forcefully than instructions relayed through his parents.

Doctors should take pains to help their young patients understand their disabilities and put themselves out to win the child's cooperation, because the patient is the focal member of the medical partnership.

REFERENCE

1. Jacob J. Feldman, Paul Sheatsley, and Odin W. Anderson. *What the Public Knows, Thinks, and Does About Health and Medical Care.* Health Information Foundation, Research Series No. 23. Chicago, University of Chicago Press, 1963.

8

YOUR CHILD IN THE HOSPITAL

Young children are apt to be upset by hospitalization. So good doctors and nurses protect them as much as they can from unhappy experiences. Children are strongly influenced by their parents' attitudes. It will help if you understand what the hospital is trying to do, positively, for your child and communicate some of this feeling to him. It will also help if you can understand how he will react to his experiences there.

The Anxiety of Separation. The chief worry of the child under three or four years is not so much about what they are going to do to him in the hospital but about separation from his mother. At five and six and seven his greatest fears are of the pain and injuries which he imagines the doctors will inflict on him. As he grows older still, a child may focus on the anesthesia, the fear of losing consciousness, of losing control of himself.

According to an English observer, Dr. James Robertson, who has studied the effects of hospitalization,[1] the child of three or less who is left in the hospital may go through several stages. Too young to understand why he is there, he knows only that he is in a strange place and that his mother is not with him. He is apt to keep asking where she is and to cry sadly. He may cry again each time the nurse comes because he wishes she were his mother. He may not want to eat. He clings to his favorite toys he has brought from home. After a while he becomes quieter, but not happier. When his mother does come back, his grief may break out again, because of his realization of how much he has missed her.

If a young child's stay in the hospital is prolonged beyond a few days, he is apt to make a partial adjustment. He accepts the attention of the nurses, he smiles a little, he plays a little, and he eats better. When his mother visits him, he may for a few minutes seem more interested in the toy she brings than in her. This is because, though he is really glad to see her, he is also angry too that she has left him and must show this at first. If a young child has been in a hospital or convalescent home for many months, he may even pretend he doesn't know his mother throughout the whole visiting hour. This means he needs her more, not less.

Whether or not a child has seemed disturbed in the hospital, he may act very upset when he gets home. He may have outbursts of temper, particularly against his mother, because separation from her was so painful, or he may cling to her excessively for fear that she will leave him again. He may begin to wet or soil himself again, sleep badly, have nightmares, or develop erratic eating habits. It will help the child to get over his troubled feelings if his mother can show that she understands how angry he sometimes feels and that she loves him just as much as ever. This doesn't mean, though, that she should take abuse from him.

Anxiety about the Unknown.   To a child of any age there is much that is strange and alarming about a hospital, entirely aside from the painful experiences: being taken away from his parents, being put to bed by a strange nurse, having x-rays in a dark room, seeing doctors and nurses in gowns and masks, being examined by numerous strangers, using a bed pan.

Many painful or uncomfortable things happen to the child, such as certain methods of giving anesthetics, the return to consciousness after surgery, the discovery that some part of the body hurts, the use of the hypodermic needle for injections, spinal taps, intravenous feeding or blood transfusions, the application of casts, the changing of burn dressings. The child may learn to expect to be hurt.

The older child who understands more about why he is in the hospital may still be worried over some questions about the results of his treatment. "Can I play ball when I go home? Can I go to dances when I'm better? Will the gang forget me while I'm away? Will I fall behind my class at school?" Or, more serious, "Will I be able to walk? Am I ever going to get better? Will I be helpless all my life?" An anxious child wants you to listen to his questions without belittling them; at the same time, he needs your support to maintain his optimism.

PEACE OF MIND IN THE HOSPITAL

Hospital personnel are aware that the way children are handled during hospitalization can make a big difference in their reactions. Changes have been made in many hospitals and have proved to be effective.

One study compared two groups of fifty children each, ranging in age from two to twelve years.[2] In one group, parents were allowed to visit the children only once a week; there was no play program for the children and no special psychological preparation for their hospital experiences. In the other group, parents visited the children daily, a special play program was arranged for the youngsters, and the children were prepared for each hospital procedure with appropriate explanations. When possible, the hospital assigned one nurse to take care of the child's total nursing needs during her hours of duty, instead of a series of nurses with each doing different things for him.

Eighteen children in the first group developed behavior difficulties. Some acquired feeding problems or slept poorly. Others wet themselves or reverted to thumb-sucking, rocking, head-banging, or masturbation. Some showed excessive activity, restlessness, and irritability. Others were homesick, anxious or withdrawn, or developed special fears.

In the second group, only seven children—all under five years of age—had severe reactions. This study shows that separation from the mother was the main cause of the *younger* child's misery and that her more frequent visits, along with the other measures, helped a lot but were not always enough to offset his grief. The older children were better able to tolerate separation, but they still were helped by daily visits, play programs, and the advance explanations of hospital procedures. Six months after leaving the hospital few children in either group showed any kind of behavior disturbances.

The children's conscious attitudes toward the hospital experience varied with age. The preschool children commonly believed that they had been placed in the hospital as a punishment. They made such remarks as "If my mommy will take me home I'll be good." The children of primary-school age were less confused but were still inclined to think of pain or discomfort as punishment for having done something bad. They also tended to be worried about bodily mutilation or death. The still older child was more aware of the nature of his disease and of the future implications of his disability, but he sometimes tried to deny its extent or existence. A child with severe paralysis, for example, might make plans for a summer of mountain climbing. This seemed to be a way of holding off reality until he gradually gained the ability to face it.

What Some Hospitals Are Doing. Because the mother's presence is the greatest guarantee against emotional disturbance, a few hospitals now permit her to stay with her young child day and night. Sometimes she is merely given a chair and a folding bed. In other hospitals, rooms are set aside especially for mothers with young children. The charges vary.

This arrangement usually works best when the mother shares responsibility with the nurse in taking care of the child. She does for him just about what she would do at home: bathes and dresses him, toilets him, feeds him, plays with him and comforts him, and makes use of the floor kitchen as necessary, if invited to do so. Sometimes she also takes the child's temperature and perhaps holds him on her lap when the doctor examines him.

Many other hospitals, which have no provisions for parents to spend the night, have liberalized their visiting hours so that parents are allowed to visit their child at any time during the day. In some of these hospitals mothers are encouraged to help with their child's care. A few hospitals encourage the mother to be present when her child is examined and treated by the doctor, if she can keep her own feelings under control.

Some hospitals allow children to wear their own night clothes, and some supply gay, attractive things for them. The child is urged to bring several of his own toys or favorite belongings and is encouraged to feel that his bed or his room is his very own place. In some pediatric wards a great effort has been made to have an informal, homelike atmosphere where children have considerable liberty to roam around, to go to the kitchen for a snack, or to visit other children. A planned program of play and recreation, with a trained person in charge, makes a hospital more acceptable to children. There may even be pets; one hospital even has a cage of monkeys.

Understanding nurses and doctors take care to explain to the child in advance, in ways he can understand, any procedure that may be upsetting or painful. If he is to go from one place to another in the hospital, he is told where he is going and why. If he is to have x-rays taken, the doctor or nurse explains. If he is to have an intravenous feeding, he is told in a simple way why it must be done.

Studies of quite young children who have undergone operations without emotional upsets show that they were usually told in advance the reasons for the operation and something about what would happen. They were not deceived by their parents about the reasons for going. There are ways to make anesthetics and surgery less disturbing. Children may be given an anesthetic or sedative in their own hospital room and so escape the possibly frightening experience of the ride to the operating room, seeing instruments and apparatus, seeing nurses and doctors in their strange gowns and masks. One or both parents should be at a child's side, if possible, when he regains consciousness.[4]

In the past, ether was usually given to a young child without preliminary sedation. He was often so frightened that he had to be restrained while he fought and gasped the ether. Many young children struggle desperately if forced to lie down. Sympathetic methods lessen this terror. In one hospital someone holds the little child in his arms while a stream of anesthetic gas is directed at him through a tube or a toy. The younger children enjoy Perky the Pup. When this toy is connected with the container of gas, his antics entertain the child during the loss of consciousness. The additional anesthetic needed for the operation is then given without causing discomfort. The action of the anesthetic is explained to an older child and he is given a tube to hold while gas is directed through it. In some hospitals, the anesthesiologist visits the child the day before the operation and explains to him and his parents how the anesthetic will be given and how it will help the child. Sometimes he brings along a small bottle to let the child sniff the strange smell.[5]

Hospitals have been able to improve their routines. One hospital found by count that some children who were admitted for diagnostic tests were exposed to as many as 52 persons—nurses, doctors, and technicians—in the first 48 hours. The assignment of duties was changed so that the number of people who had dealings with one child was cut to about a dozen. Two nurses shared the care of a child in shifts, and one of them always went with him for his tests. These nurses took full charge of him, so that he could develop a secure, trusting relationship with them and could feel that they were "his" nurses.

Because the application of these principles is still in the early stages, there is little uniformity about rules and regulations. So it's a good idea to find out what the practices are in your hospital before your child enters. In this way you are better prepared to smooth his path. If you should have a complaint or suggestion make it to your child's doctor and let him carry it to the proper authority. Nurses and technicians are not responsible for hospital regulations but are obliged to follow them.

Deciding When to Go to the Hospital. Some hospitalizations have to be carried out promptly whether or not the child is at a sensitive age or stage. In others there is considerable choice about the timing. Then it is better to perform the operation either during the first few months of the child's life, when he is least apt to be upset by separation from his mother, or when he is past three years. When hospitalization is "elective," it is usually wise to delay if there has been a recent crisis in the young child's life that may have upset him already—a move to a new community, the birth of a new brother or sister, absence of father or mother from home for any length of time, or a death in the family or in the child's circle of friends. Better to wait until the child is on an even keel again.

Physicians, like everyone else, vary a lot in their awareness of children's emotions. Certainly it is a part of your job to tell your doctor about your child's state of mind so that he can balance this against the purely medical factors.

Realizing that home is usually the best place for a child, doctors do their best to keep the length of a child's stay in the hospital at a minimum. If your child must go to a hospital or rehabilitation center for therapy and training in self-care, his doctor may recommend that the training be concentrated in a relatively short period, perhaps three months, after which he would come home. Should further training be needed, he might go back again another year. In this way, ties with family and friends suffer less strain.

WHAT PARENTS CAN DO

Naturally any child will adjust to hospitalization more easily if he has been a secure person at home and if he has learned to look on his doctor as a trusted friend. But he also needs to be reassured that he is going to the hospital to get better, that you want him to go there to get better because you love him. In other words, you try to make it clear that there is no punishment in it. In addition, he needs to know the specific reasons, so far as he can understand them. Apparently many parents fail to explain them; one investigation showed that only 25 out of 100 children knew why they were in the hospital.[6]

Preparing Your Child for the Hospital. You may be tempted to tell your child, to allay his fears, that he is going just to be examined, or that he won't have to stay overnight. If he then has surgery or any painful treatment and has to stay for days, his trust in you will be shaken. It's better to tell the truth right from the start, emphasizing your confidence that the hospital treatment will help him to get better.

It's difficult to explain much to children under two-and-a-half or three. Some of them have quite a good command of language and may seem to understand. But the idea that his mother might leave him in a strange place without her is usually so foreign to the small child's experience that he can't really grasp its full significance. But partial preparation can be given by telling a story about how someone else was hospitalized or by playing out the situation with a doll, including the farewells when the mother leaves for the night and the greetings next morning. The best safeguard lies in keeping as much actual contact between mother and child as possible during hospitalization.

A child of three or four can be prepared fairly well by a simplified but truthful account. You could tell a child who is going to have surgery that the doctor is going to fix his leg (or whatever part of the body is involved) so that he can walk more easily. "He'll give you something to make you sleep, and while you're asleep he will do an operation to help your leg. When you wake up, Mother or Daddy will be with you. Your leg will be sore for a while, but it will keep on getting better." It's best not to burden him with technical details.

There's no point in telling a small child several months before an operation, because he has little sense of time and will keep thinking that tomorrow is the day. A week or two is usually right. But if a child of any age hears rumors or asks questions, be honest.

Even more important than what you tell your child is giving him plenty of chances—day after day—to ask questions. It's only when you know what puzzles him or frightens him that you can reassure him. You'll be surprised how different his worries are from what you had imagined. If he asks questions that you aren't qualified to answer, say frankly that you don't know and then make sure that he or you have a chance to ask his doctor.

Some hospitals encourage parents to bring their child for a preliminary get-acquainted visit, during which the medical social worker or a nurse takes the youngster on a tour of the children's ward and introduces him to some of the nurses. If you have this opportunity, make use of it.

"Playing hospital" is another way that helps young children learn something about hospital experiences in advance. They like to dress up as a nurse or doctor, get a doll ready for bed, give it a bed-bath or a meal in bed, and take its temperature. Giving the doll "something to make it sleep" helps explain the anesthetic. The child may not be sophisticated enough to introduce some of the other medical procedures into his play—injections, transfusions, or operations—so you will have to feel your way on the basis of what you anticipate will happen to him, taking care not to arouse too many fears that may prove groundless.

It's a good idea to let him pack his own suitcase and put in one or two favorite toys. If he likes to sleep with a favorite cuddly blanket, he should pack that too and you should tell the nurse about it. Perhaps he'll feel reassured about his return home if you suggest that he put some of his toys in a special place to wait for him.

There are several good books describing a hospital experience, which can be read to young children, and there are others for older age levels. Ask at your library, or bookstore, or supermarket. Your child will probably be very interested in learning about life in a hospital. If he hasn't seen the building, arrange to show it to him ahead of time, or at least describe it. Try to find out whether he will be in a big room with many children, with only two or three others, or in a room by himself, and tell him about it. (Unless your doctor advises against it, he may be happier in a room with other children.) You can describe the uniforms worn by the various members of the hospital staff, and you can satisfy his curiosity about being bathed in bed, how meals are served in bed, cranking the beds up and down, and so on. To some extent this sort of information may stimulate him to take a lively interest in hospital life once he is there; this interest may relieve him of some of his worries.

On the other hand, it would be a mistake to lead him to think that being in the hospital is a picnic. If he is going to have painful treatments, he should know that some of the things that will be done to him are going to hurt, but they will help him get better. The fact that you have forewarned him is comforting; when disagreeable things do happen, he remembers that you know about it and that it is part of your plan for helping him.

An older child's pride is easily hurt when those close to him don't consider his wishes. As he approaches his teens, he will want more information about the diagnosis and about what is going to be done to him. If there is a choice of timing or procedure, he may have strong preferences. A high school student may be eager to complete the school term before going to the hospital and should have a chance to discuss his wishes with the doctor as well as his parents. If reasons against delay are urgent and the doctor explains them carefully, the youth will feel that he is being treated as a mature person and will, in most cases, want to be cooperative.

Keeping the Home Ties Strong. A child's need to feel that he's very much a part of his family is particularly strong during prolonged hospitalization. He needs constant reassurances that he hasn't been forgotten or abandoned. Visits should be made just as often as possible by both parents. If the child is young and the hospital allows rooming-in by mothers, it is worth trying to arrange for the care of the rest of the family in some way so that you can stay with him, at least for a few days while he's getting used to the hospital.

The way you handle your good-byes makes a difference. Remember that a young child's concept of time is still very vague. When you are leaving him, your promise to return means very little. He knows only that you are going.

One device that is helpful to some children is to leave some personal belonging, such as a glove or a purse. It makes the departure seem not quite total, and is a reminder that you will come back. Even so, he will probably cry. But it's better for him to express his anguish than to suppress it. It helps him then if a familiar, friendly nurse comes soon to comfort him.

With the somewhat older child who understands "tomorrow" or "next Thursday," parents should explain their plans for a return visit. If you have told your child when to expect you and for any reason you can't get there, it's important to send a message to let him know why.

Some parents find parting so distressing that they try to slip away without saying good-bye. But when you tell a child that you are just leaving the room for a short time and then fail to return, his confidence is shaken. It's much better to be honest about it even though he will be temporarily more upset.

As a rule, visits should be cheerful. Most children are interested in hearing about events at home, getting messages from friends and teachers, and being kept up-to-date on neighborhood developments. But take your cue from the child himself. There may be days when he is thoroughly miserable and wants a chance to pour out his distress. Grown people usually urge a child to be brave and stop crying, especially a boy. When a child is sick or in pain, crying it out may help him relieve his feelings, and he should know that you understand his need to cry. On the other hand, when your child feels that it is important for him not to cry, to prove that he is grown up, you can show your appreciation for his self-control. Even then you can add, "I know you feel sad underneath," so that he won't try to train himself to be a person without any feeling.

If the hospital is far away and your visits must be few, send him lots of mail. Frequent letters, cheerful cards, surprise packages, snapshots of the family and family pets, all keep him in touch.

Frequent telephone calls help reduce homesickness. Some hospitals arrange for children to make or receive home telephone calls at certain hours. In one convalescent home for children with heart trouble, most of whose families lived far away, friends of the hospital provided a special fund to enable children to call their homes for good-night talks with their parents. If there is no telephone in your child's room or ward, there may be a jack to plug a phone into at pre-arranged times. Children who can walk or ride in a wheelchair may use a public telephone in the hospital corridor. In that case, they will need a supply of small change for making the calls.

It's a good idea to check with the nurse or therapist in charge of the hospital's play program before you choose gifts for your child. They'll be glad to tell you what toys, books, or games will be most welcome without duplicating what is already available in the hospital play materials. You may also be advised what *not* to bring! Simple gifts that put a child's imagination and skill to work usually give him more lasting pleasure than elaborate toys that have only one limited action. Naturally the choice depends upon the child's age and interests, but drawing materials, scrapbooks, puzzles, sewing and building sets, games, possibly a phonograph and records, or a radio, are fun for children of all ages.

Helping with Your Child's Hospital Care. Nurses appreciate having certain kinds of information about a new young patient, especially if he cannot tell them himself. If he still uses baby talk, what special words or signs does he use when he wants to go to the toilet? What does he say when he wants a drink of water? Does he have a nickname? When he goes to bed at night, does he want something to cuddle? Does he want the light out? Does he want to say his prayers? The nurse should also know what signs an older child uses to communicate his wants when he cannot speak or write. If he cannot hear, the nurse needs to know whether he can lip read.

If your child is in a hospital where mothers are encouraged to assist in their children's care, you will want to be useful to the nurse as well as your child. This means following exactly the directions of the doctor and nurse. They will tell you what foods and drinks your child is permitted in addition to his hospital meals, whether he is allowed to get up to go to the bathroom, what games or other activities he is permitted.

Come prepared to make yourself comfortable for the long hours you will spend in the hospital. You need comfortable clothing, easy fitting and preferably washable, and really comfortable shoes. Rubber soles will keep your steps quiet. Bring bedroom slippers, a housecoat, and toilet articles if you are to spend the night. Find out whether there is any provision for your meals. If not, ask whether you may bring your own lunch and whether you may eat it in the room with

your child. Find out what your kitchen privileges are and try
to be modest in your demands. You will want to bring reading matter and a supply of small change for telephone calls.
If you spend the night but no bed is provided, a blanket
adds to your comfort.

If the hospital is not organized to use help from mothers,
try to be patient and fit in with it as well as you can. It may
embarrass your child to have you try to get around the rules
if the parents of other children are observing them and it will
rightly antagonize the staff. Whatever the exact arrangements, there must be a thoroughly cooperative spirit on the
part of both staff and parents. For if the parents begin to
think that the nurses and doctors are being inconsiderate
toward their child or toward themselves, or if the staff
come to feel that the parents are interfering with treatment,
all the relationships deteriorate rapidly. Even if you are convinced that some of the hospital people are callous or rude,
try to win them around by your thoughtfulness. It's for your
child's benefit.

When Your Child Comes Home.   After prolonged hospitalization, the doctor may arrange for your child to make some
short visits home first, in preparation for his final return. The
short visits test his adjustment to his home and that of the
family to his problems. They also give you a clearer idea of
what your child needs at home and of questions you may
want to ask the doctor, nurse, or therapist. Even if you have
had instruction, you may find, for example, that you are not
quite sure how to help him in and out of an automobile or the
bathtub, or what he can do to dress or feed himself. This
gives you a chance to clarify your uncertainties and stimulates you to think of further questions.

A child may have become adjusted to a hospital schedule
that is very different from the one at home, particularly with
respect to meals, mealtime and bedtime. He'll get through
the first days more smoothly if routines are not too different.
You'll have to feel your way, taking your cues from his behavior and sensing when he is tired or ready for a snack.
He'll gradually shift back into home routines.

The emotional adjustment, however, may take longer.
Most children react sharply to their return. Often a child will
slip back into earlier, babyish habits, such as finicky eating
or wetting himself or displaying his temper. It may help

him to talk about his hospital experiences, or to act them out with him in play, and to have you sympathize with him about his disagreeable experiences.

After months away, the child is apt to feel that he and his family have grown apart and to resent it. Perhaps the family has changed; there may be a new baby; brothers and sisters are older, have new friends, may be in new schools. In spite of your efforts to tell him all that has happened while he was away, home may now seem so strange that he feels unsure of his place in the family circle. He may show a lot of temperament and respond unreasonably to unimportant things. Most important of all, a child shows the unconscious resentment that he is bound to feel underneath for being kept away from the family for so long.

What's the right course for the parents? They will want to make their child feel very welcome at home. But it won't do him any good and it will wear out their own patience if they allow him to be disagreeable or tyrannical hour after hour. It will help to clear the air if a mother can show she understands his feelings: "I know how unhappy you were in the hospital all the time. You feel mad at me and Daddy because we brought you there." But she can also say firmly, "I still don't want you to be rude to me." But even if the parents have to be firm, they still have to be understanding, particularly if the child's disability has been newly incurred and he is coming back home to a life that is going to be limited in ways he isn't used to.

REFERENCES

1. James Robertson. *Young Children in Hospitals*. New York, Basic Books, 1958.

2. D. G. Prugh, E. W. Staug, H. H. Sands, R. M. Kirschbaum, and E. A. Lenihan. "A Study of the Emotional Reactions of Children and Families to Hospitalization and Illness." *Amer. Jo. Orthopsychiatry*, 1953. 23: pp. 70-104.

3. D. G. Prugh. "Emotional Reactions to Surgery," in *The Nonoperative Aspects of Pediatric Surgery: Report of the Twenty-Seventh Ross Pediatric Research Conference*, Ross Laboratories, Columbus, Ohio, 1957.

4. D. M. Levy. "Psychic Trauma of Operations in Children, and a Note on Combat Neurosis." *Am. Jo. of Diseases of Children*, 1945. 69: 7-25.

5. Orvar Swenson. "Play Programs for Surgical Patients." Report of the Twenty-Seventh Ross Pediatric Research Conference, Ross Laboratories, 1957.

6. H. Gofman, W. Buckman, and G. H. Schlade. *Am. Jo. of Diseases of Children*, 1953. 93: 137.

9

SPECIAL THERAPIES IN REHABILITATION

If you should visit a rehabilitation center, you might see a child who hadn't been able to hold his head erect or sit alone until he was long past infancy but who now could stand and take a few steps without help. Another child, for years unable to hold a glass, now holds it steadily enough to drink his milk by himself. Another youngster whose legs were paralyzed as the result of accidental injury gets around independently on braces and crutches. A child who was born deaf and has never heard speech is speaking well enough for his playmates to understand him. These near miracles have been accomplished by the special therapies used in rehabilitation.

Physical therapy, occupational therapy, training in self-care (the vital "activities of daily living"), and speech therapy are the most widely used methods of rehabilitation. Play therapy often is used with young children and your own child may encounter other therapies: music, art, gardening, and recreational therapy are used for their restorative values. Even games and sports are modified for therapeutic purposes.

PHYSICAL THERAPY

Physical therapy is used to help a person who is restricted in certain fundamental *motions* of his body. Joints may be stiff or deformed so that he can't stand erect, or use his arm or his hand. Muscles that are weak and flabby from disease or disuse may need strengthening. Or certain parts of the body may need unusual development to enable them to compensate for paralyzed or missing parts. A child who has little coordination must learn how to balance himself in sitting, standing, or walking.

Physical therapy is the name used for treatment by exercise, massage, heat, cold, water, light, and electricity. Many kinds of equipment are used. There may be pools large enough for swimming or for underwater exercise of weakened muscles, because the warmth and buoyancy of water make it easier for patients to use the affected parts of the body. There may be smaller baths for the immersion of a part of the body in moving water, of a desired temperature. Parallel bars, a walking ramp, practice steps, and curbs of varying heights are used by patients who are learning to walk with braces and crutches. Wall pulley weights and other kinds of apparatus may be used to strengthen weak muscles. There are infra-red lamps and diathermy to produce heat, and ultra-violet lamps.

The Uses of Therapeutic Exercise. Physical therapy places particular emphasis on exercise. There are several kinds of benefits. Exercise enlarges, strengthens, and toughens weak muscles. It also heightens their efficiency and skill. It enlarges their blood supply and thus increases their endurance. For instance, a child's hand, arm, or shoulder muscles may need to be strengthened, or their coordination may need to be improved, before he can learn to use crutches.

Physical therapy also improves the flexibility of joints. To control every joint there are sets of muscles which oppose each other. When the biceps muscle, for example, contracts and shortens, the opposing "triceps" muscle on the back of the arm must relax and lengthen so that the forearm can be raised. But in a limb which has been affected by polio, for instance, one set of muscles is much weaker than its opponent. Then the stronger set of muscles continually outpulls the weaker set, and the limb is held in one position only—always flexed or always extended. Eventually the stronger muscles become permanently shortened because they are never stretched. For example, if the shin muscles that raise the foot are paralyzed, the calf muscles will hold the foot pointed down continually, like a toe dancer's, and will become shortened. Then it will be impossible, even for another person, to raise that foot. Exercises help the patient strengthen the weak muscles, stretch the contracted muscles, and thus improve the action of the joint.

Even when there has been damage to portions of the nervous system that control the movement of muscles, physical therapy can often bring improvement. Muscles move only when activated by nerve impulses, so they fall into disuse and grow weak when the controlling nerves are damaged. If the damage to nerve cells is temporary, the muscle is restored to use when the nerve cells recover. Physical therapy may aid in the restoration of the strength of the muscle. Sometimes only part of the controlling nerve cells are injured, leaving enough healthy cells to activate at least some of the muscle fibers. Then therapeutic exercise may strengthen the *remaining* functioning fibers, enabling the child to use the affected part of the body despite partial paralysis.

Occasionally damage to the nervous system is so extensive that paralysis of the affected parts of the body is permanent and complete. Then physical therapy may help the patient to compensate for that loss by increasing the strength and skill of unaffected parts of the body. For example, if a child's legs are paralyzed, he may strengthen his trunk, arm, and shoulder muscles so that he can use crutches. Or if his right arm is paralyzed, he may develop great skill and strength in using his left arm.

Exercises help cerebral-palsied children conquer some of the "simple" motions that so often frustrate them. They may help such a child learn to sit or stand alone. If he lacks the backward-and-forward sense of motion that is essential to walking, in the arms as well as the legs, exercises teach him "reciprocal" motion. There are exercises to develop hand control, others to control chewing and swallowing. Some children learn to control the rate and pattern of their breathing, which is often essential for speech improvement.

Sometimes the therapist massages weak muscles. Or she uses "passive motion," in which *she* moves a joint through its range of motion without help from the child. When he has improved, he will begin to give the therapist help in the movement and eventually he may perform it entirely by himself. (This is called "active motion.") In some exercises the child develops strength through "resisted motion." The resistance may be provided by the therapist's hands or by some apparatus, such as a system of weights, ropes, and pulleys. When a child has learned to control the motion of individual joints, he may have to learn to make combined motions, as when he closes his fingers over the handle of a comb and bends his wrist, elbow, and shoulder in order to comb his hair. Some children must be taught how to relax tense muscles.

OCCUPATIONAL THERAPY

Whereas physical therapy is intended to improve fundamental body motions, occupational therapy attempts to teach useful *skills*. Through its psychological effects it also hastens recovery or fosters the adjustment to disability. It is called occupational therapy because it provides healing occupations for mind and body, not because it prepares the patient for a particular occupation, although it might help to do this also.

The tools of occupational therapy for children are play, games, and what are called the creative and manual arts. Many educational toys are used with younger children— large wooden beads, blocks, peg-boards, construction sets, hammer and nail sets, erector sets. There are dolls and dollplay equipment for little girls and cars, trains, and planes for boys. Older children make greater use of handcrafts and skills such as drawing, painting, clay modeling, weaving, leatherwork, or papercraft. With the teenager, the program may include vocational skills such as printing, typewriting, metalwork, carpentry, or other shop work.

There are three distinct ways in which occupational therapy is effective: improvement in the child's emotional adjustment, improvement in the functioning of muscles and joints, and, in the case of an older child, preparation for vocational education or a return to employment.

Occupational therapy helps to reduce a child's anxiety or restlessness or boredom. If his illness rules out all physical activity, he may listen to stories or the radio and play guessing games. As soon as he is permitted some activity, he may be encouraged to play cards and anagrams or do simple weaving on a light hand loom. As his strength increases, he exerts himself more until he gradually reaches the peak of his tolerance. If he can be kept interested in things to do, and if he can divert his mind from his pain and problems, his recovery will be speeded.

Most occupational therapies help a child learn to manage his disability and are enjoyable and instructive at the same time. Playing ball with a therapist will increase the movement in a paralyzed hand or arm. Playing marbles can improve the child's use of fingers, hand, or arm. The boy who pulls down the lever of a hand-operated printing press improves the movements of an injured arm. Typesetting may increase accuracy of finger movements. Using a kick wheel and treadle in making pottery is fine exercise for the feet, knees, and ankle joints, while clay modeling, basketry, and leatherwork are good for the fingers. Drawing and sketching, which require both large and fine hand and arm movements, help develop coordination. Arm muscles can be strengthened by typing, sawing, hammering, or sanding at a carpenter's bench.

If your child is old enough to be thinking ahead to a job, his occupational therapy program may emphasize the things that will contribute most to preparing him for going to work.

SPECIAL TRAINING IN "ACTIVITIES OF DAILY LIVING"

This is the long-winded name of the most important therapy of all. The hundreds of motions that physically normal people perform unconsciously, day in and day out, may present mountainous difficulties to a person with a crippling disability. Merely getting out of bed or taking a coin from a purse may require painstaking effort.

An entire branch of rehabilitation has been developed to help disabled people cope with the activities of daily living, familiarly referred to as "A.D.L." Exercises are carefully chosen for their effectiveness in teaching self-help in getting about, self-care in bathing, dressing, toileting, or eating. The hand activities which are given preference are writing and typing and the use of ordinary household equipment.

A good rehabilitation center or school for disabled children has special equipment for training in A.D.L. One school has a room equipped with a bed, chairs, a chest of drawers, and a telephone. The children practice getting in and out of bed, sitting down and getting up from a chair, transferring from bed to wheelchair or crutches. There is also bathroom equipment in an alcove—tub, toilet seat, and wash basin. Here the children learn to maneuver their wheelchairs into position to use the basin and to transfer themselves to the tub or toilet seat. On a large wall there is a "gadget board" fitted with ordinary household equipment. The children practice using different kinds of light switches and electric sockets, doorknobs, doorbells, faucets with handles of different shapes, several types of locks and keys, jars with screw tops, and a coin box with a slotted opening. A fully equipped kitchen provides practice in working at a stove, sink, or refrigerator, opening and closing cupboard doors, and storing pots, pans, and groceries so that they are accessible to a physically limited person.

Steps in Teaching A.D.L. When the therapist finds out just what tasks the child cannot perform, she analyzes them and breaks them down to their simplest motions. Then she selects the exercises that teach him to perform those motions. Sometimes the exercise simply consists in actual practice of the activity. But some children need physical therapy to improve the use of a specific part of the body before they can practice the task itself. If a child can't use his legs because of his disability, the therapist may begin his training with such a simple thing as learning to roll over from his back to his side while lying in bed. From this he may move slowly through many stages until he can walk on braces or crutches. First things must come first.

If a child's disability severely limits his use of his hands, the therapist may decide that he needs considerable training in the elements of reaching, grasping and letting go, or placing objects where he wants them before he can begin to use eating utensils to bring food to his mouth. Some children don't know how to remove food from a spoon with their lips; some even need exercise to improve their ability to chew and swallow.

Buttons have to go through buttonholes, zippers must be pulled open or shut, hooks must go into the right eyelets, and shoelaces into the right holes. The therapist often encourages a child to dress and undress large dolls. Shoelacing is practiced on a dummy shoe that has stable sides and large eyelets, with stiff-tipped, long laces. Buttons and buttonholes of different sizes are mounted on frames for the child's practice.

Learning to write depends on other abilities. A cerebral-palsied child, for example, must first improve his shoulder control and finger skill. Crafts requiring rather large movements (fingerpainting, coloring) are used to increase shoulder control. Finer crafts (bead-stringing, leather-lacing) will improve finger action. Then the child begins to write with large pencils or crayons that are easily grasped, sometimes using large graph paper. Tic-tac-toe is good beginning practice.

Many children with limited use of their hands can learn to typewrite; in fact, many cerebral-palsied persons type more easily than they write. A child may need first to learn to relax his shoulders or to move his fingers independently. If he can't use his fingers, he may be able to depress the keys with a rubber stick on a holder fastened to his hand. Some of those who can't use an ordinary typewriter are able to use an electric machine, as it requires less effort.

Physical Education in Rehabilitation. Some children undergoing rehabilitation are able to play at active sports, but the games are usually modified to suit the special problems. Baseball, basketball, archery, table tennis, and shuffleboard are popular. Swimming is recommended for many children with disabilities because it is good therapy and good fun.

Some children have to be restricted in their physical activity to avoid fatigue. But the problem for most of the handicapped who are in good general health is to find enough opportunities for enjoyable exercise, especially exercise with other children. If your child can't participate in the play and recreation programs in your schools and community because of his disability, you will have to do what you can to create opportunities for him. (See Chapters 18-20.)

How You Can Help. The first step in helping your child with his therapy program is to understand what it means to him. What seems to you a very simple thing may be quite frightening to the child when he first attempts it. There is a cartoon on the wall of the Institute for the Crippled and Disabled in New York, drawn by a patient to show "How it looks to the therapist" and "How it looks to the patient." The patient in the cartoon is learning to use his crutches to step off a curb two inches high. To the therapist, it looks only two inches high. But to the patient with paralyzed legs it looks like a mountain cliff. Even if a handicapped child isn't afraid physically, he may be anxious that he will spill his food or look awkward. You try to show him that you understand his feelings, whether he wants to talk about them, ignore them, or joke about them.

Of course the results of therapy come slowly, often over a period of months or years, and even then they may not seem spectacular. Your child may find his exercises tedious and even painful. He needs your encouragement. It helps him to know that you have confidence in the treatment.

One way of showing your confidence is to make sure that the child follows the schedule worked out by the therapist. If you allow appointments to be broken without good reason, or home exercise periods to be skipped, your child will find it hard to believe that you place much value in the therapy.

If you think results are too slow, raise your objections with the therapist or the doctor. He will explain. He may point to progress that you haven't noticed. But wait until you can talk it over when your child is not present so that he won't be upset by your doubts.

The importance of helping the child to help himself needs repeated emphasis because good parents have a natural, strong impulse to run to their child's aid the instant he is in trouble. It's natural, but often not helpful. He probably needs to get up by himself. He surely needs to learn how to handle himself in all the situations he'll meet. You may show your love better by suggesting or demonstrating a more effective way to accomplish what he is trying to do than by helping him directly. Sometimes it's best to pretend that you don't see. Then he'll work it out himself or call for help if he really needs it.

You may be asked to help your child with his exercises at home. To be effective, you have to know the correct position the child should take for an exercise and just how it should be performed. Also know how many times he should repeat the exercise and how long his practice periods should be. The therapist will give you instructions. If she asks you to take your child through the exercises in her presence, don't feel shy about it, for this is your chance to learn to help correctly. If the therapist's instructions are not clear, ask questions. She may occasionally forget that terminology which is A-B-C to her is unfamiliar to you, but she will gladly explain when you ask her.

Sometimes parents are embarrassed to let their child discover their own ignorance. After a series of treatments by the therapist, your child may know more than you do about his muscles. If he wants to brag because he knows where the *quadriceps femoris* is, that's fine. If you are proud of what he knows and can laugh about your own ignorance, it may draw you closer together.

A patient is expected to apply regularly in his living what he has learned in therapy. If the therapist has helped him maintain good posture when he uses his crutches, it is for all the time, not just for practice periods. On the other hand, every child has times when he needs to let himself go, out of protest and rebellion or just for relaxation. You'll have to use your judgment about the circumstances.

SPEECH THERAPY

There are many kinds of speech disorders. They occur most commonly among children who have cerebral palsy, impaired hearing, or cleft lip or palate, or who are retarded. Some children with speech problems have no other disabilities. If you can't find a professional therapist nearby, refer to the directory of clinically certified speech therapists published by the American Speech and Hearing Association, 1001 Connecticut Avenue, N.W., Washington 6, D.C.

The speech therapist is trained to understand the complex psychological, physiological, and anatomical factors generally involved in the causes and correction of faulty speech. For one thing he helps a child relax physically. Speech is easier if speech muscles are relaxed but they cannot relax if the rest of the body is tense. The therapist has to teach some children to inhale and exhale correctly and to control tongue movements. Better control of the face and throat muscles that are used in speech is sometimes achieved by sucking, chewing, and swallowing exercises. The question of right-handedness or left-handedness and the establishment of the dominance of one side or the other is in some cases related to speech problems.

Often psychological factors are involved. A child may not have been motivated to speak clearly. A child may not bother to speak clearly because his every wish is gratified anyway. Or perhaps he lacks self-confidence. Parents often jump to the conclusion that a severe language limitation is probably due to a low I.Q., but this isn't usually true. Children who suffer from absence of language (aphasia) or improper speech need a careful investigation of hearing, speech organs, intelligence, and various aspects of emotional and social adjustment.

Children with cleft palate must learn to breathe out through the mouth instead of the nose; the therapist uses blowing exercises, such as blowing a candle or ping pong ball. Other exercises teach the child how to close the passage between the back of the mouth and the nose.

Children who are hard of hearing usually have sufficient residual hearing to benefit by speech therapy, whether or not an aid is used. The child who is born deaf, however, since he has never heard speech, must be taught to speak by entirely different methods. He depends upon what he can see as he watches the face, lips, and tongue of the therapist and what he can feel as he touches her face, nose, and throat. He may be taught sign language, too. (See Chapter 11.)

How You Can Help. The speech therapist will certainly suggest things you can do to help your child. The family's general attitude is important. Children want to be included in conversation, but adults have a natural tendency to ignore them when they are young because they are often boring to listen to. It's doubly hard for the child with a speech problem to interrupt. His urge to communicate with people is constantly being frustrated, except when they listen to him patiently and calmly. When you correct a child's mistakes and take him through speech exercises, try to do it without nagging or making him feel embarrassed. Relaxation is of prime importance in speech therapy. Tension is utterly self-defeating.

You can see to it that your child has interesting things to do. You can share experiences with him so that his comments will fall on sympathetic ears. When you read stories to him, or sing or read poetry, you share with him a sense of pleasure in language. This is one of the happiest ways of helping him with his speech. The gains he makes will be a continuing source of enjoyment to him throughout his life.

PART III

Education

You want your child to have an education that will enable him to make the very most of his talents. As he approaches school age, you'll be worrying about many questions that don't even arise with the average child: Will he be physically and mentally able to go to school? Will the public schools accept him? If not, how can he get an education? Must he go away from home for his schooling?

"Tommy's four and he doesn't walk yet. Whatever will he do about going to school? Would they let him come in a wheelchair? But how could he get up all those steps? He doesn't talk very well, either. I wonder if the teacher could understand him. I just know he's smart enough to go to school, but the teacher may not think so. What if the school won't let him come?"

The answers are much more favorable today than they were in earlier generations. Where the school program for disabled children is best developed, the teachers are specially trained to work with handicapped children. Each child is placed in the class or school that is best for him. The curriculum and activities are adjusted. School equipment and buildings are modified according to the special needs of the children, whether they have crippling disabilities, are blind, partially sighted, deaf, hard of hearing, retarded, or have serious emotional or social problems.

Unfortunately, though, in a great many areas there are still no special school facilities for the child with disabilities, and in others they are very limited. The parents in such communities may not even know what a good program of special education could do for their child. But some parents in this situation have banded together to organize their own special classes or schools (particularly for retarded children), and the public schools have been led to incorporate the special classes within their system. In other cases, parents who have learned what special education can do for their child have managed to send him to a community where the schools provide it. Occasionally the whole family has moved.

Solving your child's educational problems involves three steps. The first is to find out the facts about your child's ability to learn and to achieve, and to understand his physical, mental, and emotional needs. The second is to find out what kinds of schooling actually will be available for him, particularly in your local community but also in your county and state or, if necessary, farther away. The third is to work out a practical, long-range plan based on the realities of the first two. It may be helpful first to think over some of the attitudes about education frequently held by parents of handicapped children.

10

YOUR FEELINGS ABOUT YOUR CHILD'S EDUCATION

What is educationally best for normal children may or may not be good for a disabled child. If plans are to be worth anything, they have to be based on the child's real abilities. You can go astray by either underestimating or overestimating them. It takes careful evaluation to know just what a child's intellectual capacities are.

Wanting Your Child to Excel. There is a popular belief that a physically handicapped child is likely to have special intellectual gifts to make up for his physical loss. This has sometimes led parents to jump to the conclusion that their handicapped child would go right through college and into a profession, without considering whether this was realistic or not. A child can do it only if he is intellectually, temperamentally, and physically suited. Otherwise the consequences of trying may be unfortunate.

One intelligent young man who was severely disabled by cerebral palsy struggled through law school, only to discover that no law firm would hire him because his speech was considered too slow and uncertain. A girl with a serious speech defect went through college determined to become a teacher and found, after graduation, that the schools' regulations would not permit them to employ her. These may be extreme examples but they are not really far fetched. Training for some specialized fields requires many years of hard work and often is costly. The best will in the world can't always bring success. This isn't meant to discourage handicapped people from training for a profession; it's only a warning that educational and vocational plans have to be based on a very realistic appraisal of what an individual can do, re-evaluated at each stage of his schooling.

Underestimating His Ability. You may find it hard to believe, but occasionally parents misjudge their child's educational needs because they underestimate his mental ability. This rarely happens when the child has had a proper psychological examination, but it can easily happen when the child's disabilities make testing very difficult.

The story of a boy named Frank is a case in point. Because he was deaf and couldn't speak, his family assumed he was incapable of learning anything. They didn't even try to teach him how to dress or feed or toilet himself. When he was about three years old a psychologist who tested him concluded that he was retarded, and a few months later he was placed in a school for retarded children.

There he was housed in a dormitory with forty teen-aged girls who were made responsible for him as part of their own training in child care. The girls were delighted with the chance to mother a real live child. In this atmosphere of loving attention he began to thrive. A year after his admission he was able to dress and feed himself and keep clean and dry. He showed a keen sense of humor and an ability to communicate his ideas, even without speech. Because of his steady progress the school officials thought that his intelligence was probably normal and they had him re-examined. To get to the happy ending, he was eventually enrolled in a school for deaf children of normal intelligence.

Resisting the Need for Special Education. By special education is meant a special school or a special class suited to the needs of handicapped children. Some parents resist special education because they can't bear to admit that their child has a permanent disability. Others fear that a special school or class will limit the child's educational opportunities. They attribute too much importance to the academic subjects and forget the importance—to the handicapped child—of the nonacademic aspects of special education.

Special education differs from conventional schooling because it pays so much attention to the handicapped child's individual needs. It doesn't turn him down, with all kinds of excuses. It takes him as he is. It accepts responsibility for helping him manage his disability so that he can go on from there. Physical or occupational therapy, for example, may bring the child's muscular coordination up to the level for writing or typing. Speech-and-hearing therapy may make it possible for him to communicate with other students and with teachers. Then he can get on with his school subjects. You may not at first think of these therapies as a part of schooling but they are as basic to academic progress as arithmetic is to algebra.

The Child with Retardation and His Schooling. Of all defects, mental retardation is often the most difficult for parents to accept in our society where school ability has acquired such importance. Yet it is one that most demands special schooling. Parents may readily admit that their child is "slow." But if the school tests show that he will never be able to go far in formal schooling, they may not be at all ready to understand this. Perhaps they say, "He may be a little slow, but he'd get along fine in a regular class if he had a different teacher"—or if he hadn't been absent so often, or if he didn't tire so easily.

Other parents accept the diagnosis for the time being but can't believe it is permanent. Some break their hearts and bank accounts going from clinic to psychologist to doctor, and then making the rounds again, trying to find a specialist who will bring about a magic cure. Or they continue to believe that the child will grow out of it. One group of parents who worked hard to establish a special class for retarded children in their community were entirely willing to send their children to the class when it opened, but the next year several of them repeatedly asked the school psychologist, "How soon will my child be ready for the regular school?" It took them a long time to realize that children who are more than mildly retarded will *always* need a special kind of education.

Some parents assume that if they could only give their child a long enough time in the regular school he would overcome his need for special education. The fact is that the school progress of a child with mental retardation will be much smoother and happier if he is placed in a special program from the beginning. He shouldn't be subjected to the daily frustration of failing in assignments that he can never master. It's good for parents to talk with teachers and others who have seen how well retarded children do in a school program planned especially for them.

Many parents are understandably distressed because there is less emphasis placed on academic subjects than they expected. The curriculum for *educable* retarded children does not omit academic subjects, but it gives at least equal attention to practical living skills. The educable retarded child learns how to take care of himself, how to be a useful member of his home and his community, what is expected of him if he is to hold a job, how to enjoy his leisure hours. This knowledge will make a vast difference in his life. Perhaps he can't achieve more than third- or fourth-grade reading ability and can master only simple arithmetic. But he can learn to write, and his academic instruction will probably include social studies and science. If he learns to use his ability to read, write, and figure in practical ways, if he learns to make satisfactory social adjustments, he is better prepared to live a happy, useful life than if his schooling placed all the emphasis on academic learning, much of which would be beyond his ability.

The *trainable* retarded child, in contrast to the educable, can do very little, if any, academic work. He may learn to read signs such as "Stop," "Men," and "Women." A few can learn to read at first- or second-grade level. His training is directed almost entirely toward improving his abilities in self-care, in speech and language, in getting along with other people. The emphasis is on forming good work habits and enjoying recreational activities.

Even parents who appreciate the retarded child's need for special education may not realize how simple it has to be. He requires countless repetitions and concrete experiences in order to learn what the average child grasps immediately. If parents don't understand this difference, their child will sense their constant disappointment.

Almost all parents are reluctant at first about placing their child with retardation in a boarding school, and more so when a state school is being considered. The state school is usually thought of as an "institution," sight unseen, whether it is large or small, excellent or indifferent. But the question is not really whether the school is an "institution" or whether the parents will be criticized or will be unhappy because their child is in an "institution." The question is whether the school offers the right kind of educational program for the child and can make him happy. There are excellent state schools for retarded children, and parents shouldn't shy away from them just because of the label.

Judging His Chances for Happiness at School. A school plan always involves the question whether the child will be happy in the proposed situation. But when parents ask the question they are often asking an entirely different question: "Would *I* be happy in this school?"

Probably you wouldn't be happy in a special school, whether day or boarding, and there is no good reason why you should be. The child's point of view is the one that counts. The retarded child is happy in a school where he associates with other children of his own level, provided the atmosphere is generally warm. There his companions enjoy the things he enjoys. He has a chance to do things in which he can succeed. He has a chance to be important. He is not always left out of things because the brighter children take the limelight.

The physically handicapped child, too, may be happier in a good special school, day or boarding. One epileptic girl who was subject to very frequent seizures that couldn't be medically controlled found the state school for epileptics a haven. "I'm happy here. People outside are scared of me, but people here like me," she confided to a teacher. The child with a crippling disability may find greater satisfaction—and more fun—in a special school or class where games are adapted to his requirements, where there is space to move around on crutches or in a wheelchair, where a program of physical or occupational therapy helps him improve his physical skills. Of course it is essential that a boarding school particularly have an adequate staff of kindly people who can give children affection and security as well as training.

Obviously not all children with disabilities should be in special classes or special schools. The real point is that parents should judge the suitability of a school plan from their child's point of view, putting his progress and his happiness ahead of their own feelings about the strangeness of the school.

11

KNOWING YOUR CHILD AND
HIS EDUCATIONAL NEEDS

If a friendly teacher said to you, "Now tell me about Johnny," you might think she was primarily interested in his I.Q. But wise educators realize that it's more important —more helpful—to think of a child as a whole person. They must appraise his emotional and social development and his home background and the community in which he lives. They must understand how a child's physical limitations affect his ability to learn and to achieve.

Diagnostic Evaluation. The handicapped child's schooling requires unusually careful study because it is vital that he receive the best he can use. Your own observations and those of his teachers need to be supplemented by specific examinations by experts. The kinds of experts will depend on the type of disability. A psychological examination to determine the child's mental age and his rate of intellectual growth is commonly included.

If the child's hearing is impaired, for example, audiologic study would reveal the nature as well as the degree of impairment. His speech should be evaluated. Psychological testing would indicate not only the mental ability but any emotional disturbances or problems of learning. Certainly his adjustment to his home environment and the feelings of his parents about sending him away to a residential school or keeping him at home are part of the picture. The medical diagnosis has a bearing on the educational program. If the hearing loss is permanent, the child's education must include skills to compensate for it.

Whether the child is deaf or only moderately hard-of-hearing may determine the kind of school situation he needs. If he is hard-of-hearing, the usual recommendation is that he attend a regular school, probably with a hearing aid. The child who is born deaf, however, generally needs to attend special schools or classes for deaf children, at least until he has acquired enough skill in lip reading and speech to be able to adjust satisfactorily in a regular school. The evaluation might provide a basis for deciding whether he should go to a residential school away from home or to a day school with classes for deaf children in his home community. The parents' preferences and the child's adjustment to brothers and sisters would enter into such a decision.

Before reaching any decisions about education for the young deaf child, a parent should know something of the advantages and disadvantages of the various methods of communication that are commonly taught. First, there is oral speech. This involves lip reading to "hear" and kinesthetic speech to "talk." (The child learns to form sounds by imitating the lip and tongue motions of his teacher and by trying to reproduce the quality and character of the throat vibrations produced by speech, since the congenitally deaf child has no other way of perceiving the quality of the voice, intonation, or the shape of words.) This method is difficult to learn, and it is not effective when the speaker is too far away to be seen clearly or when the context of what is being said is unfamiliar. But it is the only way to communicate with the hearing-speaking world, and its advocates claim that it is very effective.

Secondly there is finger spelling, or sign language. This is learned easily later in life, after the skills of reading have been mastered. Obviously deaf people can communicate only with each other in this way, although hearing members of the family can learn it too and thus make home life a great deal more satisfying for everyone.

Informal gesticulation—basically just using the hands, arms, and shoulders and facial features as most people do when they want to lend emphasis or indicate direction or strong feelings—is another way of communicating, one that develops quite naturally and comfortably. There is some danger, though, that the child who becomes highly skilled in a private language of gesticulation that he uses with his classmates may become less motivated to learn oral speech or formal finger spelling.

These methods are not mutually exclusive and there are obvious advantages to the child's using all of them. The important thing to keep in mind is that oral speech—the first method discussed—is best learned early while vocal cords, throat and facial muscles are supple, and especially before finger spelling has become so comfortable that the child just gives up the effort because he has no motivation.

Since the congenitally deaf child should begin his schooling early, the year between three and four is commonly suggested for entrance to a residential school, but the evaluation should help to determine the appropriate age for a particular child. It may show that a program of home training in speech and use of a hearing aid would be very successful. Or it might reveal that the child is also somewhat retarded intellectually and needs to be placed in a school for the deaf where there are classes for mentally slow children.

An increasing number of hospitals, clinics, and medical centers offer diagnostic evaluation services. Some schools have developed their own systems for analyzing the needs of handicapped children through psychological and educational tests, though they may depend upon the cooperation of health centers and clinics for medical appraisals. If your school has not worked out a plan, perhaps information about your child can be forwarded to his school from the family doctor or from a hospital or clinic where he has been examined.

Psychological Testing. Broadly speaking, psychological tests fall into four groups: tests of intelligence, tests that throw light on personality and emotional reactions, tests of aptitudes and interests, and tests of the child's educational achievements.

Intelligence tests measure the child's inherent *ability* to learn, not what he *has* learned from experience and education. The standardized intelligence tests have been tried out on thousands of children, so that the average performance of children of different ages is known. A child's performance on the test is used to express his mental age, which may be quite different from his chronological age. For example, if a child of eight performs in a test at the level of the average six-year-old, his mental age is said to be six years. His I.Q. or intelligence quotient, is found by dividing his mental age by his chronological age and multiplying by 100, to avoid decimals. Thus, the eight-year-old with a mental age of six has an I.Q. of 75 ($\frac{6}{8} \times 100 = 75$).

Intelligence tests may also reveal a child's specific difficulties in mental functioning. Children who suffer from brain damage, for example, may have a short attention span, be easily distracted, or have a tendency toward continued repetition of words or acts. Some don't understand spatial relationships, others have visual reversals. Some children with cerebral palsy show a time lag between their mental response and their muscular response, whether in speech or writing. Psychological evaluation helps parents and teachers understand the problems of such a child.[1]

"Projective tests" are used to study the child's personality and emotions. They explore the world of the child's imagination and provide clues to his anxieties and inner conflicts. The Rorschach Test, which consists of a number of variously shaped ink blots, is a well-known example. The child is asked to describe what he sees in each blot but is not prompted as to what he "should" see. The objects he sees in the ink blots give clues to his inner worries, antagonisms, and obsessions.

Aptitude and interest tests give good indications of the child's particular abilities and weaknesses. The tests are designed to show whether he works well with his hands, what his coordination is like, how well he relates to other people. In this way, they help to predict his chances for success along the lines of his special interests. They are often used in vocational counseling.

Educational achievement tests measure the child's mastery of his school subjects. They help to point up his educational needs and thus indicate what his future schooling should be.

Testing the Handicapped.   Some parents distrust psychological testing, particularly I.Q. scores, feeling that the disabled child is at a disadvantage. It is obviously difficult to appraise the intelligence of the child who has special problems of hearing, seeing, speaking, or using his hands, but psychologists have long been experimenting with methods that take these into account.

Some psychologists prefer to report the child's mental ability simply in terms of general levels—superior, average, borderline, or deficient—rather than in exact I.Q. scores, especially when a child's disability makes it impossible to give the tests in the usual ways. A number of them emphasize that a sensible evaluation can only be made through highly individual appraisal tempered with judgment: the psychologist selects appropriate tests but also takes into account significant observations of the child's behavior.

Group intelligence tests are economical because a large number of children can be tested in a short time. They will pick out children with superior intelligence. They also reveal mental retardation in children who are not otherwise handicapped. They are much less reliable in indicating the intelligence of children who are emotionally or socially maladjusted or who have speech, vision, or hearing disabilities, cerebral palsy, or serious orthopedic impairments that interfere with taking the test.[2]

If your child makes a superior mark on a group intelligence test, you can follow your natural inclination to accept it happily. But if he has a physical or emotional disability that may interfere with testing, and if the group tests give him a low score that seems unjustified to you, you'll want to arrange for an individual psychological appraisal by a psychologist who works with exceptional children. If there is still doubt, repeated testing at a later date will be wise.

If you are wondering about the validity of mental testing for a child with cerebral palsy, this report from the Children's Hospital of Boston should throw light on the question.[3] Here the practice of individual psychological appraisal has been followed for years. Recently, evaluations were repeated for 214 children and young people, and the results of the earlier and later appraisals were compared. The comparison showed that about three-fourths of the children were in the same category of mental ability (superior, average, borderline, or defective) in both the earlier and the later examinations. The doctors felt that these individual appraisals had been very much worthwhile and had enabled them to give the majority of parents reliable guidance in planning for their child's treatment and education.

Your Own Observations. Your own observations about your child's abilities and limitations can be extremely useful to the diagnostic team and to school officials. A mother usually has a record or remembers the ages when her child first sat up, crept, stood, walked, held his cup, said his first words, began to use short sentences, and so on. In fact this sort of record sometimes provides the first clues to a disability. Records of the child's health history can be very useful to doctors and educators who are studying his educational needs. Don't hesitate through shyness to share such information with them.

Some Special Questions about Mental Testing. If mental retardation is suspected, the main emphasis is placed on careful psychological examination. A school program would be quite different for the "educable," moderately retarded child, whose I.Q. ranges between 50 and 75, and for the "trainable," more severely retarded child, who I.Q. falls between 25 and 50. A physician on the diagnostic team will probably make a neurological examination to find out whether the central nervous system was impaired. If there has been brain injury (the effects vary, depending on which areas of the brain have been damaged), the kind of schooling recommended would depend on his specific problems. For example, the cerebral-palsied child who is also mentally retarded must have physical therapy, special methods of teaching, and special equipment. On the basis of his I.Q., the child is placed in a regular or special class or will go to a special school. Occasionally it is better for a child to be excluded from school.

Experienced educators and psychologists are able to gain a very good idea of the child's intelligence in most cases, through tests and observation, even when there is a bodily disability. But some children are born with a type of physical defect that makes it difficult to measure their intelligence. The child who is born deaf, for example, may give the impression that he is retarded. Because he can't speak he hasn't been able to take advantage of opportunities for learning. The congenitally blind child may be considered slow because his parents have been very protective and he hasn't learned to feed or dress himself and isn't toilet trained. It may be particularly difficult to determine the real intelligence of the cerebral-palsied child, especially if his speech is poor and his physical handicaps prevent him from writing or taking the tests in the usual way. However, a skilled examiner who has had experience with children of this kind can, as a rule, make a reasonably sure evaluation, one that can at least serve as a starting point. Educators who know something about handicapped children recognize that such an evaluation is tentative. They are ready to change the child's school program in the light of later testing and observations.

Occasionally a child's school achievements may not measure up to his mental abilities. Testing can bring this situation to light. The child's teachers can then try to find out why his progress in school has been slowed down. It may be that illness or special treatments have taken time away from school. Some children perform below the level of their ability because they are discouraged or worried. Sometimes a long period of severely restricted activity lowers their initiative and encourages excessive dependence. Conferences with the parents and further psychological testing can help the school to get at the root of the problem. The purpose of testing, you can see, is not to get a number or pin a label but to be sure that a child receives all the help he needs. You can't know what adjustments need to be made in his schooling or home life until you know what the causes of any educational problem are. On the other hand, some students achieve more than could logically be expected from their I.Q. score because their drive to succeed is so strong.

Many special classes or special schools now exist for the "educable" retarded child. There is a much smaller but increasing number for the "trainable" retarded child. Educable children develop mentally at about half to three-fourths the speed of children of average intelligence, whereas trainable children develop at one-fourth to one-half the speed of children of average intelligence. Considering this difference you can readily understand that each group needs a different type of schooling.

Although there is often suspicion of mental retardation in a child's first year or two, it usually isn't possible to be sure or to diagnose the degree of retardation with any certainty before the child is two or three or four. Even in the case of the mongoloid child it may take three or four years before the examiner can determine whether he will be educable, trainable, or completely dependent.[4] Repeating the tests several times over a number of years gives the most reliable information.

Both physical and mental growth stop sometime during the teens. If the child has developed mentally at a more rapid rate than most children, he will reach a mental age that is higher than average. If his development has been slower than average, he will have a lower-than-average mental age when his mental growth stops. Of course he will continue to learn new facts after that, but there will be no further progress in his capacity to understand subjects that are more complex.

I.Q. Isn't Everything. A child's I.Q. naturally isn't the only factor to be considered in making decisions about his schooling. For one thing, there is no sharp difference between children in the upper ranges of one intelligence category and the lower ranges of the category just above. For practical reasons schools have used the I.Q. quite arbitrarily as a basis for classification of pupils, and this has sometimes confused parents whose child is on the borderline. It is particularly confusing when parents think of a certain I.Q. as really marking the difference between a "normal" and a "retarded" child.

The following example illustrates the point. A child was found to have an I.Q. score of 76 on a test. For purposes of classification, a person is called retarded if his I.Q score is 75 or below. So when this child's parents pressed the examiner to know whether their child was "normal" or "retarded," they were told that she was not retarded. Eager to have her attend a regular school instead of a special one for retarded children, they so enrolled her. As several years went by, the child became increasingly unhappy at school, behaved badly, and fell further and further behind. Finally her parents consented to have her transferred to the special school. After several months she became a very much happier and better behaved girl, and the parents realized that she belonged there. The difference between the so-called "normal" I.Q. of 76 and the so-called "retarded" I.Q. of 75 was insignificant. What was vital was the child's need to be in a school environment where she was not under pressure to compete with much more intelligent children.

Incidentally, most psychologists will give parents only a rough idea of the test results, not the exact I.Q score. This is because they know that figures give a misleading impression that the testing is more accurate than it really is.

Periodic Evaluations. Sometimes it seems that the handicapped child is always being examined and tested. But the child with a disability really does need periodic re-examination to be sure that his school program continues to suit him. This is particularly important for the child handicapped by chronic illness or any disability that is not static. Though the I.Q. of a majority of children stays fairly steady (mental ability increasing as age increases) there is a minority in which it can change quite a bit, depending on how life is treating them. Sometimes a child improves to the point where he can move from a special class to a regular class; in other instances, the child needs still further simplification of his school program.

If your child is in a school that makes special provision for handicapped children, the school will probably re-evaluate his educational achievement and give periodic psychological tests of intelligence and emotional adjustment as these seem to be needed. If you aren't satisfied that your child is in the right school situation, and if you think that retesting might indicate that a change is in order, ask your child's teacher or school principal for a conference.

Facing the Truth. Some professional people are very vague themselves in telling parents what their conclusions are. They may soften hard facts at first because they find it so painful to tell a parent that his child is retarded, or that his faulty speech is evidence of cerebral palsy, or that his disability will grow worse. And most parents are naturally unable to face the full force of bad news at once. They can only accept it gradually, as the evidence accumulates and as they realize that their child's welfare and happiness depend on their making constructive plans. Professionals are usually able to tell parents the truth more frankly if they sense a readiness to accept it.

REFERENCES

1. Wm. A. Phelps, T. W. Hopkins, and R. Cousins. *The Cerebral Palsied Child.* New York. Simon and Schuster, 1956. 237 pp.

2. E. T. Newland. "Psychological Assessment of Exceptional Children and Youth." *Psychology of Exceptional Children and Youth,* Wm. M. Cruickshank, ed. Englewood Cliffs, New Jersey, Prentice-Hall, Inc., 1955. 594 pp.

3. Edith Meyer Taylor. *Psychological Appraisal of Children with Cerebral Defects.* Cambridge, Harvard University Press, 1959. 449 pp.

4. S. A. Kirk, M. B. Karnes, and W. D. Kirk. *You and Your Retarded Child.* New York, The Macmillan Co., 1957. 184 pp.

12

EXPLORING EDUCATIONAL FACILITIES

Just as soon as your child's disability has been diagnosed, it's time to begin finding the available facilities for his education even if he won't be using them for some time. But he may be able to benefit as early as three or four years. The staff at the clinic may be able to tell you a good deal.

Where to Look.   The most important place to inquire is at your local Board of Education. Large cities have a department of Special Education that is responsible for the schooling of physically and mentally handicapped children. If your local community doesn't offer what your child needs, write to the Department of Education at your state capital. Every state now provides some type of educational service for handicapped children. In some states you may be referred by the Department of Education to other departments for certain services. Sometimes, for instance, the mental health department is responsible for clinics for the diagnosis of mental retardation.

If your public school system doesn't provide the right school situation, you will want to investigate private schools for handicapped children. There are a considerable number of them, established or sponsored by private organizations such as the Cerebral Palsy Associations, branches of the National Association for Retarded Children, and the National Society for Crippled Children and Adults. Your state or local health or education departments can put you in touch with any group of this kind that has an educational program for handicapped children in your community; or you can write to the national headquarters of such organizations. The nearest Council of Social Agencies is another source of information.

Your Child's Right to Education. If your community doesn't provide education suited to your child, you may rightly wonder why your schools aren't living up to their obligations. By all means you should talk with responsible school officials to find out the reasons and to learn what they suggest should be done. Theoretically at least, public schools have long recognized their obligation to provide education for the physically handicapped and for the educable mentally handicapped. But it often takes parental pressure to get the tax funds that will be necessary.

The picture is even less satisfactory for the severely retarded who can't be educated in the academic sense of the word. In recent years, some public schools have been persuaded to provide school programs for the trainable mentally retarded children. All agree that the state should accept responsibility for training the mentally deficient child. Some educators view this as a part of the school's legitimate business. Others suggest it could be done better by the state department of health, mental hygiene, or social welfare.

The Gap between the Real and the Ideal. It is estimated that only about one-fourth of the handicapped children in this country who require special education are being served by special school programs, and there are only about one-fourth as many special teachers as are needed.[1]

You should work with other parents for increased community awareness of this problem. It is impressive how much has already been accomplished by parents' groups. Meanwhile you may have to make the best of an unsatisfactory choice between a far-from-ideal local school program, a school to which the daily trip is long and inconvenient, or a residential school away from home.

TYPES OF SCHOOL PLANS FOR HANDICAPPED CHILDREN

There are half a dozen basic plans for providing special education. All have their uses and no one plan is best except insofar as it is best for a particular child. Not all of these plans are likely to be found in any one place unless it is a large city or metropolitan area.

The Regular Class in a Regular School. Attending a regular class in the neighborhood school and being with children of the same age has great advantages. It works well for a great many handicapped children—*if* there are provisions for modifying the program to suit individual needs. That "if" is important. The advantages are lost when the regular class puts too great a strain on a child or when he learns less readily than he would in a special situation.

The use of a "resource room" is one method for providing for the special needs of handicapped children in regular classes: the child spends part of his time in his regular class and part of his time in a resource room where there is a special teacher and special equipment. The resource room has been widely used for children who are blind, for partially sighted children, and for the hard-of-hearing, the deaf, and children with crippling disabilities who need physical or occupational therapy.

A resource room for blind children, for example, contains Braille books, Braille writing materials, typewriters, special equipment for teaching arithmetic and geography, and record players for recorded books. The teacher has been trained to teach Braille and typing and provides special help in other subjects to any child who needs it. She may arrange special activities and games, since blind children can't take part in the competitive sports of seeing children unless the rules are changed. She may teach some handicrafts and give special instruction in Braille music.

Special help from "itinerant teachers" is another way of serving handicapped children in regular classes. The itinerant teacher, trained in special education, goes from school to school advising the regular teachers. She also provides special instruction directly to some children. An itinerant teacher can cover several schools, but of course she is not able to give as much service to the individual school as a resource room teacher. The young blind child who is just beginning to read Braille usually needs more concentrated instruction than the itinerant teacher is able to provide. But the blind child in high school who uses Braille easily may get along quite well with occasional assistance.

All kinds of modifications in regular classes have been worked out on an individual basis for thousands of physically handicapped children who don't require special instruction but whose physical condition requires consideration. A child who wears leg braces has no need of special teaching methods, but he may have to be excused from school regularly to attend a clinic for physical therapy. A child who uses a wheelchair may need help in the bathroom or on stairs, but if he has no other difficulties he can get along perfectly well in a regular class. So can many children with chronic medical problems such as diabetes, heart trouble, or epilepsy, provided their daily routine is adjusted to accommodate their medical requirements for rest, treatment, or modified activity.

If your child is in a regular school that has no special provisions for the handicapped, make sure that his doctor provides school officials with whatever information they need for his protection. If he is subject to epileptic seizures, for instance, his doctor will probably feel that his teacher should know what situations are likely to induce them, how he characteristically behaves before and during a seizure, what to do for him if he has one, and whether he needs medication during school hours. If your child has diabetes, his teacher should know whether he is to take insulin during the day, what rules of diet he must observe, and what to do if he is threatened either with insulin reaction from too much insulin or with diabetic coma as the result of too little.

The Special Class in a Regular School.   A regular class is unsuitable or impractical for many handicapped children. The child with a severe orthopedic handicap who needs daily physical therapy treatments, for example, or the cerebral-palsied child whose lack of muscular control is combined with poor vision, hearing, or speech, can't profitably attend a regular class. Nor can the mentally retarded child, since he learns more slowly than other children, needs different methods of teaching, and soon feels lost and unhappy in a class where he is constantly failing.

There are special classes for many kinds of handicapped children, including the blind, the deaf, the hard-of-hearing, and children who have crippling disabilities or chronic medical problems. Most numerous of all are classes for the mentally handicapped. There are also classes for partially sighted children.

Often the handicapped child is enrolled in a special class where he is given the attention he needs, but he goes to as many regular classes as he can. He may also mingle with the nonhandicapped children in the auditorium, the cafeteria, or in school clubs. This arrangement is sometimes called the "cooperative plan." The mingling of all children in suitable school activities is good for both groups and is considered one of the major points in favor of the special class in a regular school. But in some schools the participation of handicapped children in regular activities is so slight that they have no opportunity to establish themselves among the others, and this segregation may reinforce the tendency of normal children to regard them as "different."

Going to School with Nonhandicapped Children: Advantage or Disadvantage? Going to a regular class enables a handicapped child to mix with nonhandicapped children and to count himself among them. After all, most handicapped children will live in a world of nonhandicapped people and they need to learn how to get along with them without too much self-consciousness.

On the other hand, the mere fact that a child with a disability attends a regular class with nonhandicapped children doesn't guarantee that he will be really a part of the group. The vital element is that the activities he shares with them must have value for them as well as for him. A skillful teacher can do much to help him win acceptance through giving him opportunities to assert himself. If he can't play on the team, perhaps he can write a story about the team for the class paper. If he can't dance, he can serve on the decorations or refreshments committee for the school party. The teacher who helps a child find the jobs he can do for the group is doing him a real service.

The value of mingling for part of the day becomes less when the handicapped children have little to contribute to the others, as with the very retarded children. And mingling has no advantage if it means that a handicapped child has to be deprived of the very special education he needs. So the various needs of the individual child must be balanced against what types of schooling are available in each case.

The Special Day School. Special day schools offer a greater concentration of services and equipment than most special classes can provide. The child who needs extensive special teaching, equipment, or therapy, or who just can't cope with the hustle and bustle of a regular school, may be better off in a special school. There, too, all the personnel, including custodians and bus drivers, are oriented toward helping him.

Some of these schools serve only one type of handicapped

child; others take children with many kinds of handicaps. In the latter, those who have similar handicaps are usually placed together in classes for certain types of study or therapy but join the other pupils for general school activities.

The severely handicapped child is often happier and more comfortable in a special school than in a regular school, especially when he is young. The playground, the lunchroom, and the school clubs, as well as the classes, are his territory, in contrast to the same areas in a regular school where the other children are more likely to take over. Many handicapped children need this sheltered environment until they have developed enough skill in managing their disability to meet the outside world with confidence. Some children need it throughout their school years. But the child who remains in the protected environment of a special school beyond the time when he is ready to attend a regular school loses valuable experiences and stimulation.

A disadvantage of the special school—or the special class in a regular school, for that matter—may be that it is far from home and transportation presents difficulties. Naturally if the trip is a strain for the child, you will want your doctor's advice. If it is very inconvenient, you will have to decide whether it can be undertaken without sacrificing the welfare of the rest of the family. Sometimes the solution is to move.

Some special day schools have worked out a way to serve children who have to live too far away to make a daily trip. The child is placed in a foster home in the school community for the school year. Careful choice of foster homes and special efforts to help the natural parents and the foster parents become friends have made this plan quite successful.

The Residential School.   For some children the residential, or boarding, school offers the best opportunity for development. Because residential placement is such a big step from the point of view of the emotional wrench to both parents and child, particularly when there is great dependency, the final chapter in this section deals with it exclusively.

Education in the Hospital.   Many hospitals and convalescent homes provide educational programs for children from preschool years through high school; there may even be arrangements for college courses. The educational programs in convalescent homes or in hospitals for chronic diseases are more extensive than those in general hospitals because confinement there is much longer.

Your child's schooling in the hospital may enable him to keep up with at least some portion of his regular school work. But as a rule you can't expect that he will be taught as many subjects or make as rapid progress as if he were well and in regular school. In a hospital or convalescent home, the child's medical care comes first; his educational program is often interrupted, either by hospital procedures or by ups and downs in his condition. His hospital teachers will do their best to prepare him for returning to his normal place in school, but they may not always be able to achieve this goal. Many children become anxious about falling behind in their work and need help in getting some perspective on their needs.

A parent may wonder whether school work is too demanding of a child while he is in the hospital undergoing treatment or recuperating from an operation. Usually there is no need to worry, for he is under constant medical supervision. As a rule, the school program adds interest to his day and is good for his morale. It may relieve his anxieties about his future and lift his spirits. Doctors may insist on it for this reason as much as for education.

Instruction at Home.   Many school systems provide home teaching for the handicapped child who can't leave home, usually three to five hours a week although it may be less. Some children need home instruction for only a relatively short time and are then able to return to their usual school; others may require home instruction for years.

When a child needs only a short period of home training, the teacher's principal efforts are likely to be concentrated on preparing him to return to school. If he will be taught at home for a long period, she will try not only to instruct him in academic subjects but also to provide experiences that enrich his limited daily program. She may plan for social contacts with other children, help him develop his talents, encourage his interest in hobbies, try to stimulate his desire to learn about the many things that will add interest to his life. She will also help him take a realistic view of his disability and his plans for the future.

The home teacher may make considerable use of radio and television, especially when educational programs are offered. New York City has a television program, "The Living Blackboard," to supplement home instruction. A radio program, "High School of the Air," has been conducted since

1949.[2] The children who are enrolled in it use home-study guides and textbooks and mail their completed assignments to the "High School of the Air" for correction. Papers are then returned to the students. Such instruction can't replace the home teacher, but it does give her valuable assistance.

Several thousand children in their homes or in hospitals have used the wonderful school-to-home telephone for part or all of their education in elementary school, high school, or college. This service provides two-way communication between the classroom and the child at home. The system consists of two speaker-microphone units looking rather like portable radios. The home unit is connected by a private telephone line to the school unit, and the school unit can be taken from one classroom to another and plugged into a jack. The child listening at home hears the discussion of the teacher and the class at school and can signal the teacher when he wants to enter into the discussion or ask a question. In this way, discussion includes the child almost as if he were present with his class.

Not every shut-in child can use the school-to-home telephone.

Are the classes small enough so that teachers can give indifunction effectively at fourth-grade level or better. Unusually mature children are able to use it even more successfully. The handicaps of some children prevent them from making good use of this system, especially if they can't speak clearly or if they are physically unable to maintain pressure on the "Talk Bar" long enough to finish speaking. Sometimes the telephone company is able to make helpful adjustments.

The school-to-home telephone is not a substitute for the home teacher, but when a child uses this system his home teacher can work closely with the teacher at school to dovetail the programs. The child can have many more hours of instruction per week than when he depends solely upon the home teacher's visits. The plan also gives him more vital contacts with other children of his age; in many instances both the school teacher and members of the school class visit the child at home.

In order to find out whether this system is suitable for your child, consult the school officials in your community who are responsible for special education. Most state education departments now accept teaching by telephone as an approved method for homebound children. The majority of states reimburse the local schools for part or all of the cost of the service or allow the homebound child to be carried on the average daily attendance rolls for regular state-aid reimbursement. If you can't get information about this plan locally, write to your state division of special education. Information can also be obtained from the Special Education Division, Executone, Inc., New York City.

Whatever kind of home instruction the child uses, parents should plan his day so that a regular part of it is set aside in a quiet part of the house for school work. Meals and therapy should be scheduled so that they don't interfere.

As the half-dozen principal types of special schooling have been described, you've probably been thinking about your particular child and what would be best for him. The next chapter suggests points to consider as you work out a plan that suits his abilities.

REFERENCES

1. Wm. P. Richardson. *Teamwork Practices with Handicapped Children.* Proceedings of Seventh Annual North Carolina Conference on Special Education. The Nemours Foundation, 1957. pp. 37 and 60.

2. Wm. M. Cruickshank and G. O. Johnson. *Education of Exceptional Children and Youth.* Englewood Cliffs, New Jersey, Prentice-Hall, Inc., 1958.

13

LAYING THE GROUNDWORK

School is a child's first real venture into the world. By the time the average child is ready for it, he has come a long long way. He knows how to take care of his personal needs. He can pay attention to directions and stick to a job. He can separate from his parents. He has become a social creature. Almost everything you do during your child's early years to encourage his growth and development can be considered as preparation for school.

Probably the most useful single preparation you can give a handicapped child is to encourage him to do things for himself. He'll need independence in school, and he'll also need to be accustomed to getting along without you. If he has never been left in anyone else's care, he may be very uneasy at first—if not totally unwilling—when you leave him with strangers at school.

A school with a program for handicapped children may accept certain children who would probably be rejected by a regular school. You should know as much as you can about the school situation your child will enter. Visit the school in advance. Find out what your child will be expected to do for himself. Observe the physical setup. If your child is receiving therapy, the therapist may be able to adjust the therapy program to prepare him for the conditions he will meet. It will be useful to know whether the child will have to climb stairs, what the bathroom facilities are, whether he will have to manipulate a wheelchair through swinging or revolving doors, whether he will eat lunch at school, and so on. You may be advised to concentrate on the development of his skill in self-care and in manual activities.

Find out what information to have ready for registration, such as birth certificate and smallpox immunization record. You may need a report from his doctor of a recent physical examination, including information about his disability. If he is to enter a program of special education, the school may require him to be examined by the school physician before his placement can be authorized. Some schools provide special transportation for handicapped children and you may have to supply information showing that your child is eligible. These matters may take some time.

It's helpful if you can meet your child's teachers and the school principal. It's also reassuring to meet the school nurse and the school doctor, since they may have rather close responsibility for your child. If the child travels by school bus, you will feel more comfortable about his safety if you know the driver; his attitudes and remarks can make a big difference in your child's frame of mind each morning. If the driver is to lift him on and off the bus, he should follow a method recommended by the doctor or therapist. On the other hand, if your child is to be encouraged to move independently, the bus driver has to know that he shouldn't be helped.

The Proper Time to Begin School. The fact that your child is handicapped may mean that his schooling should start either earlier or later than usual. Circumstances combine to bring about an unfortunately late school start for many handicapped children. Hospital teaching or home instruction may not be available. Parents may not know about special facilities or not realize that their child can use them. A late beginning adds to the burden of the child's handicap.

Professional people who work with handicapped children are placing increased emphasis on educational and therapeutic services for them earlier than the usual age of school entrance. Many states are revising their laws toward that end. When special schools can serve handicapped children as young as one, two, or three with nursery school programs, children will be much more ready to profit by regular classroom work at six.

Children who have been deaf or hard-of-hearing since infancy will benefit particularly from early training in speech development, lip reading, and the use of a hearing aid. The natural years for the development of speech and language are the preschool years, and if the child doesn't lay the foundation then, it will be much harder for him later. Many parents are able to carry on early, informal training at home under the guidance of a speech and hearing therapist or an audiologist. A considerable number of universities now have audiology centers. You can get information about them from The Volta Bureau for the Deaf, 1537 35th Street, N.W., Washington, D.C. The Tracy Correspondence Course, available from The John Tracy Clinic, 806 West Adams Boulevard, Los Angeles 7, California, has been used with satisfaction too.

There are now many nursery school programs for deaf children, some of them in schools for the deaf, others associated with university audiology centers. If you are fortunate enough to have such a nursery school in your community, your child might benefit by attendance as early as two-and-a-half or three. If, however, he must leave home to go to a residential school, he probably shouldn't go until he is at least four, because separation from home is very difficult for the younger child.

If you lack a preschool program for children with impaired hearing, you might consider a regular nursery school that will accept one or two handicapped children. The experience of being with other children in a supervised group will certainly broaden a child's interests and advance his social adjustment.

A young blind child can also benefit from a regular nursery school provided he himself is ready for it and the teachers understand his needs. The nursery school might well be his first new environment, one in which he can test and extend his independence. The other children will soon accept him. They learn that he has to be guided when he walks, or else must hold his hands in front of him to avoid running into things. They learn that he "sees" by touching and feeling and that they must tell him when they are offering him something to take into his hands. They also learn that he can play with them on the jungle gym, ride a tricycle, and do many other things they do. In such an environment, the blind child can develop self-confidence about the things he can do and be unembarrassed about his limitations.

Whether he can move about easily and has a fair sense of direction are important considerations in judging whether a blind child is ready for nursery school. To some extent he has to be able to find his way in new surroundings and to take separation from home and mother without being too unhappy. Readiness for nursery school may come somewhat later than in seeing children and, because his development in general is often slower, he may be happier with younger children.

There are many nursery schools for mentally handicapped children, some of them organized by parents. Nursery school gives the retarded child a chance to enjoy and play with other children. Through their example and the guidance of an understanding teacher, he may form better habits in taking care of himself and his possessions. In these ways the educable retarded child can become better prepared to adjust in the organized school setting later.

A number of cerebral palsy associations have set up development centers for cerebral-palsied children who are severely retarded, and there are some nursery groups for trainable retarded children. Some of them accept children as young as three. These children seem to make better progress after they have joined the group, showing improvement in self-care and personal cleanliness. Some improve a little in speech and in their ability to follow uncomplicated directions, and play very simply with other children. This is helpful to the child and to his parents. But parents shouldn't expect too much. Mentally deficient children learn very slowly, and even though they may benefit by being in a supervised group, an early start will not enable them to "catch up" with less retarded children.

Nursery school greatly enriches the life of the child with an orthopedic handicap. For one thing, it has a wider variety of play materials and equipment than he can have at home. More important is the encouragement to do things for himself that he receives from watching other children. This gives him a strong motive to cooperate in his therapy. Participation in the care of a pet, a field trip to the fire house, the chance to be part of a rhythm band—all these call forth his eager effort. By widening his experiences, they help him to become ready for kindergarten and first grade.

The Schools' Point of View. Actual authority for placement in the public schools lies with school officials, but they are glad to discuss the placement with you, especially if you have expressed your interest. It is helpful to the school, as well as to you and your child, for you to understand the reasons for a particular placement and to ask questions and state your own views.

You may be told that, because of existing shortages in special education in your community, the recommended placement is not the absolute best but simply the best one available. Perhaps the very best class for your child is already overcrowded. Or there may not even be one that is really suitable. In these situations you may want to discuss with school officials the relative advantages of a private school. When the best placement is quite far from your home, they can sometimes help you solve the transportation problem, thereby overcoming one big obstacle.

So far as possible, the placement for a child will be based on his individual needs, but you should understand a few general priorities that educators consider. Other things being equal, an effort is made to keep a child in his regular neighborhood school if it can meet his special needs. This is particularly important for the young child, because it enables him to remain close to his home and friends. It is most feasible of all for children with mild physical disabilities.

Another general principle is that the handicapped child should be in a school situation where his specific problems of learning receive attention. This may seem obvious, but it is not always clearly understood. There have been instances in which a partially sighted child was placed in a class with blind children. The blind child doesn't make use of visual methods. The partially sighted child does, so he should be placed with seeing children. The hard-of-hearing child should be educated with children who hear, not with deaf children, because the child with even partial hearing needs to be encouraged to use it. Sometimes children with crippling disabilities who have normal intelligence and those who are retarded attend the same special school or class because treatment facilities and special equipment are concentrated in one place. However, they should not be grouped together for academic work, because their educational needs are different.

School officials may advise you that the best thing for your child is a residential school because there is no suitable day school nearby. Then there are some children for whom it really is the first and best choice. Sometimes this is because the child can't receive proper care at home; perhaps one parent has died or the home is broken by divorce. In other instances the continued presence of the handicapped child in the home is clearly too much of a strain on other members of the family. The mother may be ill, or his care may be so demanding that other children are neglected. The child himself may be miserable because of a lack of playmates or activities.

A program of home instruction or hospital schooling is recommended only when no other plan of education is possible. Although both programs have many benefits, they lack the advantages of group experiences. They should be considered as temporary expedients until return to school is possible.

Placement for High School Children. If your child is of high school age and has average intelligence, he will probably attend regular high school classes with whatever individual modifications are necessary. For one thing, it's likely that he will have mastered the special techniques he needs well enough so that he can get along in regular classes. For another, the public schools have provided fewer special classes and special schools at the high school level.

The realization has been growing, however, that a mentally retarded teenager belongs in a school environment where he associates with children of his own teen age, teen size, and teen social interests, even though he can't study the regular high school subjects. At the same time he must have a chance to learn and to be useful at his retarded mental level. Some public high schools now have special classes for mentally handicapped children. Instead of a regular academic curriculum, they are given a program that helps them to develop socially and to form the habits of promptness and reliability necessary for holding an unskilled or semi-skilled job. The program also teaches some skills of home living, health, and safety. There may be considerable emphasis on practical vocational education with opportunities for shop work, laundry, housekeeping, gardening, and instruction in similar occupations. This type of program for mentally handicapped teenagers may also be found in good residential schools and special day schools for the retarded.

Is the School Program a Good One? Even when you are satisfied that a school generally answers your child's special requirements in teaching methods and physical care, and that transportation problems have been solved, certain questions still remain. Are the teachers well trained in the techniques of special education? There is a scarcity of certified special teachers, but some school systems offer in-service training. You can feel reassured when you find a teacher who is alert and interested in her work, interested in the children and sensitive to their needs.

Is the total evaluation of your child reviewed at intervals to assure that his program will be adjusted as his needs change? Does the school have the services of a psychologist experienced in testing and evaluating the development of handicapped children and who can be called upon to talk things over with the children when necessary?

Is the physical setting of the school favorable? You may want to look over the school plant itself to see whether it has such facilities and equipment as ramps, side-rails, elevators, rooms for special therapies, standing tables, parallel bars, etc.

Is there a school nurse available, with a doctor on call? This may not be vital to most handicapped children but it's reassuring to parents.

Are the classes small enough so that teachers can give individual attention to each child? A class for mentally handicapped children should not have more than fifteen or twenty children. Classes for children who are cerebral palsied or emotionally disturbed should have no more than six to ten pupils. For retarded children of nursery school age, usually one teacher is needed for about eight children of three or four years, or one teacher for twelve to fifteen five-year-olds.

Are the parents welcome in the school? Is there a good working plan of home-school cooperation? Many schools for the handicapped have active parents' groups that assist the school by giving volunteer services, helping crippled children move from class to class, helping them to the bathroom, to put their wraps on, and helping at lunch time. Parent-teacher organizations in some schools have an active study program to help them understand handicapped children better, and some parent organizations raise money to supply equipment.

You are not likely to find all the best of everything in any one school. However, if you are satisfied on most of these points, you have good reason to be pleased. If not, you and other parents will know what to work toward. Keep in mind, too, that an important indication is how happy the children in the school are and how comfortable the general atmosphere seems to be.

Should He Go to College? The intelligent but physically handicapped youth has as much interest in college as anyone else, maybe more. If his handicap limits the scope of his activities, the intellectual stimulation and the rich cultural interests found in college will help fill those gaps.

If your child and you are thinking of college primarily as vocational or professional preparation, however, both you and he will have to be quite realistic about the limits imposed by his handicap. Young people with handicaps are strongly tempted to disregard their limitations and to think that a college education will solve all their vocational problems. If this is your child's attitude, he should certainly have the advice of a guidance counselor who is familiar with the employment problems of the handicapped. (See Chapter 17.)

You should also realize that some colleges do and some don't take the problems of handicapped students into consideration. Before your child sets his heart on entering a particular college, and certainly before he makes formal application, you and he should find out whether that school is prepared to accept a student with his physical limitations. In writing for this information he should be quite specific about the nature of his disability and his special requirements in health care, living arrangements, transportation or special aids needed to move from class to class, and about any modifications of his activities that may be necessitated by his handicap.

There have been some excellent programs in universities. In 1948 the University of Illinois began a program for disabled veterans, which has continued to provide special facilities for severely disabled students. In a recent year, there were 166 disabled students enrolled, of whom 115 were in wheelchairs. The Kansas State Teachers College began to admit handicapped students in 1954, and in 1960-61 enrolled more than 60 of them. In a building without elevators or ramps, it has become the custom for the huskier men students to pick up a student in his wheelchair and carry him up the stairs. At the University of Missouri, a major center for handicapped students is being developed with the aid of funds from the Office of Vocational Rehabilitation. Other colleges and universities are following suit, and some of them are designing all new buildings with ramps and other facilities for the handicapped.

14

WHEN YOUR CHILD GOES TO A RESIDENTIAL SCHOOL

By the time a baby is half a year old he knows who his parents are, even if several other people help to care for him, because his parents show him special devotion and concern. And a young child wants to be close to his parents because he loves them much more than anyone else in the world and he draws most of his security from them. If his family is a happy one, he has the best chance of developing an affectionate, self-confident, outgoing personality by living with them.

Parents, for their part, want their children with them, at least until they are old enough to go away to boarding school or college. Ordinarily they wouldn't think of parting with them earlier.

If a handicapped child lives at home, he is apt to have a better opportunity to play and work with nonhandicapped children, to judge his own limitations realistically, to learn how he can get along in an ordinary community.

Then why do parents sometimes decide that it's better—all things considered—to send a child away to a special boarding school? There are different reasons. A child, especially a blind or deaf one, may urgently need a very specialized form of training that is not available within hundreds of miles of the family home. A child who is physically almost helpless may have grown so large that it is impossible for his mother to move him. If a family has been broken by death or separation and if the mother has to work, a child may have no one to care for him at home. A retarded child may be increasingly unhappy at home because he has no friends and no school suited to his abilities; or in adolescence he may become so hard to control or so easily led into trouble that the parents dare not take responsibility for his care any longer.

146

And there is many a handicapped child who needs such an excessive amount of attention that his mother finds she is seriously neglecting her other children and her husband. Or the child's care proves so difficult and frustrating that she is always nervously exhausted; as a result she feels she can't be a satisfying parent to any of her children.

The child's age is an important factor. If he is born with a serious physical defect like mongolism, microcephaly, or spina bifida, which are apt to be associated with mental retardation, the parents may be confronted with the question of placement right at the start. In former times it was often recommended that parents place such a baby immediately in a nursing home, if they could afford it, so that they would not become too wrapped up in him. (Most state schools do not take retarded children until they are six or eight years of age.) In a majority of cases this was not the best recommendation. Most families can't afford such an expense indefinitely. More important, most mothers and fathers are not ready to make up their minds in a hurry about a matter so close to their hearts. They shouldn't let themselves be hurried. They need time to get over the shock, to sort out their feelings, to discuss the pros and cons—for the baby and for themselves—on a number of occasions, with a relative, friend, or professional person. (A family social agency is a good place to look for counseling.) The parents also need time to get acquainted with the new baby, to learn what his presence and his care will mean. It used to be assumed that if a baby who was not going to develop normally was placed away from home, this would keep the parents from becoming too upset about him, and would make it easier for them to raise their other children. But out of sight is not out of mind. Some parents will be more upset if they place their child in a nursing home or boarding school than if they took care of him themselves, because they'll accuse themselves of shirking their duty.

The congenitally deaf child may be accepted by a residential school for the deaf at about the age of four. Some residential nurseries have been established for blind children as young as two or three, but such early separation from parents is not recommended unless the home situation makes it quite impossible for the child to be cared for there and unless the nursery can provide a very motherly, individual kind of care.

Most residential schools for mentally retarded children supported by the state will not accept them before six or eight years of age, because there are usually not enough facilities and because, other things being equal, small children make a better emotional adjustment at home, cared for by loving parents. And a good emotional adjustment is what will enable the retarded child to make the most of his limited intellectual capacities.

Sometimes parents of a severely mentally or physically handicapped child are able to keep him at home when he is small but find it increasingly difficult to give him the care he needs when he is large and heavy or if he becomes unhappy or chronically disobedient. In such cases the parents are not required at any one moment to make a decision for which they are not ready. They give the child the loving family care he needs most when young. As he grows older the difficulties of the situation help them to make up their minds. Then they may come to the conclusion that he will be happier among children with whom he is an equal and a program of activities appropriate for his stage of development. Or they may decide that they can do a lot better with their other children if they are not chronically frustrated by a feeling of inadequacy in coping with the handicapped child. If an older child is in a residential school in which he can remain as an adult, he will be protected and kept occupied even after the time when his parents will no longer be able to care for him, and after their death.

However, the fact that a child is severely retarded doesn't necessarily mean that he should be placed in a residential school or institution. A child whose I.Q. is below 30, for instance, will learn only to a very limited degree in a training program in an institution and this won't make any vast difference in his life. The more important reason for residential placement in such a case is whether his care in the home disrupts family life. If the family accepts him quite well, if they are fond of him and enjoy having him around, he will probably be better off at home. Some people automatically assume that the mongolian type of retarded child must be placed in an institution. But most of them have a happy, affectionate disposition; they are easily managed and well loved at home.

Parents who are reluctant to send their child away to school can remember that in most cases he will return home again after he has completed the educational program. The children who remain away permanently are the few who cannot live safely or independently in the community. In any case the decision can always be reversed if the child's maturity and the home conditions warrant it.[1]

Selecting the School. When you first begin to wonder whether residential placement might be best, you will want to be looking at the schools that are available to you. This will help you to make up your mind. The sources of information about special education suggested in Chapter 12 will be helpful, or a social worker at the clinic or family agency should be able to guide you. You should also speak to the superintendent of public schools in your district.

There are several things to consider in addition to the educational program: Are the housing and food satisfactory? Are the medical and nursing staff and health services adequate? The recreation program is important. You would like to know if there are any opportunities for contacts with nonhandicapped children outside the school. You will hope to avoid an overcrowded situation. A friendly atmosphere is most important of all, certainly more important than the appearance of the buildings. Of course a school which fails to score high on all these points may still be able to do a good job for your child.

Try to visit more than one school so that you can have a basis for comparison. You are more apt to get a comprehensive view of the place if you have arranged an appointment in advance. It's a good idea, too, to talk with parents who have children in the school or with members of a local group of parents of handicapped children who know about the school.

When there is an even choice between similar schools, you will probably want to choose the nearer one. Being able to visit your child and have him make visits home reasonably often is an important consideration.

You may have a choice between a private school and one that is run by the state, particularly if your child is mentally retarded. Of course the private school will be more expensive; state residential schools either do not charge tuition or charge according to the means of the parents. There are good and poor state schools and good and poor private schools.

There are usually long waiting lists for both public and private schools for handicapped children, and the school that can admit your child more quickly may take priority if he is in urgent need of a special school program.

State laws govern the eligibility of children for admission to state schools and certain procedures must be followed. Regulations vary from state to state. Find out from your state department of education, or from the state welfare department, what steps you must take. Usually the first step is an appointment at the clinic or agency through which you are to apply. Be sure to go with your child, as you will have to supply information and sign the application. In the case of children who are mentally retarded, state laws commonly require evidence or proof of actual retardation. Both medical and psychological reports may be required. You may have to show good reason why your child cannot be cared for at home. Parents are usually asked to make a statement about the family's income and the number of dependents.

There are various procedures for admission to state schools. Children may be placed there voluntarily by parents, or admitted on the certificate of one or more physicians, or, in some instances, placed in the school by court commitment. None of these makes the child's return home impossible, because the head of the school has wide powers of discretion. Many state schools are now developing programs that concentrate on preparing educable children for holding suitable jobs in the community so that they can leave the institution. However, the child can remain permanently in the state institution if he continues to need institutional care.

Many state schools arrange for a child to leave the school for a trial period at first, to go either to his own home or to an approved family in a community where a job has been found for him. He will be visited periodically by a social worker from the school. If he adjusts successfully to life outside the school, he may be discharged. If he has difficulties, he may return to the school for a while and try again when he shows greater readiness. Some states have established clubs, colonies, or hostels where young people can live under continued supervision during the period of adjustment.

Preparing Your Child for Going Away. You should prepare your child, over a period of months, for his going away to school and help him to understand the reasons—as far as possible. The first reference to it might be a very general one, before a date has been set or perhaps even before a school has been selected. For instance, "Some time when you are older you will be going away to live in a school for big boys. There will be lots of boys like you there, to play with and to go to school with."

You will want to explain to your child, on a number of occasions, the advantages for him in going away to school: companionship with children like himself, a class that will be just right for him, with activities that he can participate in and enjoy, training for taking care of himself and perhaps for holding a job some day. (You shouldn't paint such a glowing picture of the school, however, that the child will be disappointed when he gets there.) This kind of explanation may not be too difficult in the case of an intelligent child with an orthopedic defect or a visual defect, for example. But for the mentally retarded child the words must be extremely simple. You might only be able to say, "In this school, lots of children will play with Tommy." The young deaf child may have to depend on several visits for his preparation.

You can expect most children, especially young ones, to balk at the idea of being separated from parents. You explain that you will be visiting him at regular intervals, that he will come home for vacations, and that some day he will finish school and come home to live. Actually he might go on to another school or even to college if he has the capabilities, and he may get married instead of coming home. But don't mix him up with these possible complications now. The idea to get across to a young child is that boarding school is not banishment for life but a temporary stay, with eventual return home.

When a child objects to the idea of being sent out of town to school, as he is bound to do at times, it won't help for the parent to talk harder and faster, like a frantic salesman. Overly persuasive arguments sound insincere and only make the child more suspicious and balky. It's essential that the parents speak and act as if they are quite sure and comfortable in their *own* minds that the child will benefit from the boarding school. They can suggest that they and the child will have lots of chances to talk about the school again and (probably) to visit it, as if there is no rush about the child becoming convinced.

It's important for you to realize that a young child often assumes that he is being sent away to school (or to a hospital) as punishment for some actual or imagined sin, or because

152   CARING FOR YOUR DISABLED CHILD

the parents don't love him as much as they love their other children. If a mother gets hints that her child is having thoughts like these, she should bring them out into the open to clear the air and then remind him again of the true reasons. She might begin, "Sometimes a child thinks, when he is sent away to live in a school, that it means his father and mother don't love him very much. He thinks they don't want him to live at home. That's not true. They send him to a far-away school because they love him and think he will be more happy there."

Even more important than what you tell your child about the boarding school is giving him all the opportunities he wants to ask questions and express his own misgivings. It's surprising how different a child's apprehensions are from what the parents imagine them to be. But you can't begin to reassure your child until you know just what he is worrying about. Furthermore, his fears are apt to keep shifting as he gets a more concrete picture of what to expect. You can be sure that his questions will persist until he actually settles down in the school, and you should be prepared to keep on answering and explaining.

If it can possibly be done, take your child at least once, preferably several times, to visit the school. Spend the whole day. Let him get to know the housemother or teacher who will have most contact with him. Let him play with the other children. This is the most convincing way to demonstrate to him that there are interesting things to do, children who are fun to play with, adults who are trustworthy and comfortable to be with.

Making the School Experience a Happy One. If your child is very young, or if he is greatly retarded or can't speak clearly, give the nurse or attendant who will be in charge of his care some information about his habits. She should know how he expresses himself when he wants to go to the bathroom and when he is hungry or thirsty. It is helpful for the school to know about a young child's special food idiosyncrasies and special bedtime routines. You can't expect your child to receive as much individual attention as at home, but many schools welcome whatever information will help them make the child comfortable.

Any child who is away from home enjoys receiving letters, postcards, packages, and, most of all, visits from members of his family and from friends. If the school is too far away to permit frequent visits, letters and packages become especially significant as evidence of your love. Your letters should give all the interesting news from home but should not reflect your anxiety—it's unfair to spill over your adult worries and problems onto your child. Your letters should show that you think the school is a good place and that you are satisfied to have him there because it can do so much for him. In one school where some of the children are too young to read and where others cannot read because of brain damage, the school staff suggests that parents illustrate their letters with pictures cut out of magazines. The children in this school enjoy sharing their letters from home. Mail delivery is always a big event. Letters are particularly valued when snapshots of members of the family, family pets, and neighborhood friends are enclosed.

One of the pleasantest ways of adding to your child's enjoyment of school is by sending gifts that he can share with his new friends. The director of the school can suggest the kind of thing that has proved most successful and can steer you away from unsuitable gifts. They need not be expensive; one mother made her daughter and the other little girls extraordinarily happy by sending ten-cent rings to each of them. A box of cookies, crayons, toy balloons—these give great delight.

Care for the Totally Disabled. Some children have such severe physical handicaps that they are completely unable to look after their physical needs, although their minds may be normal and alert. The paralyzed child in an iron lung is one example. Even when rehabilitation has done all it can, the individual remains entirely dependent on others for his care. Many of these patients are cared for at home. But those who can't be should have a suitable educational program. Admittedly, the combination is hard to find; chronic disease hospitals and convalescent or nursing homes for children are sometimes the only available facilities. Fortunately many such institutions do provide an educational program for the children, usually through the cooperation of the local board of education.

For the very severely retarded children—those with I.Q.'s under 30 who cannot be trained in self-care, cannot feed themselves, do not develop bowel and bladder control, often cannot sit up, and who perhaps cannot even turn themselves over in bed—there is no question of education. Kindly custodial care is what they will need throughout their lifetimes. They can rarely be cared for at home. There are some public and some private schools for the retarded which provide the necessary custodial care. The idea that custodial care is the primary need of *most* handicapped children was discarded a long time ago, but there are some children whose very life depends upon it.

REFERENCE

1. Katharine G. Ecob. *Deciding What's Best for Your Retarded Child.* New York State Society for Mental Health, New York, 1955.

PART IV

Your Child's Vocational Future

*"Will my child ever be able to work and support himself?"
This may be the question that has caused you the greatest
concern. Some of your worry may be based on common misconceptions about employment of the handicapped. Perhaps
you've heard that only two or three occupations are suitable
for people with your child's disability and that none of them
seems to offer a good future. The first chapter in this section
will present the facts about employment for the disabled so
that your thinking can be realistic.*

*If your child is still young, you may think that vocational
planning should wait. It's true that choice of a specific field of
work should be deferred until a young person knows what he
can do and what he would like to do, but some aspects of
vocational preparation can't wait. Much of what parents do
or don't do for their child in the early years lays the foundation for his later success or failure. So the second chapter
will discuss some aspects of home training and how they relate to vocational preparation.*

*Eventually your child will also need your support in work-
ing out a specific vocational plan. He should have vocational
counseling. He may benefit from further medical rehabilitation to improve and broaden his opportunities. He'll probably
need specific education or training for the work he decides
on. Possibly he will require experience in a sheltered workshop to prepare him for commercial employment. He may
well need help in finding an actual job and continued counseling to help him adjust to it. In all these steps your support
is vital. These aspects are discussed in the third chapter.*

15

FACTS AND FANCIES ABOUT EMPLOYMENT OF THE HANDICAPPED

The first thing you should know is that more and more handicapped persons are going to work. There are two important reasons: improved methods of rehabilitation and greater public acceptance of their abilities.

In the year ending June 30, 1962, 102,396 disabled Americans were rehabilitated into employment. This was 11 per cent more than the preceding year, and was the seventh successive year in which a record was established.[1] These were persons whose disabilities were serious enough to entitle them to the services of the public agencies.

Section 2 of the U.S. Civil Service Act reads: "No person shall be discriminated against in any case because of physical handicap" if the individual is qualified to perform the duties of the job without hazard to himself or to his fellow employees. Similar policies are in effect in some state and local governments, including New York State and New York City. These figures don't tell the whole story, but they do indicate that the numbers of employed handicapped are substantial. Over the years since 1942, when the Federal Civil Service adopted a policy of employing qualified handicapped persons, the government has hired more than 188,000.

Despite the fact that vocational rehabilitation has been the key to employment for the handicapped, many of them delay rehabilitation or fail to consider it altogether. Among the 74,000 persons rehabilitated through the public program in 1958, the average age of disablement was 27; but the average age at the beginning of vocational rehabilitation was 36—a nine-year delay.[2]

Delay in rehabilitation lessens a child's opportunities for

good vocational adjustment in several ways. It may mean postponement of certain kinds of medical attention. It may deprive him of counseling in planning his education wisely. It may prolong his attitude of dependency so that with each passing year it becomes more difficult for him to take on the responsibilities of a job.

Many parents—and teachers too—simply don't know about the services of their state's office of vocational rehabilitation or about the services of other agencies. In 1958, the New York City school system took a census of handicapped high school students who needed special program adjustments and found that of the more than 3000 students qualified only 500 were making use of it.[3] Unfortunately, many agencies have neither the staff nor the money to publicize their work, so parents just have to make it their business to investigate the facilities in their own community.

Can He Work If He Is Severely Disabled?   The severity of a disability is only a partial indication of possibilities for holding a job. It *may* be more difficult for the severely disabled to find work, but many of them do. A study made by the Institute for the Crippled and Disabled[4] showed surprisingly little difference between the employment records of the severely handicapped and the moderately handicapped. As a matter of fact, the ability to travel independently seemed to be more significant than the severity of the disability. Even when everything possible has been done through rehabilitation, however, some persons are unable to work because of their disability.

The key to your child's employability is to be found not in the mildness or severity of his handicap, not in statistics about employment of the severely handicapped, not even in inspiring success stories. The key question is: Does he have assets that he can use vocationally? The disabled people who find and hold jobs are those who have cultivated their vocational assets. What will be your child's abilities? That is the real question. The lack of some ability or other will not be important if it is not required for the work he will do. To discover the child's potentialities is the basic step in his preparation for a vocation.

What Kinds of Work Can Handicapped People Do?   Too many people assume that there are only a few rather specific kinds of work suitable for the handicapped. Here are some of the facts:

Every kind of job has been filled at some time by a handicapped person. (The Dictionary of Occupational Titles, published by the U.S. Employment Service, defines more than 22,000 jobs known by more than 40,000 titles, so you can see how broad the choice is.) Each year, through public vocational rehabilitation programs, handicapped persons are placed in a wide variety of positions. In its Annual Report dated 1961, the Vocational Rehabilitation Administration gave these percentages of persons placed in different occupational categories:[5]

Skilled and semiskilled work	27%
Service jobs	19
Clerical and sales	17
Family workers and housewives	14
Professional, semiprofessional, and managerial	8
Agriculture	8
Unskilled	7

Of course, each one of these categories includes a great many different kinds of jobs of varying complexity.

In the early days of vocational rehabilitation, lists of jobs considered suitable for persons with the same disability were compiled—it seemed practical then. But as recognition of the vocational abilities of handicapped persons increased, these lists frequently proved to be useless and sometimes even harmful. After all, there is no reason why 100 persons with arthritis should be expected to do the same kind of work. Their vocational abilities were different before they became arthritic and they continue to be different afterwards. There is no reason why blind persons should do basket weaving or why all those with heart trouble should do sedentary work.

Outmoded attitudes toward the handicapped lead us in subtle ways to think first of the limitations, of what a disabled individual can *not* do. And so we are tempted to ask first, "Does his disability keep him from working?" Or we ask, "What kind of work is suitable for someone with this disability?" But these are not the right questions to ask first.

If your child is hired for a job it will be because *he can do something* for which the employer is willing to pay. The first question to ask about his job future is: "What work can he do?" Then if his disability sets limits within which the work must be performed, those limits should be clearly understood. Perhaps your child can qualify as a stenographer—but perhaps he can't travel on buses during rush hours. That sets limits to the jobs he can accept, because he must either take a job not requiring bus travel or one with unusual working hours. But if he is hired, it will be because he is a good stenographer. The abilities come first.

Special Employment for the Handicapped.   Many of the applicants who go to the state offices of vocational rehabilitation think that there will be a special pool of jobs set aside for handicapped persons. Actually, *special* employment opportunities are quite limited. By far the greatest number of employed handicapped persons hold jobs in ordinary competitive employment.

Relatively few attempt their own business. In 1963, for example, of the 110,136 people who were rehabilitated into employment through government programs, only 7,243, or slightly less than 7 per cent, became self-employed. Of these, by far the largest group was the blind.

A limited number find employment in "sheltered workshops." There are about 600 sheltered workshops in the United States, including about 130 that specialize in programs for the blind. Altogether, the workshops provide employment for 20,000 to 25,000 people, and of these almost 5000 openings are for the blind.[6]

A government report issued in 1955 estimated that there were about 10,000 homebound handicapped persons employed by industrial concerns or social agencies to do work at home.[7]

Although a great many more handicapped people might benefit by sheltered workshop or homebound employment (the number has been estimated at from 200,000 to 350,-000), it seems likely that for some years to come most job opportunities for the handicapped will be found in ordinary competitive employment.

The Employers' Attitude toward Qualified Handicapped Workers.   Probably a majority of employers still have to be persuaded to give favorable consideration to the handicapped applicant, but more are prepared to hire them today than some years ago. There are even a few competitive industries that employ only handicapped workers.

Employers give a variety of reasons for their reluctance to hire disabled persons. Some of them seem to believe that all the jobs in their organization require a physically perfect worker. (It is a rare job that really requires physical perfection.) Sometimes an employer merely uses this excuse as a screen. In other instances, he may not have stopped to ask himself what physical abilities are actually required by the jobs in his business.

The fear that the work of the handicapped will compare poorly with that of other employees keeps some employers from hiring them. However, many employers have found that it is good business to employ the handicapped. Their production, attendance, low record of accidents, and loyalty to the company are often outstanding. In the over-all, their record compares very favorably with that of the nonhandicapped. Some large studies have given the handicapped workers an advantage in certain respects.

Some employers are afraid that their insurance rates for workmen's compensation will be increased if they employ handicapped workers. This is simply not true. These rates are determined by the job itself and are upgraded in relation to the degree of hazard involved to the worker. Rates are adjusted periodically, depending on the number of accidents and the number of payments made. Studies show that the accident rate and the severity of accidents among handicapped workers are not very different from those of the nonhandicapped. In some studies, the handicapped have shown the better record; in others they have been slightly more subject to accidents.

Other employers offer the excuse that the unions will object to the employment of the handicapped. The fact is that today most unions actively support the principle of rehabilitation of handicapped workers and have gone on record in favor of placing disabled persons in suitable jobs.

Sometimes an employer is afraid that the handicapped worker will expect inconvenient special privileges, or that it would be embarrassing to let him go if he didn't do his job well. Experience doesn't justify this fear. Of course, there are people among the handicapped as well as among the nonhandicapped who take advantage of employers, but this is the exception in both groups.

Other employers claim that it doesn't look well to have wheelchairs and crutches around their place of business, or that it isn't safe. Sometimes the blame for rejecting a handicapped applicant is placed on the other employees: "I've had my bookkeeper ten years, and she says she'll leave if I hire anyone who has fits."

These attitudes yield slowly to education, but they are yielding. The public program of vocational rehabilitation, which in recent years has been strengthened repeatedly by congressional legislation, has helped to bring this about. Private organizations concerned with special groups among the handicapped are also working toward increased employment opportunities for them. The President's Committee on Employment of the Physically Handicapped, with corresponding governors' committees in the states, has been carrying on a program of public education. If public opinion in your community lags behind, you can get help from these sources to introduce a progressive point of view.

In spite of improvement in public attitudes, the handicapped person should be prepared to face unfair rejection and should have the courage to keep trying. This is one battle he doesn't have to fight alone; both public and private agencies in vocational rehabilitation stand firmly behind him.

There is little support for compulsory registration and employment of handicapped workers in the United States, although it has been tried in some European countries. There are many objections to it, principally the temptation of antagonistic employers to reserve the least desirable jobs for workers with disabilities, or to make up their quota of "handicapped" by including workers with mild disabilities that are not really handicapping. Opinion in this country favors education and persuasion.

Does Vocational Rehabilitation Pay?   It is difficult to measure the deep personal satisfactions that come from finding and holding the right job. A handicapped person who has struggled long and hard to overcome physical limitations, personal doubts, and employment prejudices gets profound gratification from his work. It means more than gainful occupation: it is participation in the social and economic stream of life.

The economics of the matter are worth noting. Of the 102,396 persons rehabilitated in the year 1961-1962, some 16,700 had been receiving public assistance prior to rehabilitation at the rate of $18 million a year. The cost of their rehabilitation was $17 million. The group is expected to contribute about 150 million man-hours of work each year. The group as a whole had been earning $47 million before rehabilitation. It is now earning $205 million a year. It is estimated that each will pay an average of $10 a year in federal income taxes for each dollar invested in his rehabilitation.[8]

Summary. Your child should have the benefit of rehabilitation services at an early age. His opportunities for finding satisfying employment are greater when vocational planning begins in the early years so that education can serve his vocational needs, so that he can form good work habits and attitudes that favor good vocational adjustment.

He will have a wide field to choose from, limited by his abilities and his interests rather than by the severity or nature of his disability. If you and your child can be oriented toward what he *can* do and away from what he *cannot* do, your approach to all his problems—not just those of employment—will yield positive results.

REFERENCES

1. Howard A. Rusk. "Rehabilitation Record." New York *Times,* August 19, 1962.

2. *Annual Report 1958,* Office of Vocational Rehabilitation, U.S. Department of Health, Education, and Welfare. Washington, U.S. Government Printing Office.

3. Roberta R. DeMar. "Secondary School Referrals to Division of Vocational Rehabilitation, School Unit, Division of Vocational Rehabilitation, New York City." Mimeographed report, 1958.

4. Marion S. Lesser and Robert C. Darling. "Factors Prognostic for Vocational Rehabilitation Among the Physically Handicapped." *Archives of Physical Medicine and Rehabilitation,* February 1953. Vol. 34: 73-81.

5. *Annual Report, 1961.* Office of Vocational Rehabilitation, U.S. Dept. of Health, Education, and Welfare. Washington, U.S. Government Printing Office.

6. W. Oliver Kincannon, personal communication. Office of Vocational Rehabilitation, 1962.

7. *Study of Programs for Homebound Individuals.* U.S. Office of Vocational Rehabilitation. Washington, U.S. Government Printing Office, 1955.

8. Howard A. Rusk. "Rehabilitation Record." New York *Times,* August 19, 1962.

16

HOME INFLUENCES AND YOUR CHILD'S VOCATION

"The most important thing my parents did for me was to have faith that I could amount to something. There was never any doubt in their minds that I could have a career of some sort. Sometimes other people thought it didn't make sense, but my parents never gave up." This was the statement of a young man who is now a successful editor and writer. He is a leader in many community groups working for and with the handicapped. He is cerebral palsied and confined to a wheelchair.

His wife, who is an artist as well as the bookkeeper in the family business, said the same thing. "I'm a dwarf. I'm so short that it's awkward for me to do a lot of things other people do. For example, I can't use public toilet facilities. I can't wash my hands in the ordinary basin or use the average drinking fountain. But my mother always urged me to go out and do all the things the other girls did. I went to the public schools. I was active in our church. I went to parties and to the theater with my friends. When I was old enough, I went away to college. I traveled back and forth alone, by train, and made all the changes from one train to another, and got along fine. But I never would have done all these things if my mother hadn't insisted that I could."[1]

Your faith in your child is contagious. He'll take from you the courage to have faith in himself. Without it, he is not nearly as likely to have the determination and patience to overcome the physical obstacles of his disability or the initiative to move out from the shelter of home into the hustle and bustle of school and community life.

"Johnny won't have to work; he'll always have us to look after him," some parents say with the best of intentions.

They don't realize that this attitude belittles the child's abilities. It hinders him from growing up to shoulder adult responsibilities. It cuts him off from the satisfactions of useful work.

Parents are more apt to slip into this attitude—satisfaction that the child won't have to work—if they themselves have given up all their own outside interests and devoted their lives completely to his care. What results then is a mutual absorption that's boring and narrowing.

This situation runs counter to the basic role of parenthood. Childhood is only preparation for adulthood. No one can make a satisfying life without first achieving physical and emotional independence. So a child needs to learn, step by step, to carry all the responsibilities of adulthood that are within his power.

Even the idea that "he'll always have us to look after him" is risky. The child will almost certainly outlive his parents. He isn't likely to find other people to care for him who will be as understanding as they. The financial future is never certain. The parents' money would have been spent more wisely, in most cases, in preparing the child to make his own way.

Of course there are some children who will be unable to work because of their disability. But you shouldn't assume that your child will be one of them until you get expert vocational evaluation about the things he could be expected to do for himself and the degree of financial independence he would be likely to achieve.

Widening Your Child's Horizons.   All children have a lot to learn about the obligations of workers, regardless of the field of employment. They need to get an idea of what it means to put in a full day's work. They need to realize how closely the quality of work is related to wages and promotion. They need to outgrow fantasies about quick success and glamorous careers.

The average child's daily experiences give him some preparation for the world of work. In the community he sees people at work in various occupations. Every day he rubs elbows with other children and adults and learns to make the effort to get along with them. In school he develops work habits. But the child with a disability may have had much of his schooling in a hospital or at home. He often has to be left out of the family's excursions and community activities. Perhaps he rarely leaves home.

It may not be easy to get your child out into the community, but the rewards are worth going after. Even casual contacts teach him something about the job of the grocer, department store clerk, postman, fireman, policeman, librarian, bank cashier, jeweler, shoe repairman, dry cleaner. To some extent, books and make-believe will help fill the gaps in the experience of the handicapped child, but it isn't quite the same as having a first-hand look.

Getting Along with People—A Vocational Asset. One study of 4000 workers (not physically handicapped) who had been discharged from their jobs showed that 62 per cent of them were let go because of social incompetence rather than lack of occupational skill.[2] They couldn't get along with other people. Children need to learn that they have responsibilities in friendship and in ordinary social relationships. Our social traits are always showing.

There are dozens of occasions every day in a child's early home training when he learns or fails to learn about getting along agreeably. Is he taught to show courtesy in greeting people? Does he consider their wishes and their comforts? Does he say "Thank you" and accept help graciously? Does he share his playthings? Are others always expected to give him unnecessary, special privileges? Most important, is he polite to other members of the family and reasonably helpful? If he is pleasant at home, he is apt to be so elsewhere.

Some handicapped young people lack social adaptability chiefly because they have had little opportunity to mix with boys and girls of their own age. They are polite enough but they have no idea what to say or do. They first need help in making wider social contacts. But just being in the company of other young people isn't always enough. If a boy has an attitude that antagonizes other children, for instance, being with them won't do him any good. And even if a child goes to a regular school with nonhandicapped children he may feel excluded from their circle.

The socially inexperienced child is apt to be happiest in a group where his needs—medical, social, emotional—are understood. So if a child can't be comfortable among the children of the neighborhood, he should try to join some organized group activity. If he can then find out how to establish himself with a small, well-supervised group while he is still young, and gets the feeling of belonging, he will be better able to make a go of the larger world. The attitude and skill of the adults in charge are of crucial importance. They must know how to foster mutual respect between each individual and other members of the group.

Some vocational rehabilitation centers consider social adjustment so important that they deliberately provide social and recreational activities and psychological counseling as part of vocational training. Sometimes parents of a handicapped child object to his taking part in such a program, because they don't want him to get used to associating with other disabled persons. This attitude is understandable but mistaken. A young woman with epilepsy who had always been painfully shy was a case in point. At the rehabilitation center she was included in some well-organized social groups and at the same time took training for stenographic work, which she enjoyed and did well. Medical treatment brought her seizures under better control. Through the center's group activity program she began to feel more at ease socially and was winning acceptance. But unfortunately when she wanted to bring her handicapped friends home from the center her parents couldn't bear to permit this. In fact they eventually withdrew her from the entire program.

Emotional stability is very closely related to job fitness. One vocational rehabilitation center noted in a recent year that of the 31 handicapped college graduates it had served, 13 were not placed in jobs. Study showed that in none of the 13 individuals was the physical disability sufficient to prevent employment.[3] They were rejected for jobs because of psychological problems based on poor attitudes toward their disabilities. The handicapped person who is very insecure or resentful will have a hard time adjusting to a job.

A child needs to grow up with a philosophical attitude toward his disability and a sense of personal worthiness. These he gets mainly from his parents. These are what prepare him emotionally for taking a job and performing it.

Helping Your Child to Be Realistic about a Vocation. It isn't at all easy for handicapped young people to be realistic about jobs or about their own qualifications. Of course this problem isn't confined to handicapped youth. But because finding the right job may be more difficult for them, they need to be especially well prepared.

Education is of course an absolute essential for the handicapped job seeker. He must grasp this early. If he has the mental ability to complete high school, it's vital that he do so. A high school diploma is a minimum requirement for desirable jobs nowadays. A parent's encouragement or insistence may be the decisive factor in keeping a child in school when he feels discouraged or when he is in a hurry to start earning money.

Education for a specific field of work has particular advantages for the handicapped child, because he may not have as wide a range of jobs to choose from as the average. He should avail himself—early in his schooling—of the local guidance and counseling facilities. If a trade school promises to be more suitable than a purely academic school, he should know before it's too late. Far too often the handicapped youth gets all the way through school without counseling and, in some instances, is even graduated from college unprepared to earn a living because he has majored in a field in which it is impossible for him to find a job.

All young children have fantastic ideas about what they will be when they grow up. No one is disturbed when a five-year-old announces his plan to be a cowboy or a space-ship pilot. As he grows older he gradually becomes more realistic about different occupations and about his own capabilities.

But the handicapped child may have difficulties in moving from fantasy to reality, because he has less worldly experience and he has a greater need to dream big. One small way to help him is to keep him familiar with what his father's job is, and his mother's, too, if she works. Children learn about the world by imagining themselves in the jobs of their parents. It's hard to believe but many young people—particularly handicapped children—don't know what work their parents do.

It's very helpful for a father to chat often with his son about the kind of work the boy thinks he wants to do, to evaluate his plans, and to encourage him, if this is justified. Yet a father may fail his handicapped child in this way, because of uncertainty about what he can advise. He needs to keep in close touch with the vocational guidance his child is receiving. A mother may fail to teach her handicapped daughter the elements of homemaking because she doubts that the girl will ever have her own home. The handicapped child, who longs to be treated like other children, interprets these omissions as evidence of his parents' lack of confidence in his future.

Public libraries usually have good books for young people about careers and jobs. The American Library Association in Chicago issues a pamphlet, *Vocations in Biography and Fiction,* which lists many books about real-life achievements. The U. S. Department of Labor issues many pamphlets, available at little cost from the Government Printing Office, Washington 25, D.C., which contain useful information about jobs. One of these, *Job Guide for Young Workers,* describes in detail scores of jobs for high school graduates. Another useful publication is *Future Jobs for High School Girls.* Your local librarian can suggest still others.

Discussion and reading can't replace skilled vocational counseling, but they can broaden your child's thinking and correct some misconceptions. Reading can be useful for you, too. Should the vocational counselor suggest an unfamiliar field of work for your child, you can read enough about it to have an intelligent idea of your child's prospects.

The question of how much television deserves careful thought. It may be a boon to the confined child. But since you are concerned about having your child develop realistic attitudes, you have to be careful that television doesn't become a substitute for real-life experiences. Some programs are educational and factual, but most are for entertainment only and give very little idea of the work-a-day world. The average child has enough experience in life to differentiate gradually between fact and fancy, but not the sheltered child. He may idealize a truck driver or develop contempt for the police; he may conclude that every businessman is overwhelmed by obligations; he is apt to overdramatize the lawyer's work. A parent can't always know what misconceptions a child has. He can't be expected to view television along with the child all the time. But just being alert to the problem helps.

Most children expect to choose their own programs. They don't always show good judgment, though, and parents simply have to limit the amount of viewing and occasionally be firm about refusing permission to see a show that they know is unsuitable. It is even more important for parents to make certain that their child has other, more constructive recreational interests.

Aiming for the Right Job. People find the greatest satisfaction in an occupation that gives their abilities full scope. It's just as much a mistake to aim too low as it is to aim too high. Your hope is that your child will be on target, with a career that matches his abilities. But if he is to succeed, he will have to avoid certain common pitfalls.

Many handicapped people feel a tremendous need to compensate for their disabilities, and this drive can generate enough power to carry a few of them to extraordinary success. The careers of Franklin D. Roosevelt and Helen Keller are extreme examples. But when the drive is not coupled with a realistic appraisal of his capacities, the young person will be exposed to severe frustration. He may aim for a certain occupation because it seems glamorous, or carries prestige, or promises a quick, easy way to get rich. Of course, nonhandicapped young people fall into these traps, too. But the youth with a disability is subject to unusual pressure to find, somehow, anyhow, a glorious life that will make up for his troubles.

Parents are naturally tempted to err in the same way. Out of their eagerness for their child to have the best in life, they may overrate his capacities, or at least they may forget his disabilities. Parents who are professional or business people will have trouble making the mental adjustment if they are told that their child should aim for semiskilled labor. Still others get so depressed and discouraged that they underestimate their children's capabilities.

It's usually very hard to see things realistically when so much feeling is involved, but doctors and vocational guidance experts can help you.

Developing Self-criticism. If a person hasn't learned to judge his own work honestly he may be resentful of any criticism or even suggestions on the job. A child has to learn the difference between praise for a good try and praise for quality. On the job, "E for Effort" is not enough; the product must meet all the requirements. It's more difficult for the handicapped child to learn to make this distinction, especially if he is homebound and doesn't have chances to see other children often doing better than he does.

And parents are strongly tempted to praise the handicapped child, to let him think that his achievements are better than they actually are. It's true that a child needs encouragement more than criticism. But still it's no kindness to let him get delusions about his abilities. You can praise him sometimes for what he has really done well and often for trying hard. But when he is doing average work or less, you may not need to say anything. Occasionally you can show him where he can take another step forward. He will learn to look at his own work critically and to find ways of doing it better. The cerebral-palsied girl who can type perfectly but can produce only five addressed envelopes in an hour deserves praise for her accuracy; but she also has to know that she is not yet able to type fast enough to hold a job.

A child's schoolteachers are in an even better position than the specialists in vocational rehabilitation to appraise his achievements. Their standards will be adjusted to what normal children do and this can be a good corrective. This is one more reason for you to know your child's teachers and to keep in close touch with his school.

Be sure to find out about the promotion policies of your child's school. Some schools promote children automatically, especially in the primary grades. They feel there are sound reasons for keeping a child with children of his own age, even though he has not mastered the subject matter of the grade. Other schools demand satisfactory completion of the year's work. But even in this kind of school some individual teachers may feel such a need to be kind to the handicapped child that they move him on to the next grade regardless of his achievements.

The important thing is for you to know what your child's status is in school. If he hasn't really mastered his work, you don't want to be left with the false impression that he is equipped for a given grade level. Some handicapped young people have learned for the first time when they have gone for vocational counseling that their basic skills—spelling, English, arithmetic—are inadequate.

Independence and Self-reliance. It turns out that many disabled people who can't perform simple chores have been restricted more than was necessary through their growing years. A young woman may be unable to travel alone, for instance, mainly because her mother always assumed that she had to take her. Years of unnecessary dependence have prevented her from learning the skills and becoming self-reliant. At an older age this usually takes a lot longer. And think of all she has missed in the meantime.

Experience in the management of money contributes a lot to self-reliance and is essential for the person who expects to go to work. Parents can start when the child is still quite young by sending him to the store to buy groceries, allowing him to shop for his own clothes as soon as he is old enough. He may have to go in a wheelchair or on crutches, but he can still learn to look for quality and to compare prices. He should certainly decide the spending of his own allowance. He can take part in discussion of the family budget. He may visit the bank, make bank deposits, and learn to keep a checkbook.

Encouraging independent travel is usually the hardest thing for parents to face. But it's a prime asset for the handicapped youth who wants to work. Even though it may be uncomfortable or difficult for him, he must learn to use the public transportation facilities when he has sufficient skill. The younger he learns, the less self-conscious he'll be. You may be quite surprised by how well he manages.

All self-care activities are desirable, but self-help in toilet needs is essential. The physically limited worker can get someone to help him with his coat or lunch tray, but no adult wants to be dependent for help in the bathroom.

Simple homemaking skills are a real asset for both young men and women, particularly when a job requires living away from home. Homemaking is a vocation for the young woman who marries, whether she is handicapped or not. Many handicapped women find employment as household workers, too. Furthermore, a disabled person who can't work outside but can help in the home may make it possible for someone else in the family to take a job and thus improve the family finances. Rehabilitation centers show how methods may be adapted to suit an individual's particular limitations and teach simplified housekeeping techniques.

Teaching self-reliance around the home is particularly hard for parents because these are the things they could easily do for their child and would be glad to do. They feel sorry for his suffering, they feel responsible for his disability. They naturally want to make it up to him. Theoretically they know it would be good for him to do things for himself, but at the moment it always seems easier and kinder to do them for him. This is why parents need the opportunity to consult regularly with rehabilitation workers who can be objective about the child's capabilities, and with a social worker who understands the parents' feelings and conflicts.

Good Grooming and Personal Hygiene. Since the physically limited person usually has to overcome a certain amount of prejudice, it is common sense for him to put his best foot forward. Personal attractiveness is sometimes hard for him to achieve. Braces or crutches make it difficult to keep clothing neat and may cause rubbed places or holes so that garments soon look worn. One who wears braces or walks with crutches, or whose gait is awkward, expends a great deal more physical energy than others in the performance of work which ordinarily does not cause excessive perspiration. Deodorants and anti-perspirants are helpful to both men and women in keeping well groomed. They don't take the place of basic personal cleanliness, but they give added assurance.

Many disabilities make it hard to brush teeth, to shave, to comb hair, to handle a washcloth, or, in the case of girls, to apply makeup. Some of the devices that assist the physically limited person in his grooming are described in Chapter 24. However, the first essential is the individual's own desire to be personally attractive and to be willing to take the trouble.

The handicapped girl about to enter her first job may need some good advice about how to manage her menstrual periods when she is at work. She may not know that sanitary napkins are available in almost every public restroom and are probably available in the restrooms where she works. She may need to be told about protective clothing or shields. Young girls who have not known about these conveniences have sometimes stayed home from work several days each month and have unnecessarily handicapped themselves on the job by these absences.

Good Work Habits. The humdrum demands of everyday life contribute to the development of good work habits. School attendance requires children to conform to standards of punctuality, following an expected routine, carrying through an assignment and completing it on time, doing homework. The parents should back up the teacher in seeing that these demands of school life are met, without special considerations unless they are absolutely necessary.

Young people learn a lot from part-time jobs during out-of-school hours. Handicapped boys and girls are likely to have fewer opportunities because they are not physically equal to the work or can't spare the time from a program that is crowded with therapy. But others are held back only because their parents fear the neighbors' criticism. The experience of doing useful work and being paid for it is of course more important than what the neighbors say, when you stop to think of it.

REFERENCES

1. Mr. and Mrs. Gil Joel, Rye, New York. Personal communication.

2. A. C. Rennie, G. Swackhammer, and L. E. Woodward. "Toward Industrial Mental Health: An Historical Review." *Mental Hygiene,* January 1947.

3. (Miss) Sonya LeBeaux (social worker), Federation of the Handicapped, New York City. Personal communication.

17

STEPS TOWARD A VOCATION

Discovering Vocational Abilities. You constantly take stock of any child of yours. You notice, perhaps only subconsciously, whether he is happier when he works with his hands or when he explores ideas; whether he prefers to work with people or alone. If he is keen about music or art or a hobby that might develop into a career, you judge whether he is really good at it or whether he is strictly an amateur. If he is a poor student, you begin to think about careers that don't depend on book learning.

But a homemade estimate is not enough in the case of the handicapped child. He needs a professional evaluation. The term "vocational evaluation" means a study of the person by a team of experts to determine whether he can benefit vocationally by rehabilitation services and what those services should be. We can use the Institute for the Crippled and Disabled in New York City as an example of how a large center proceeds.

First the staff gathers as much information as possible from those who have previously known the patient—about his medical history, his social adjustment, his education, his work experience if any. They interview the patient directly. They might also ask him to take some psychological tests. A rehabilitation medical examination comes next, to determine whether vocational services would be fruitful in view of his physical condition and whether he needs any kind of medical or surgical treatment to improve his ability to work. Physical or occupational therapists may test his abilities in the activities of daily living.

Then the team of professional staff members reviews all the information gathered so far to determine whether rehabilitation would be vocationally helpful and, if so, whether further evaluation procedures seem necessary. Depending upon the child's needs there might be more psychological tests, additional medical examinations or consultations, psychiatric interviews, vocational counseling and testing for vocational aptitudes, speech and hearing examinations, or a study of his adjustment to his home situation.

It may become clear by this time that the child should have further schooling to prepare him for a particular field of work. Or the team may conclude that he is ready to be placed in a job without further training. Or that he needs the experience of employment in a sheltered workshop. Or a few months of specialized training.

There are quite a few handicapped persons whose vocational abilities are not clearly enough shown by just the usual examinations and tests. For these people, the Institute uses the "work sample" method, or "reality testing." The tests consist of samples of real work selected from thirteen occupational fields, with about ten tests in each field. They call for the performance of actual tasks as they would have to be done on the job, and they are given under simulated working conditions. The tests are called the TOWER system, the name made up of the initials from the words Testing, Orientation, and Work Evaluation in Rehabilitation. It usually takes about three weeks to complete all the tests, and the person must come daily and put in a full day's work. The TOWER tests cover 13 broad categories: clerical, drafting, drawing, electronics assembly, jewelry manufacturing, leathergoods, lettering, mail clerk, optical mechanics, receptionist, sewing-machine operation, welding, and workshop assembly.

The standards for both the quality of the product and the rate of production are the same as those in industry. As a result, the tests provide a realistic basis for judging the individual's employability.

Your child may not need such extensive vocational evaluation. Many people who are only mildly disabled are able to fit themselves into suitable jobs quite readily. On the other hand, many of the seriously handicapped who once would have been considered hopeless are now being restored to active life through improved evaluation and rehabilitation.

Vocational evaluation should take place early enough so that it can guide your child's education. If you expect to use your state's program, find out from the state office of the Vocational Rehabilitation Administration at what age your child may apply. In New York, for example, the state program does not serve boys and girls under fourteen.

Health and Vocational Evaluation. The doctor is often called upon to decide whether the health of a handicapped patient is equal to the demands of full-time work. Some people need time to build their work tolerance by beginning with a short work period each day and gradually increasing to full time. Others have to continue to limit themselves to part-time work. Also, certain kinds of work may have to be ruled out on medical grounds, and this should be reckoned with early in vocational planning.

The doctor can sometimes suggest practical ways to protect the health of a disabled worker. The paraplegic may be advised to avoid long hours sitting in certain positions, for instance.

Psychological Tests. There are many kinds of tests: intelligence, achievement, aptitude, work sample, interest inventories, personality tests. Any of these may be given in the course of vocational evaluation. These have been discussed in Chapter 6, but they belong in this discussion too.

A person's I.Q., taken by itself, cannot predict vocational success or indicate exactly what field he should choose, but it does help to rule out certain kinds of work. It is fairly reliable in judging how well he will do in school, since I.Q. scores and grades usually parallel each other. It's safe to say that the person with a low I.Q. shouldn't plan on a career that requires college preparation.

Aptitude tests reveal an individual's special strengths and point up his potentialities. Aptitudes are studied by means of a series of tests that concentrate on several different areas: intelligence, verbal ability, numerical ability, spatial ability, form perception, clerical perception, motor coordination, finger dexterity, and manual dexterity. Aptitude tests can suggest the *range* or *type* of occupations for which a person is suited, but they do not usually specify any one particular kind of job. Tests may show, for example, that he possesses great verbal ability; this aptitude is a fine asset in many occupations—the law, the ministry, and all kinds of writing.

Interest inventories are used to find out the pattern of a person's special preferences. They are not really tests and they don't measure abilities. The Kuder Preference Record, for example, indicates whether the individual favors out-of-door, mechanical, computational, scientific, persuasive, artistic, literary, musical, social service, or clerical activities.

WHAT TO FIND OUT ABOUT AN OCCUPATION

Your child has to be pretty well informed about an occupation before he can consider it intelligently. The vocational counselor will help him get the necessary information, but the counselor can't make the decision. The following questions will give you an idea of what to look for.

What is the work like? What are the usual duties? How is the work done? What are the physical demands? Your child needs enough information of this kind to be able to relate the facts to his own abilities. One young man who had lost a leg came to a rehabilitation center determined to go into a phase of optical mechanics which, unknown to him, required constant standing. This was not for him.

In what fields of employment is the work found? If he is considering a job as operator of a certain kind of office machine, he must know in just what kinds of offices those machines are used. He should also know whether he can find the kind of job he wants in his own community.

How does a person get into the field? Some fields are especially hard to break into. This certainly seems to be true in radio and television, journalism and publishing, and the theater, where it is difficult to prove your abilities without showing past experience but where real experience can be had only through actual employment. Often the approach must be indirect—through related experience or through personal contacts.

What are the going wages, licensing requirements, and union requirements? Tales of high wages may lead the inexperienced youth to expect much more than the job pays; misinformation about high license or union fees may discourage him.

What are the promotional opportunities and the usual scale of salary increases? People can get very unrealistic notions about speed of promotion and salary increases. One young worker on his first job asked for a raise after ten days of employment.

Does the field offer a good future? Some jobs are almost inevitably dead ends and some industries seem likely to suffer a gradual decline.

The questions listed so far are of interest to *all* young men and women trying to decide on their futures. But there are other questions of particular significance for the disabled. The U. S. Department of Labor has collected a great deal of special information in a volume entitled *Estimates of Worker Trait Requirements for 4000 Jobs.*[1] A brief summary of the headings used will give you an idea of the complexity of job requirements.

Training time, or the amount of specific vocational preparation and general educational development required for average performance. The training time might vary from a short demonstration for a job impersonating Santa Claus to more than ten years for an orchestra conductor.

Aptitudes in such categories as verbal, numerical, spatial, form perception, clerical perception, motor coordination, finger and manual dexterity, eye-hand-foot coordination, color discrimination, and intelligence. Requirements for numerical ability, for example, vary from the simple ability to count and weigh fur pelts to the use of the most complex mathematical formulas in chemical or engineering research.

Temperamental traits such as the ability to carry on a variety of duties with frequent change, ability to do repetitive work according to set procedures, ability to deal with people, ability to work alone, ability to take instruction, ability to take initiative, and so on.

Interests required by a job cover the following kinds of categories, in which the worker's preferences are an indication of job adjustment and probable success: working with things and objects vs. people and ideas; routine activities vs. creative work; business dealings vs. scientific; social vs. nonsocial activities; gratification in prestige vs. tangible results. As an illustration, examining and testing electrical installations requires a preference for dealing with things, whereas writing news stories requires an interest in people.

Physical capacities such as the amount of lifting, carrying, pushing and pulling that are involved, and such *working conditions* as whether the work is done indoors or outdoors, extremes of temperature, moisture, noise, presence of fumes, toxic conditions, dust, poor ventilation, or other hazards.

For the handicapped worker, knowledge of working conditions and their possible effects has to be unusually detailed, with information that relates specifically to his individual problems. The worker who is prone to dizziness, for example, has to know whether the job he is considering requires him to work near dangerous equipment or in high places.

The *physical* demands of a job can be analyzed to take into account the following factors:

Lifting, carrying, pushing, and pulling require varying amounts of strength, depending on the nature of the work and whether it is sedentary, light, medium, heavy, or very heavy.

Climbing and balancing require agility and equilibrium.

Stooping, kneeling, crouching, and crawling require full use of the lower extremities as well as back muscles.

Reaching, handling, fingering, and feeling involve the ability to extend the hands and arms in any direction; to seize, hold, grasp, or turn objects with the hands; to pick, pinch, or manipulate with the fingers, or to perceive the size, shape, temperature, or texture of objects.

Talking and hearing are specifically required in jobs in which the worker must give oral information to others or must receive detailed information by oral communication, or must make fine discrimination in sounds.

Sight is an important requirement for many jobs, particularly so when vision defects might result in injury to himself or to others or when precision is demanded.

Naturally, the physical capacities of the worker have to match the physical demands of the work. But the fact that the two don't always match doesn't necessarily mean that that field of work is automatically ruled out; there may be a possibility that medical treatment, therapy, or training will vastly improve a disabled worker's capacities. Many amputees, for instance, have developed so much skill in managing their prostheses that they have been able to work successfully in jobs where you would never expect to find them. They have succeeded as fliers, electricians, printers, auto repairmen, dental technicians, glass blowers, and so on through a long list of skilled and professional occupations.[2]

Many minor but ingenious job modifications can be devised for the handicapped worker: handles can be lengthened or shortened, a block of wood can be attached to a ruler for easy grasp, etc. However, when extensive modification is demanded, a child should probably think twice before embarking on such a career. His chances for landing a job are probably much better in occupations where major adjustments are not necessary.

Making the Choice. At the crucial point of deciding on one field or another, certain questions that may not have been given much thought before must be faced squarely. They have to be asked, and they have to be answered—honestly. Is it work that the individual really wants to do? Many handicapped people settle for work they don't enjoy simply because it's hard to find any job at all. If your child makes this compromise, will the salary, the social values, or just the satisfaction of holding a job compensate for his boredom?

Are the opportunities for the future hopeful? Of course advancement depends upon the skills of the employee. But if the job itself holds no promise of advancement, it should at least be stimulating or pleasing enough to hold his interest.

Can the child obtain and follow through with the rehabilitation, education, and training that would be essential for the job? Good intentions are valuable but they aren't enough unless backed up with financial resources, availability of schools or workshops, acceptance by the schools, and so on.

How will family and friends feel about the kind of work? Unless the family can appreciate the value and dignity of work—even humble work—and can give strong moral support, his adjustment won't be very satisfying. On the other hand, the determined young man or woman who is willing to brave initial disapproval must be prepared to withstand persistent criticism, be able to take pride in having the courage of his convictions.

Your child naturally can't expect all the answers to these questions to be favorable. He will weigh the pros and cons and will probably have to make some compromises. What's more, he will have to accept the consequences of any compromise choices he makes. But it's far better to be prepared for them than to be embittered by disappointments when it may be too late.

The Search for a Job. No matter how much preparation he has had, the young person about to apply for his first job is bound to have some anxious moments. His greatest fear may be that he just won't find a job. But he also may be worried about some practical steps: telephoning to request an interview, and the interview itself, can be quite frightening, especially for someone who has had little experience in approaching strangers. He may be surprised and flustered by some questions and forget to ask his own. It's not a bad idea to have some pretend interviews at home.

The handicapped applicant has to be able to answer questions about his job skills and ask questions about the work. It's better still if he can show the employer a positive interest in the job and confidence in his own qualifications. But he also needs to be able to talk honestly about his disability and what effect, if any, it has on his work. His attitude will impress the employer more than his exact words.

He will probably first fill out a job application blank, including the section that asks for a description of his disability. A vocational counselor can be very helpful with this.

Finding the Job. When he is job hunting, your child should take advantage of any contacts through relatives or family friends. Every sensible person uses such advantages, not because he is seeking special privilege but because he wants to leave no stone unturned. Some young people are very reluctant about asking such referrals from personal friends. They want to get the job on their own. But they need to understand that the job is the important thing, not how they found it. Besides, people in a position to be helpful are accustomed to requests and are very glad to feel they have done a service.

Most agencies that do vocational rehabilitation will help find jobs. State offices of vocational rehabilitation do some placement and often cooperate with the state employment agency or with other agencies qualified to place disabled workers. The state office of the Vocational Rehabilitation Administration and the state employment agency usually know which employers in the area employ handicapped workers.

If your child applies for a job through a private employment agency, make sure that he understands the terms of any agreement he may sign. Nowadays the fees charged by properly licensed private employment agencies are high and, since they are regulated by state laws, they vary from state to state. An applicant may be concerned about the loss of the fee when the job doesn't work out. In New York, for example, each placement is treated as a separate negotiation. If employment is terminated by the employee, the agency is entitled to 50 per cent of the gross wages earned to date up to the amount of the maximum fee. If the employment is terminated by the employer, the agency may keep 10 per cent of the gross wages earned to date, provided that amount does not exceed the maximum fee.

When your child locates his job through a newspaper advertisement, he should make sure that the employer is responsible and reliable. If he is under 18, it is important to know whether the employer complies with state and federal regulations for minors. If there are any doubts about whether the job is right for him, he should consult a vocational counselor or the state employment service.

Help Along the Way. The long, uphill road to a job is sometimes made easier by getting together with other handicapped young people who have similar problems and are working them out together. The following account (an excerpt from "Ability Counts" by Stella Matza which appeared in *Club Larberec in Action,* published by Federation of the Handicapped in New York City) tells how some of them feel:

". . . after going through a vocational rehabilitation training program, as well as a program of socialization, we believe it is time to look for a job. Now disappointment is ahead for many of us. We go to many private agencies all over New York City, filling out applications for jobs which have been advertised in the newspapers. Employment interviewers are very courteous when we walk in. They hand us an application blank, which we fill out and return. Some inform us that the position has been filled. Others say that they do not think we would be able to fill the position satisfactorily because of our disability. We really don't mind when they are honest and tell us that, but when they tell us that a position has already been filled, and two minutes later someone else is interviewed for the same position and gets it, because he is not handicapped, that hurts even more. This goes on day in and day out. Rejection hurts. But, the fact that in a group such as Larberec we can frankly discuss these rejections with our group leader and other club members makes them more bearable. We find that there are others in the same boat as we are. This does not give us jobs but makes us feel like less of a failure. . . . Together we stand a better chance of figuring out how we can tackle the problem of employment. . . . How do I know all this? I have cerebral palsy. For the past four years I have looked for a job. I have been fortunate enough to get a few temporary positions, but I'd like to be self-supporting. I need a permanent job."

Fortunately, thousands of handicapped workers do find permanent jobs each year, but they need a lot of courage and they have to keep at it. They also continue to need all the moral support and understanding they can get.

Group discussion gives to young people who are just starting new jobs the opportunity to air their grievances and to clarify mistaken notions. Here are a few questions raised for group discussion by one counselor in a rehabilitation center:

"Your working hours are from 9 A.M. to 5 P.M. The employer asks you to drop off a package at the post office on your way home. This has occurred on several different occasions after 5 P.M. and takes you somewhat out of your way. What would you do?"

"What would you do if your employer asked you to come in and work on Saturdays?"

"You were promised a wage increase after working six months. If your employer failed to give it to you, what would you do?"

Questions about duties and privileges are quite perplexing to young people on their first jobs. There is no one answer. Discussion gives the group a chance to hear several points of view. Naturally the vocational counselor can be of great help in guiding the discussion and resolving some of the conflicts.

COMPETITIVE VERSUS "SHELTERED" EMPLOYMENT

Although most job opportunities lie in ordinary competitive employment, some disabled workers cannot meet the requirements. For them some form of "sheltered" employment is better, at least temporarily. If sheltered employment seems best for your child, he should know what it can do for him and how it differs from competitive employment.

In *competitive employment*, the handicapped worker is hired for a particular job and is expected to meet the accepted standards of quality and rate of output. He receives a fair return for his labor on the same basis as any other employee. On the whole, he won't find many special provisions made for his handicap, although some firms that have an active policy of employing the handicapped are prepared to make adjustments. A small number of competitive industries, operating for profit, employ only handicapped workers, and naturally they make more extensive special provisions. There are also a few nonprofit companies that employ only handicapped workers.

Some states issue a limited certificate of employment that allows an employer to pay less than the minimum wage to the handicapped employee whose work is below par. Under careful regulation, this provision gives employment in competitive fields to some handicapped people who couldn't otherwise get it. If your child accepts a job under a limited certificate of employment, he should understand that his wages are lower because he produces less.

Self-employment generally involves competing on the open market and it appeals to some handicapped persons because it allows them to adjust their working conditions and hours to their needs and convenience. But in other ways self-employment is very demanding, and success takes a lot of know-how. State rehabilitation offices are authorized to provide tools, equipment, licenses, and initial stock and supplies necessary for a small business or for homecraft production and marketing to those who meet the qualifications.

Because self-employment seems so attractive, and other jobs so hard to get, many people are taken in by fraudulent schemes that manage somehow to be advertised to the public. The Better Business Bureau has compiled a list of about a dozen basic types that have victimized the public, particularly the handicapped and the aged. Some of them require an investment in supplies in order to make articles which the company will market—*if* they meet quality standards. But there is always some excuse why the product is "not up to standard." Other schemes offer a high-priced course of home instruction. The "course" turns out to consist of a couple of pamphlets containing information available in any public library. Others try to attract writers, artists, or musicians. The advertisement may promise that for $50 "we will compose music for your poems" and submit the song to a music publisher. They'll submit it—but since the company sets any "poem" to music, regardless of merit, the result finds its way into the waste-paper basket, where the $50 might as well have been dropped in the first place.

Get the advice of an experienced vocational counselor or check with the Better Business Bureau about any "get-rich-quick" scheme that sounds tempting before you plunge in. The National Better Business Bureau, 230 Park Avenue, New York, N.Y. 10017, issues a pamphlet entitled "Facts You Should Know about Earning Money at Home Schemes."

A *sheltered workshop* is a nonprofit organization for the rehabilitation of the physically, mentally, or socially handicapped through paid employment. The purpose of the first sheltered workshops was to provide permanent work for disabled persons who couldn't find regular jobs. More recently, however, they have also come to serve as a temporary, transitional stage in which the individual is prepared for competitive employment. While there, he can form better work habits, improve his social adjustment, develop greater physical strength and work tolerance, or explore his vocational abilities. Some sheltered workshops also provide educational, spiritual, psychosocial, and therapeutic services.

Working conditions can be adjusted to meet individual needs. Some handicapped persons may be able to work for only a short time each day in the beginning but may eventually be able to do a full day's work after their endurance has been increased. Few jobs in competitive industry can offer such an adjustment in working hours. The workshop may also give the handicapped individual an opportunity to develop special techniques that compensate for his impairment.

Some people think of the sheltered workshop as the complete answer to the vocational problems of the handicapped. It really is the best for some—those whose disability precludes all other employment and those who prefer the security of the noncompetitive atmosphere. Opportunities for advancement are limited. Laws make it possible for workshops to pay on the basis of the actual amount of work performed, so long as payment is based on piece rates paid to nonhandicapped employees in the same field of work in commercial industry. The slow worker may earn only a very few dollars a week.

Most sheltered workshops obtain contracts or subcontracts from industry. The industry supplies the materials and the workshop provides the labor. Some workshops produce manufactured goods on their own account, but this practice is less general. A few large organizations operate workshops that are national in scope. Goodwill Industries, for example, has workshops in more than 90 cities. They repair and sell in their own retail outlets such salvaged materials as clothing, appliances, and furniture, all of which is contributed free. There is more variety of opportunity and greater possibility of advancement in such large organizations than in most workshops, which operate as separate, private organizations.

Despite relatively low pay and small opportunity for advancement, the sheltered workshop serves a great purpose and many more of them are needed. But anyone who is considering the workshop as a vocational goal should be clear about what he can expect.

Homebound employment is another type of sheltered employment. Even after extensive rehabilitation, many of the handicapped are unable to go regularly from their homes to an outside job. Stairs alone may be an impossible hurdle. Many are not physically well enough to go out, and some can't take the emotional pressures of working, where they must constantly adjust to other people.

Homebound employment (sometimes called "industrial homework") is regular employment, at a regular wage, in which the work is done at home. Agencies authorized by the state (there is quite rigid state control) take the responsibility for instructing workers, for pickup and delivery of materials, for inspection, and for payment of wages. The agency attends to the financial details of withholding taxes, social security, and workmen's compensation. Payment is usually by the piece, at rates comparable to those paid in industry. Some agencies subcontract with industry for such work as light assembly, packaging, sorting, or finishing that can be done in the worker's home; others take the sole responsibility for the manufacture of the item. Detailed information about homebound employment can be obtained from your state division of vocational rehabilitation.

Even if there is a well-organized program of homebound employment in your community, your child would not want to choose this work if rehabilitation could improve his working capacities enough to enable him to take regular outside work. Being isolated from other people makes for loneliness, and loneliness sometimes fosters self-pity. Even the most resourceful among us need social stimulation. Your child should not settle for homebound work unless evaluation and counseling confirm the fact that this is the best kind of employment for him.

SOURCES OF VOCATIONAL REHABILITATION AND COUNSELING

New rehabilitation programs are developing constantly, but they vary a great deal from one community to another. The listing that follows will simply give you an over-all picture. You'll have to explore the situation in your own city, county, and state.

Schools. Some public schools have comprehensive vocational guidance programs of testing and counseling. If your child's school doesn't have a full program, the teachers who know him best may have some good suggestions about his further education and choice of work. If you live near a college or university, you might look for a vocational counseling service in one of its departments, psychology, for instance.

Many public schools offer training courses for skilled or semi-skilled occupations, but they are not usually intended for students with disabilities. In school systems that make special provisions for handicapped children there may be programs of counseling and training geared to the needs of those who are served by the school.

There are a few special vocational schools for handicapped persons, of which the Bulova School of Watchmaking is an outstanding example. It is nonprofit, and the Bulova company has a strict policy of not employing its graduates. Students there are trained to become instrument technicians and go into private employment in a variety of jobs where these skills are in demand. It accepts students only after careful testing and evaluation to make certain that this field of work is suitable for them.

Rehabilitation Centers. In Chapter 5 (page 65) there is a brief description of how various and broad the services are in these centers. If there is one near you, it is certainly one of the resources you should investigate first for vocational guidance and possible training. In 1962 there were more than 200 of them, scattered across the country in 27 states.[3] Few of them make vocational (as opposed to physical) rehabilitation their primary purpose but most of them include some vocational services. In 1959 these vocational services were offered to the following extent in about 100 centers that were surveyed:[4]

Vocational evaluation: about 90 per cent of the centers.

Vocational counseling: more than 85 per cent.

Prevocational experience (work-sample testing): about 75 per cent.

Special education (consisting of schooling by regular teachers for children who remain in the center and adult education in subjects related to finding and holding a job): more than one-third.

Vocational training (systematic instruction for a special trade): more than one-third.

Sheltered employment with pay: just under 30 per cent.

Job placement was part of the program in a little more than 60 per cent.

Public (Governmental) Programs of Vocational Rehabilitation. Every state now has a program of vocational rehabilitation, supported by funds from both the state and the federal government. This public service is available to everyone who meets certain requirements and is in no sense "charity" or "welfare," though many people mistakenly think so.

There are several qualifications for eligibility. Medical examination must show that the person has a substantial, permanent, or long-term disability. The handicap must be one that prevents him from doing the best he could but, at the same time, one that will show improvement through vocational rehabilitation and thereby improve his job possibilities. The type of disability doesn't make any difference, nor does age, so long as the individual is at least close to working age.

These public agencies don't usually supply services directly themselves. Instead, once they know the person's physical abilities, his work skills, his interests, etc., they will recommend to him some or all of the following services, refer him to the proper sources, and help him pay the costs:

Medical services to improve the ability to work. The agency pays part of the bill, you pay whatever you can.

Physical aids, such as braces, artificial limbs, or hearing aids. The agency may pay part or all of the cost.

Vocational counseling, to guide the child into the field that's best for him, and preparation for the work. There is no charge for this service.

Education or job training, which varies from study in a university to actual work on the job. There may be an appropriate trade or technical course or even a correspondence school course. The agency may help with expenses.

Board, room, and travel during rehabilitation may be paid for by the agency if financial help is needed.

Aid in finding a job may be given by a counselor, either through cooperation with the state employment agency or through other channels. This is a free service.

Tools and licenses are required for certain kinds of work. The agency helps the individual get whatever he needs and pays part or all of the costs if necessary.

Counseling on the job, free of charge, to iron out the initial problems.

Every state has an office of the Vocational Rehabilitation Administration and most states have several local offices. You can get the address of your nearest office from the local, county, or state health department or department of education. You may also get addresses, along with any other information you seek, from the Vocational Rehabilitation Administration, U. S. Department of Health, Education, and Welfare, Washington 25, D.C.

There are separate offices for vocational rehabilitation of the blind in many states. If your child is blind you should mention it in making your inquiries. It's wise to mention the nature of the disability in any case.

State Employment Services for the Handicapped. There are more than 1700 local public employment offices across the country, administered by the states, with standards set by the U. S. Employment Service of the Department of Labor. Their primary purpose is job placement for all kinds of workers, but they also have a special program for the selective placement of the handicapped. Because services vary, your child will have to find out just how much service the state employment office is prepared to offer to disabled persons in your state. Some of the offices are not able to place severely handicapped persons, especially those who are homebound or confined to wheelchairs.

The state offices make counseling available to applicants who have problems in choosing, finding, or holding a job, and they are prepared to give certain aptitude or psychological tests where they seem to be called for.

Private Rehabilitation, Health, and Social Agencies. Some private agencies provide vocational rehabilitation services for persons with the particular disease or disability in behalf of which they operate. Some local or state affiliates of national organizations (for example, The National Society for Crippled Children and Adults, The United Cerebral Palsy Associations, the American Heart Association, the National Association for Retarded Children, or organizations concerned with tuberculosis, arthritis, or diabetes) provide medical services or physical aids to improve the individual's vocational abilities; others sponsor or operate sheltered workshops or provide vocational counseling or job placement services. You can write to the office of the national organization or consult your local council of social agencies The American Red Cross provides transportation for the handicapped.

Counseling or placement services are also offered in some communities by the Y.M.C.A. or Y.W.C.A., special clubs for boys and girls, and various sectarian organizations. These services, however, are not usually meant specifically for the handicapped.

New York's famous J.O.B., Inc. (Just One Break) is exclusively concerned with job placement of handicapped persons. It has five or six offices in other cities. If you are interested in locating the one nearest to you, write to their New York City office at 717 First Avenue. Some other fraternal groups, service organizations, and unions take an active interest in vocational rehabilitation by giving either financial support or volunteer assistance to existing rehabilitation or placement programs. Your local council of social agencies is probably the best source of information about the activities in your area.

If your child is still very young, his vocational future may seem too far off for you to be greatly concerned. If his condition is slow to improve, you may find it hard to believe that rehabilitation will eventually enable him to be socially and financially independent. But if your child had been born a generation ago, his chances of independence would have been infinitely smaller. The picture of the orthopedically handicapped waif who could expect little more than occasional help from charity is no longer accurate.

Today physical handicap is recognized as a social problem, and both the government and the public are actively engaged in doing what is possible for the alleviation of disability. There is an army of professional personnel at work on all aspects of the problem. Your greatest obligation is to see that your child has the full advantage of such care.

REFERENCES

1. *Worker Trait Requirements for 4,000 Jobs.* U.S. Dept. of Labor, Bureau of Employment Security, U.S. Employment Service. Washington, U.S. Government Printing Office, 1958.

2. Henry H. Kessler. *Rehabilitation of the Physically Handicapped.* New York, Columbia University Press, 1953. pp. 59-60.

3. W. Oliver Kincannon, Chief, Publications and Reports Service, Dept. of Health, Education, and Welfare, Office of Vocational Rehabilitation. Personal communication.

4. Henry Redkey. *Rehabilitation Centers Today.* Rehabilitation Service Series, No. 490. Office of Vocational Rehabilitation, U.S. Dept. of Health, Education, and Welfare. Washington, U.S. Government Printing Office, 1959.

PART V

Enjoying Life

Parents aren't usually aware of what a large part they play in their children's recreation. It's they who generally choose toys and play equipment. They keep an eye on the child's more hazardous projects. They try to steer him, occasionally and tactfully, in his choice of friends. They help him and his friends to get over their fights and to see one another again. They arrange family picnics, excursions, vacation trips. They worry about television and comics. They cheer from the sidelines when their child is on the school team and they give birthday parties and chaperone their teenager's school dances. They find someone to teach their children music, art, dancing, or swimming. They choose a camp. They act as scout-master or den mother. They drive him to meetings, parties, lessons.

You provide the same things, in a general way, for your disabled child. Of course, the details of his play may differ, but he needs toys, equipment, and a chance to try his wings in adventurous play. He needs friends and family fun, a chance for games and sports, for parties, special skills, camping, or scouting. You may feel less sure about how to guide him because perhaps he can't walk or run or see or hear, but you really know a great deal about children and their play just the same.

Unfortunately, many children with disabilities suffer from a starvation diet of fun and play. Mistaken ideas are at the root of much of this deprivation. It is realistic to admit that a child's disability may keep him from certain activities, but, until your child has tried, he and you won't know how much he can do or how much pleasure a new venture may bring. There is no kind of play that some disabled person hasn't enjoyed.

The capacity for enjoyment is built into every human being, whatever his condition, and will come out on top if given half a chance. So the nonhandicapped person has to be on guard against assuming that disability necessarily destroys happiness; that a child's "whole life is ruined" because his face is scarred or he can't walk. A child's disability does not naturally get to be the biggest thing in his life. If it becomes so, it is because the family just can't see it any other way. Your handicapped child will be able to enjoy most of the good things of life as other children do if he is managed sensibly. This has been shown in tens of thousands of cases, even with severe disabilities. Your child will also gain pleasure from being loved and from the feeling of belonging. He will take pride in achievement and the recognition it brings. Each good experience will enrich his spirit.

The Essence of Play. Play is what a child does because he can't resist it. But it often involves a terrific amount of work, as in building a tree house or giving full care to a doll; so there is no distinction between play and work as long as it is something that challenges him.

Through play the child also gains physical strength and skill and develops alertness. He learns a lot about living, too. He expresses emotions in ways that aid his adjustment. He sorts out his feelings about the members of his family and his friends. He experiments with grown-up activities that he sees in the world around him, and this is one way he matures. In play he discovers friends, learns how to get along with other people. He tests himself out in relationships with his peers. His self-knowledge grows as he learns about what he can do and what he enjoys. His self-confidence grows as he

develops new skills just as much as he n
Special Need for,
subjected to unusu
and from emotions
fascinates and ab
Even temporary fro
and give relief fro
developed in tha
all childre

grow up

oungster may be
cal pain or discomfort
can take part in play that
he minimizes his disability.
ns contribute to his good health
anxiety or self-pity. In a play program
Children's Memorial Hospital in Chicago,[1]
had a period of play before surgery. They went
to the operating room more confidently, took the anesthetic
more quietly, and recovered more tranquilly following the
operation.

A child whose life is restricted particularly needs the sense
of freedom that play brings into his life. He is free to play or
not to play; free to choose this game or hobby instead of that;
free to move into worlds he imagines for himself; free to
laugh and shout and make noises.

If his disability has sharply curtailed his physical activity
—running, jumping, climbing—he needs opportunities for release of aggressive feelings in other kinds of play.

Isolation and the Need for Socialization. Play is the main
road to a child's socialization. He learns his first lessons about
getting along with other people, sharing his toys, taking
turns, being considerate, but particularly the joy of companionship. Later he learns about getting hurt and taking it
bravely, quarreling and making up, obeying the rules of the
games, being a good winner or loser, planning and carrying
out a project, cooperating, competing enjoyably.

A child who has had to be deprived of these lessons may be
way behind. Ned was like this at the age of seven when he
joined a club of nonhandicapped boys.[2] Because he had
hemophilia he had become so preoccupied with the fear of
death that he didn't even take part in activities that were
quite safe. It required three and a half years of slow progress
before he was playing with boys his own age after school,
enjoying hobbies, making regular use of the swimming pool.

Every child longs to be included in group play. You can
help your child by familiarizing him with the rules and the
vocabulary of the games that other children play. You can
help him keep up-to-date on popular sports and sports heroes.
This way he's in the swim of things even though he can't be
active in all the games. Most important is to get him used to

he [...]

child [...]
find [...]
can buil[...]
ment, the [...]
hobbies offer these opportunities.

Harry was a young man whose hands were so deformed by arthritis that he was ashamed to accept his brother's invitation to visit his home for a weekend away from
the hospital. "I wouldn't want my brother's kids to have to
look at my hands," he explained to the hospital recreation
director. But she pointed out that he played the harmonica
beautifully and that if he played for the children they'd just
think of him as the uncle whose music they loved. This is how
it worked out, of course.[3]

Play as Stimulation.   Play can mobilize the child's mental,
physical, and emotional forces when nothing else will. The
child who was "too tired to do homework" responds with
sudden energy to the call of friends to come out and play. In
the same way the child with a disability may accomplish in
play what otherwise seems impossible to him. Every therapist knows the child who can scarcely master his limp in
doing exercises but who forgets all about it in the excitement
of a game. Therapists use this principle and parents can use
it too.

Billy was five when his legs were severely burned. After
this recovery, he had to do exercises. He complained that
walking and his exercises hurt him, but his mother found that
he would gallop happily around the room to music when he
imagined that he was a high-stepping horse.

At the age of twelve, May went to the hospital for orthopedic treatment.[4] She had been so isolated at home that she
could not—or would not—talk and was considered retarded.
But after she took part in the hospital's play program she
began to talk. Within a few months her play level jumped
from that of a six- or seven-year-old to that of a nine- or ten-
year-old. On her way to join other children in games, she
forgot the dragging shuffle she used when she practiced walking as an exercise and would swing along quickly on her
crutches. Her speech, her physical activities, and her school
work all improved.

Restrictive Att...

sume that a disab...
it truly does. ...
who wears a brac... Chil...
a classmate in a ...
ents assume that ...
can change when ...
is made of.
A scoutmas...
time in his ...

...ple often as-
...much more than
...nclusion that the boy
...in vigorous games, or that
...can't enjoy a party. Some par-
...can't go camping. Such attitudes
...hild has a chance to show the stuff he

...er tells of his misgivings when, for the first
...experience, a boy with cerebral palsy asked to
join the troop.[5] The scoutmaster thought that it would be
unfair to burden the patrol with a member who couldn't do
his full share. At first, he saw the boy chiefly in the light of
the things he could *not* do. But, encouraged by the experiences other scoutmasters had had with handicapped boys, he
admitted the boy to the troop. Later he wrote: "Well, he had
his Tenderfoot tests down pat before you could say 'square
knot,' and is now well on his way to Second Class." The boy
was elected Patrol Scribe and did a fine, all-round job of
scouting.

Insistence that everything the child does in his play must
be performed in the "normal" or usual way restricts his
play. A more flexible attitude encourages the child to adapt
the conventional techniques or equipment to his needs.
Specific kinds of adaptations are discussed further in Chapters 19 and 20.

Exploring the Choices. The recreation specialists who
plan programs for the handicapped don't limit their choices.
They draw on their knowledge of the entire world of play.
The school for children with orthopedic disabilities will probably have swings and jungle gyms, swimming, active games
such as dodgeball, relay races, badminton, baseball, and an
active scout program. Some of the sports may be adapted,
but this isn't always necessary. In a camp for children with
handicaps, the program will include activities found in
camps everywhere.

The program of the Lighthouse, operated by the New York
Association for the Blind, includes bowling and swimming;
many arts and crafts; singing, music appreciation and the
use of musical instruments; dramatics and play production;
social, folk, and square dancing; Braille reading, Talking
Books, and reading aloud by volunteers; creative writing;
club activities, discussion groups, charm courses. Camping

prob-
                                        uld with a
                                   games and may
                              in shooting baskets,

                     activities that he can enjoy if some ad-
              ade? In ordinary neighborhood games, he will
         ly discover his own adaptations quite naturally, and
his friends will help him as they are able to. One mother tells
how her son, Anthony, played tennis.[6] He was born with certain bones missing in forearms and hands, but bone grafts
made both hands partially useful. He was determined to play
tennis, though it seemed impossible for him to hold his racket
and throw the ball for the serve at the same time. He learned
to hold the racket between his knees while he threw the ball
high in the air with both hands. Then he grasped the racket
with both hands as the ball came down and swung his arms
with a strong movement from the shoulders. He became so
skillful that he played in the doubles finals of his school, and
his mother had the joy of seeing him receive the prize.

Many adaptations of team games and sports have been developed. Wheelchair basketball is played widely enough so
that there is a National Wheelchair Basketball Association
that issues rules and regulations for the game. They may be had
by writing to T. J. Nugent, Commissioner, National Wheelchair Basketball Association, Student Rehabilitation Center,
University of Illinois, Urbana, Illinois. Paraplegics have found
that they can take part in many other sports as well from a
wheelchair, and there have been international paraplegic sports
festivals similar to the Olympic Games including such events
as archery, javelin-throwing, table tennis, wheelchair polo, and
wheelchair basketball.

The third question is: What activities interest your child
so much that he will go all out to develop skill? Perhaps your
child should answer the third question first. When his heart is

every...
judgment a...

Usually ove... opportunity to give ... adults in a rehabilitation cente... three months of weekly social meeting... then became interested in organizations th... handicapped people. Through a bingo party they ... $35, which they gave to the Cerebral Palsy Association. One of the youths said, "This is the best therapy in the world. It's the first time in my life that I have ever been able to give something rather than be on the receiving end."[7]

Suitability for Stages of Development. Naturally play should be suited to a child's stage of development. This isn't always easy to accomplish for a handicapped child. If he has very limited use of his hands he may not be able to handle the small toys that are normally used by children of his age. He may require jigsaw puzzles with large pieces. But these are usually intended for very young children and are uninteresting to older boys and girls. However, someone who is handy with a jig saw can mount on plywood pictures that suit the child's age and interests, cutting them into sizes that he can handle.

Of course, the disabled child often lags behind other children of his age in his play. He goes through the same stages of development as other children, though, and in the same order.[8] He does not skip over a significant phase, but he is likely to remain longer than usual in one stage before going on to the next.

Discovery and Challenge. If your child's heart is set on some recreational accomplishment that seems impossible for him because of his disability, you may be in doubt about whether to encourage him or to urge a substitute. It's usually best not to prejudge his ability but to let him try out the beginning steps of what he wants to do. Perhaps he can draw on resources you didn't know he had. If not, the experience will teach him to be more realistic. (Unhandicapped children have to learn the same thing.) One blind Boy Scout who learned to swim wanted to try for his Merit Badge in Life Saving. He had difficulty in judging distance and depth and in keeping his sense of direction in the water, but he persevered until he overcame these obstacles and passed his tests to the complete satisfaction of the official examiner.[9] And more than one cerebral-palsied person has learned to paint by holding the brush in his teeth. In fact, there is an association of artists who use either mouth or foot to hold the tools as they paint.

Doing It Himself. The young child needs to be introduced to a new activity in a way that gives him confidence and helps him to enjoy it. He may have to have a demonstration or try a very small step first. However, an important function of play is to encourage the child to find out what he can do for himself. When he is experimenting with a new toy or a new activity it is better not to give him help unless he definitely asks for it, even though you may be tempted to because of his handicap. The baby will probably learn to grasp his toy sooner if his mother simply puts it within reach.

One mother hung a string of bells just out of reach to encourage her two-year-old daughter with spastic cerebral palsy to sit up and reach for them. For several days the child watched another child in a nearby crib playing with his string of bells. Then one day she was found sitting almost upright, hanging on to one of the bells and smiling happily.[10]

Play Is for Fun. The best test of play is whether the child is really having a good time. A hospital recreation worker tells about a group of boys whose life in the hospital was transformed when they had a chance to do just what was fun for them.[11] They were making bookends in occupational therapy but were not much interested, either in books or bookends. She asked if there was something else they wanted to do.

"We'd like a swing band," they told her right aw "We've been saving money for it and we've got forty lars."

To their delight, she found second-hand instrume them. Then they needed music stands. "Why don't your occupational therapist if you can make the The therapist agreed, and the boys made the st learned to read music, actually formed the band" wonderful time. In working together toward a dream of their own they accomplished more than they or anybody else had ever expected.

MAKING HOME A GOOD PLACE TO PLAY

The spirit of a home is more important than all its schedules, rules, virtues, and accomplishments. Your child will develop more soundly and his friends will come more often if your home has an atmosphere in which laughter is welcomed and children are enjoyed. If the parents can't enjoy life, their children won't either.

Some lucky parents have the knack of getting the spirit of play into many of the small things that go on in the course of a day. All mothers of young children are busy, especially with a handicapped child, but playing isn't necessarily an "extra." Sharing a joke and laughing with your child isn't time consuming. Paper plates and hot dogs can transform lunchtime into a picnic. Straightening a bureau drawer may become a game when your child works with you sorting things out. The gaiety of the shared companionship makes chores less burdensome.

It's easier to create a home where children play happily if you have some fun of your own. "What do you do for fun?" seems a harmless question. But it brought sudden tears to the eyes of the mother who replied, "My husband and I haven't been out together to a movie or party for years. How can we leave our child?" Parents need fun and recreation, both for their own sakes and for the well-being of all their children.

Parents need to keep their roots in the community, to stay ʼert and responsive to the ideas of others, to preserve their ʼndships. When they withdraw from community contacts, ʼly life becomes progressively ingrown and narrow. Then ʼandicapped child and his brothers and sisters also ʼnore difficult to reach out.

ʼaluable by-product of the parents' social contacts is ʼ people get to know and understand the handi-ʼd. If they understand, they can help their children ʼoo.

ʼlay Equipment. Selecting toys and play equipment requires only the same common sense that you'd use in choosing them for any child. Perhaps the doctor or therapist will suggest toys that encourage certain kinds of movements that are important.

Play materials that the child can use imaginatively, in many ways, are much more fun in the long run than elaborate toys that have only one use. Blocks, dolls, trucks, crayons, clay, building and sewing sets, for example, hold interest longer because the child can go on doing different things with them every day. Versatile play materials are especially good for the child whose mental interests have outpaced his limited physical skills. Finger paints, for example, can be fun for a young child or for an adult whose hands function poorly.

If your child's disability interferes with body control or balance, the toys that he sits in, rides, or pushes should be exceptionally stable. If his hand control is poor, playthings should be hardy enough to withstand rugged treatment. Follow the usual safety precautions in choosing toys. Flammable materials should be avoided, as should sharp edges, or very small toys or those with removable parts that the baby or child of two or three years may swallow. What is hazardous for the toddler is often reasonably safe for the older child. Electrical toys should carry the seal of the Underwriters' Laboratories, but the child of eight or ten should use them—and dangerous tools as well—under supervision until he has developed reliable skill.

Every household has all kinds of items that the child can use for fun. One book about children's play[12] devotes six pages of small type to listing household equipment that can be used as play material. From the kitchen come milk cartons to make tunnels for trains, macaroni for stringing into necklaces. The writing desk supplies paper clips, rubber bands, scotch tape, paste, a magnifying glass, and the stapler, a very versatile tool in play with paper or cloth. Bedroom and closet offer old clothes for dressing up, old stockings that make wonderful dolls, discarded junk jewelry, and so on. Try an Odds and Ends Box, putting into it all kinds of discards and oddities that a child might improvise with.

A convenient place to keep toys and play materials is important. Open shelves may be more convenient for some children than cupboards with doors, especially if it's difficult for a child to operate a latch. If other space is lacking, sturdy cartons will do quite well.

Fun for the Child in Bed. If a child has to be in bed for a long time, the choice of the room is important. It should be a cheerful room and, if the view from the window makes it possible for him to keep up with what's going on in the neighborhood, so much the better. He can watch people and street traffic and the birds, trees, and stars more easily if his bed is near the window.

Your child's view of the world can also be enlarged by several strategically placed mirrors. A mirror outside the window may show him a part of the neighborhood he couldn't otherwise see, and inside mirrors help him keep track of what happens in other rooms of the house.

To make the room itself more interesting, you might try decorations that can be changed frequently, along with your child's changing interests. The room should be attractive to the child rather than to adults. The expensive bedspread will just be a nuisance to a young child, although it may bring great pleasure to a girl in her teens. The young child can use an old sheet for a spread and have his visitors write their names or messages in brightly colored crayons, just as friends' names and messages written on a plaster cast turn it into a prized badge of distinction.[13]

A large bulletin board (a piece of beaver board or one side of a large carton that takes thumb tacks easily) has many uses. Pictures or posters can be tacked up and changed frequently. Clippings, radio and television programs, snapshots of pets or friends, get-well cards, crossword puzzles, or anything else that interests him can go on the board. If it is on a wall beside his bed, blank paper can be tacked up so that he can draw.

The child will need a good light over his bed, arranged so that it shines on his work and not in his eyes. He will need a backrest if he is allowed to sit up. You may want to buy one, but comfortable backrests can be improvised. A canvas backrest, like those used at the beach, plus one or two pillows, may be satisfactory. A large carton, cut diagonally in two with the open side placed down, provides support in the shape of a triangular pillow. Edges can be bound with gummed paper.[14] The weight of the covers can be lifted from his feet and legs by some sort of footboard or by pillows that support the bedding.

A bed-table is another necessity. The adjustable breakfast trays used by adults are usually not large or secure enough for a child's play with blocks, puzzles, or paints. Adjustable tables such as those used in hospitals are splendid but expensive. An old-fashioned kitchen table on casters, wide enough to span the child's bed, provides good play space and stability. An old card table, with its legs cut down to about eight inches, gives good play space and can rest all four legs on the bed. Someone who is handy with tools can made a bed-table, sized according to the child's needs, by using double plywood fastened firmly to two plywood sides. It is an advantage to have a recess in the table top that will hold a drinking glass securely.

Bedclothing, floor coverings, and the child's clothing can easily be protected. Two yards of plastic material, about the weight of a plastic shower curtain or table cloth, can serve both as apron for the child and cover for the bed. A round hole near one end of the child's head, and two smaller holes for arms, give him freedom to paint, model clay, and enjoy other messy activities. Oilcloth or plastic on the floor around the bed protects rugs or floor.

A handy place to keep toys and play materials within the child's reach saves steps for Mother and is pleasant for the child. For the young child, it is better to have a selected few of his toys within reach and to change them when he is ready for others; the older child may want to have a larger selection at hand. A set of shelves next to the bed is one possibility. Shelves on casters, or a small storage cupboard on wheels, can be rolled alongside the bed or pushed back against the wall when not needed. Or a carton under the bed may serve for storage if a cord is attached to it so that the child can draw it out. Small boxes, egg cartons, sandwich bags, baby-food jars, and many other containers are handy for keeping small toys sorted. A sturdy shopping bag fastened to the side of the bed can be used for a wastebasket; ordinary paper bags, pinned to the mattress, can hold disposable materials to be burned.

The Uses of Accomplishment. The disabled child often has to work hard to be accepted by other children. A warm, friendly personality goes a long way, but there are other powers of attraction. Children are notoriously awed by skills and superior knowledge, and it isn't difficult to excel in one or two things.

A playground director tells the story of Teddy, who suffered a 40-per cent loss of muscular control of the left side of his body following an automobile accident.[15] Although Teddy couldn't perform well, he knew his stuff, and when he explained to the smaller children how to kick a football, or slide into base, they really listened. Accordingly, the playground leaders made Teddy an instructor for the younger boys. He did so well for them that the older boys soon recognized him as an authority and came to him for advice.

There are many different ways a child can be a good companion. Children his age may admire his skill at games or his ability to think of interesting things to do or his enthusiasm in following the suggestions of others. They may prize his sense of fun, or his ability to make things or to play a musical instrument. They may appreciate him because he has fine toys and lets them play with them, or interesting books, or stamps to trade. Or his mother always has fine cookies to offer.

Putting Friends at Ease.   Your child helps other people feel comfortable about his disability when he accepts it matter-of-factly and acknowledges the adjustments that he and others must make. (This is quite different from a child's trading on his disability to take unfair advantage.) When new companions are curious, it is good if he can give a casual explanation. Mrs. Killilea describes how her daughter, Karen, explained her disability to another child on her first day of kindergarten. A schoolmate asked her if her braces were broken at the knees.

> Karen explained that her braces had joints where her legs had joints so that she could move right, and then added very matter-of-factly, "I have cerebral palsy, you know. I'm a spastic. Are you hungry? I am."[16]

Your child's companions may be puzzled about how to behave toward him at times. Perhaps he uses a wheelchair and other children don't know what help he needs. If your child tells them simply, there is no embarrassment. "You don't have to push the chair. But I'd like some help at the curb, please. It's easier to take this chair down the curb backwards." The child who has diabetes may be invited more confidently to a party if the hostess knows that he is used to accepting a sugar-free soft drink instead of a sweetened drink, or that it's all right for him to have a small serving of ice cream if he doesn't eat cake.

When a disability interferes with social customs, such as shaking hands, a child must find simple adjustments that put other people at ease. A blind person may take the lead in extending his hand for a handshake. One who has lost his right arm may take the lead by extending his left hand. The left hand should be offered with the palm of the hand facing outward rather than inward as usual so that it falls readily into the outstretched palm of the righthanded person.[17]

Similarly, the one-handed child will need to be prepared with techniques for eating meals or refreshments when away from home, or else be ready to ask for the help he may need. A one-handed person can cut his own meat, for example, by gradually easing the point and the cutting edge of the knife into the meat, provided his hostess gives him a sharp enough knife. When he has made a small incision, he makes one more to form a wedge-shaped bite.[18]

With Whom Should He Play? Arguments fly thick and fast about whether handicapped and nonhandicapped children should be integrated with each other in recreational groups. You must find the answer for your own child in terms of his needs and the available opportunities. What is available may, in fact, decide the matter.

Many disabled persons have found security and happiness in a recreational group where everyone has the same handicap or various ones. The disadvantage is that it does not prepare them for existence with the unhandicapped. Other parents and children will shy away from a recreation program for the handicapped. There are several things to think about before you take a position on the question. If your child has lived in isolation from other children and seems socially immature, is he ready to be comfortable in a group of nonhandicapped children? Or will he be better off, for a time, with other handicapped children where there may be less exposure to curiosity?

One child may do well in the handicapped group. Another may have social strength to get along in a nonhandicapped group as long as he is somewhat protected, as in a scout troop with a scoutmaster who knows how to teach the other boys to be understanding. But this same child might not be comfortable at first in the uncontrolled roughhousing of a neighborhood gang. Still another child will have the social ability to make his way anywhere in the neighborhood.

If your child has a chance to join a recreation group for children with disabilities, you may wonder what will hold them together. Is the disability the only tie they have in common? In the beginning, the answer may be yes. If there is good leadership and the program appeals to your child, he may be drawn into genuinely pleasurable companionship as time goes on. Without a good program, the fact of disability may be too slender a tie to hold the group together.

In some groups, the recreation program is so much fun and goes on with such enthusiasm that it is hard for any child to hold back. The verve and abandon of a group of square dancers in wheelchairs can equal that of any group of dancers. A good game of wheelchair volleyball can be played with a balloon as a ball and a "net" made of string with colored streamers dangling from it.

If your child plans to enter a group of nonhandicapped children, you should find out something about the leadership. In one instance, two cerebral-palsied boys were invited to join a Cub Pack, but so much fuss was made over them, with pictures for the local newspapers, that they were made to feel their difference in spite of good intentions and soon dropped out. More harm than good can result if the nonhandicapped children take the attitude of doing something "for" instead of "with" the child who has a disability.[19]

By contrast, a group of youngsters attending a day camp for cerebral-palsied children developed a natural relationship with neighborhood children who were not in the camp. When the campers were playing in their rhythm orchestra, some young outsiders were attracted by the music. They were invited in, given instruments, and became part of the group, returning day after day. The children accepted one another and formed friendships irrespective of the handicaps.[20]

The Baltimore Hearing Society has carried on a program of placing children with impaired hearing in recreational and social groups with children who hear.[21] In this project, each child with impaired hearing was placed in two or three small group activities each week on a year-round basis. These were the normal neighborhood groups, such as the Scouts, the Y's, or church groups. Many of the children went to camps with children who could hear.

The children with impaired hearing generally performed on a par with the others, although they had difficulty in learning the vocabulary of the games. Their adjustment to the non-handicapped children varied. Some took to group life at once; others required weeks or months before they tried to communicate with the children who could hear.

The nonhandicapped children tended to be reserved with the deaf children at first. Lack of understanding of deafness led one child to express surprise when a deaf child did lettering for a sign. "Look, Jimmy can write!" one child exclaimed. After misunderstandings were cleared away, they began to accept the deaf child as a boy or girl like themselves, who happened not to hear or talk very well.

Some of the children profited by a readiness program. A group of deaf girls were enrolled in a class of basic rhythmic skills, taught by a staff member from the YWCA. After ten weeks they felt at home with their teacher and gave a dance recital at the Y. Their experience gave them confidence to join other Y programs with nonhandicapped girls.

Some of these children were not ready for resident camping with nonhandicapped children because they lacked previous group experience or adequate vocabulary. A day camp provided supervised recreation and speech therapy as preparation for social contacts.

The parents were happy about their children's progress in these supervised recreational groups but were still disturbed because their youngsters were often ignored by neighborhood children. Consequently, the Baltimore Hearing Society intensified its educational program to increase community understanding of speech and hearing impairments.

If your child is not yet ready for extensive social activities with nonhandicapped children, a lot can be done to help him. Additional therapy may increase his skills in the activities of daily living. First-class instruction in some special skill may give him an "in." Still you may feel that, for a time, he will be happiest in a group of children with limitations like his own.

Ideally, every child needs to reach a stage of social maturity when he can feel comfortable with both the handicapped and the nonhandicapped. The presence of a disability will become less important to the child as he achieves greater self-acceptance and learns to value friendships wherever he finds them.

REFERENCES

1. Anne Marie Smith. *Play for Convalescent Children in Hospitals and at Home.* New York, A. S. Barnes & Co., 1960.

2. Richard J. Bond, V. M. Burnes, R. L. Kolodny, and M. C. Warren. "The Neighborhood Peer Group." *The Group,* Vol. 17: No. 2, October 1954.

3. Alice Burkhardt, then of the staff of the National Recreation Association, New York. Personal communication.

4. Anne Marie Smith, *op. cit.*

5. *The Crippled Child,* June 1952.

6. Josephine Burton. *Crippled Victory.* New York, Sheed and Ward, 1956. pp. 38-39.

7. Abbie S. Burger. "Group Work in a Rehabilitation Center." *The Group,* April 1955.

8. June Frantzen. *Toys, the Tools of Children.* National Society for Crippled Children and Adults, Chicago.

9. Harry K. Eby. "Scouting with Physically Handicapped Boys." *The Crippled Child,* June 1951.

10. Verna-Marie Miller. "Recreation for the Physically Handicapped." Thesis (Bachelor of Science in Physical Education), University of Wisconsin. 1930.

11. Alice Burkhardt, then of the staff of the National Recreation Association, New York. Personal communication.

12. Ruth E. Hartley and Robert M. Goldenson. *The Complete Book of Children's Play.* New York, Thomas Y. Crowell, 1957.

13. Marjory D. McMullin. *How to Help the Shut-In Child: 313 Hints for Homebound Children.* New York, E. P. Dutton, 1954.

14. *Ibid.*

15. Arthur B. Candell. "The Misfits." *Recreation.* Vol. XLIX: No. 1, January 1956.

16. Marie Killilea. *Karen.* Englewood Cliffs, New Jersey, Prentice-Hall, Inc., 1952.

17. Aaron L. Danzig, *Handbook for One-Handers.* Federation of the Handicapped, New York. 1957.

18. *Ibid.* pp. 26-27.

19. *Day Camping for the Cerebral Palsied.* Program Bulletin No. 11, United Cerebral Palsy Associations, New York.

20. *Ibid.*

21. *Children with Handicaps—They Shall Play.* Baltimore Hearing Society, Second Annual Report, 1956-57, Demonstration Recreation Project.

19

PLAY ACTIVITIES
FOR YOUNG CHILDREN

When you spend friendly time with your baby—talk baby talk with him, call him beautiful, teach him little games, hug him occasionally—you do a lot more than just give him pleasure. This is how you show him that you love him and this is what builds lovingness in him. It also builds trust in people generally and self-confidence about his own appealingness—qualities that will make all the difference in his ability to get along with others the rest of his life. You are also stimulating the development of his body and his mind. All this may seem like too much to claim. But scientists have learned that the baby who doesn't receive any affectionate care stops developing in every way. His body and his mind become stunted. He doesn't try to do things any more, just lies on his back, even at a year of age. He's uninterested in people. He grows up to be a shallow character with nothing to give to others. He's first a poor student at school and then becomes an irresponsible worker on the job.

These things are not said to scare you but to show you that, whatever your child's limitations are, he needs your attention, your love, your enjoyment of him—right from birth. He needs the stimulation of playthings and the stimulation of talking and playing with you.

If your child's handicap delays the development of his ability to use his hands or to walk, he still needs to be encouraged to do what he can in his play and to feel your pride in his progress. If he can't hear, it's still good to laugh and talk naturally with him. When you teach him some new skill, such as putting on his shoes, you can explain in words as you show him so that he begins to form a visual picture of speech. If he is blind, he can still learn from the same kinds

211

of everyday experiences, use many of the same play materials, and benefit by the same kinds of teaching, respond to encouragement and endearment like the child who sees. A blind child particularly needs help in trying new activities like walking, crawling upstairs, pushing a carton, which the seeing child is stimulated to try by imitation.

Having Fun Around the House. Most young children, whether or not they have handicaps, spend the bulk of their time at home, where they find endless opportunities for play, or create them. In the kitchen there are containers and implements for pretend cooking. As the child grows older, rolling out cookie dough and cutting cookies into fancy shapes is even more fun. Perhaps he can even help mix the dough, or he might use one of the refrigerated rolls of cookie dough available in supermarkets. Even if your child can't use his hands very well, or if he can't hear or walk, there's nothing to prevent him from having this kind of fun.

His imagination will flourish when he lines up the dining room chairs or turns them over to make a train or a cave or a house. The bathroom offers all sorts of play advantages— sailing boats, washing the doll's clothes, splashing in the tub. The hose or sprinkler in the back yard is great fun for a child and is cooling and relaxing. There are more chances to have fun, all around the house, when others in the family share it.

Bringing Playmates into Your Home. If your child's disability keeps him at home a great deal and you frequently invite other children to visit, you'll want to make sure that they enjoy themselves. Your child will need to learn to be considerate of them. You'll need to help his friends understand what he can do for himself and when he needs help. You'll want to be prepared with play materials and perhaps some ideas for a good time that he can enjoy with them.

Arranging for Play with a Group. Do you know whether there is any play program for young children in your neighborhood where your child can enjoy supervised play with others of his age? Some nursery schools for nonhandicapped children accept a few with disabilities. Some organizations concerned with specific handicaps, such as cerebral palsy, have set up nursery schools for children with those handicaps. You may find a play program for young children in some parks or neighborhood centers. Sometimes the library has regular story hours for little children and some church schools have group programs for children of preschool age.

These programs are worth investigating if your child lacks companionship.

SOME SUGGESTED PLAY ACTIVITIES

In some play, the child is chiefly using his senses, as when the baby delights to feel and touch and to put things into his mouth. Other play gives him the pleasure of running, climbing, jumping, and throwing. By three years children spend a good part of their time copying adult activities, the boys building structures, driving cars and planes; the girls caring for dolls and doing housework. This is how they make progress toward manhood and womanhood. Another of the great values of play is that it teaches the joy of companionship and cooperation with other children.

The young child is not yet interested in games of skill and rules. Competitive team activities have no appeal yet. This may be one reason why preschool children seem to be less aware and less critical of the limitations of the disabled child. They often accept him readily, as a matter of course. If he needs help, they give it quite naturally.

The Tactile Sense. Babies and young children like to feel, squeeze, and handle things. Play materials that he can enjoy in these ways encourage the child with a disabled hand or arm to make increased use of it. Rag dolls and cuddly stuffed animals are fun to grab and hold. Clay and dough encourage patting, squeezing, kneading, and rolling. The young child may like dough more than plasticine. It should be soft but not sticky and may be colored with vegetable dyes. A blind child may particularly enjoy materials that can be molded, such as dough, snow, sand, or mud.

It's fun to feel different textures. A box of assorted scraps—smooth, silky, velvety, rough, and shaggy fabrics, tissue paper, slick paper, foam rubber, feathers—may encourage the youngster to stroke, crumple, and tear. Finger paints give the small child a wonderful chance to be legitimately messy; some disabled children have used bare feet to "finger" paint.

Sand encourages many activities—grasping a shovel, digging, filling a pail, emptying it, molding the sand into shapes. Sand is fun even in a dishpan. Water, too, suggests many kinds of play, from floating toy animals or boats to splashing and getting wet. It is fun whether in a big pan, a tub, or a pool.

Active Physical Play. Preschool children normally delight in shouting and laughing, in running, marching, dancing, climbing, kicking, jumping, banging, pounding, punching, throwing, and making a try at catching. These vigorous activities develop bodily strength and provide a healthy emotional outlet.

Push-pull toys at one and two years and then *pedal toys* are great favorites. Because a tricycle, for example, requires that the child use both arms, its use may improve inadequate arm control and also develop his use of his legs. At the same time, it gives him a fine feeling of accomplishment. Possibly a child who is disabled may need a backrest on his tricycle, or wooden blocks with straps attached to the pedals to hold his feet in place.[1]

A doll carriage can be weighted with sandbags so that it will not tip over. A sturdy wheelbarrow with two wheels on the front axle requires the use of two hands and arms and is fun for children who can't balance an ordinary wheelbarrow.[2] Many children with physical disabilities can enjoy pushing wagons, cars, and trucks big enough to be straddled. They can also play on rocking toys provided the seat gives secure support.

A blind child who is learning to walk can enjoy a push toy—which, incidentally, hits obstacles in front of him before he does. As he gains confidence in moving around, he can enjoy many of the wheel toys used by sighted children, such as wagons, trucks, scooters, or tricycles.

Large cardboard blocks, and medium-sized solid wood ones, which are old favorites, suggest all kinds of projects, starting with the simple tower and working up to elaborate garages, skyscrapers, bridges, tunnels. These blocks are not carried by most toy departments but must be ordered from the manufacturer. Consult a nursery for names and addresses.

Balls have such varied uses that even a severely limited child can have a good time with one. If he can't move about, he may enjoy throwing a ball that is attached to a string and tied within reach so that he can retrieve it. If his use of hands and arms is limited, he may enjoy kicking a large ball. The older preschool child who can't walk may enjoy a simplified kind of bowling. Toy bowling pins or large, long blocks can be set up in front of a wall, staggered so that as one is hit it will knock the rest over. The child can sit on the floor and use any size ball he chooses to bowl over the blocks.

Blind children enjoy simple ball games, such as rolling the ball back and forth with a sighted playmate. The young blind child may like tossing a ball into a large dishpan that makes a noise when the ball lands in it, a game that helps improve his sense of orientation.

The size, weight, and texture of a ball should suit your child's particular needs. A large, light ball which must be caught with both hands encourages a child to use a weak hand or arm. A rubber ball is good for squeezing as well as for bouncing. Balls can be bounced in a dozen different ways that aid the child's development—bounced with the right hand, the left hand, or both hands; from one hand to the other and back, passed under alternate legs, and so on.

Balloons tied to the bed or chair by a long string are a source of amusement. They are fun to throw, to bat, or to blow from place to place. Blowing games are good for the child who must improve breath control or strengthen his trunk muscles. Children enjoy competing to see who can be the first to blow his balloon across a goal line or keep a balloon in the air the longest.

Beanbags combine fun with therapy for many children with disabilities. A fairly limp, thin bag is easier to catch and hold when the child's hand control is poor. Sometimes an odd shape makes the bag more interesting, especially if a face is painted or embroidered on it. The child with poor hand control may find it easier to pile up large square beanbags than to pile blocks since they won't topple over so easily.

A beanbag in the shape of a frog, large enough to rest floppily on the child's head, was used in one clinic to help children develop steadier neck muscles and hold their heads erect. With "Freddie the Frog" balanced on his head, the game was to see how long the child could keep him there before Freddie "jumped" off.[3]

A game of "aim-the-beanbag" helps develop directional throwing. On a large piece of white vinyl sheeting about three by four feet, eight or ten spaces are marked off by wide, solid lines. An attractive picture is pasted or painted in each space. For older children, a numeral can be painted in each space to indicate points scored. The sheet is thumbtacked to the floor, and the child tries to hit each picture by throwing the beanbag.[4]

Outdoor play equipment is enjoyed by everyone. Your child may be able to use a swing, see-saw, climbing ladder, or jungle gym, a wading pool, sandbox, or big packing boxes and play planks. Instructions for making good, sturdy play equipment are given in a government pamphlet, *Home Play and Play Equipment for Young Children,* available from the Superintendent of Documents, U. S. Government Printing Office, Washington 25, D.C., for 15¢.

Some adjustments may be needed for your child's disability. A rope swing may be made with a chair protected by a bar across the front; a see-saw may be made with an upright handle in front of each seat so that the child can hold on or can be fastened safely with straps.

For the child who must work and play at a standing table, a small sandbox may be placed on the table, or a special standing sand-table can be constructed with the recesses and strap harnesses commonly built into a standing table. If the table is built for several children, it should be long and narrow so that children play side by side instead of across from each other. In this way the possibility of sand flying into their faces because of poor hand control is somewhat lessened.[5]

Parallel bars and a climbing ladder can provide good fun. Fastening the ladder to a wall makes it easier for the child to support his toes and prevents his feet from slipping forward. A flight of two or three sturdy steps leading to a platform, with strong railings, is excellent equipment for the child with an orthopedic disability.

Often a blind child can learn to enjoy play apparatus, especially if he has friendly aid in the beginning. When he is learning to jump, he may want to hold on to someone until he learns that he can jump safely. If there is heavy, moving apparatus in your yard, such as a swing or a see-saw, a fence or ground marks such as a gravel path will warn the child who cannot see that he is entering a danger zone.

If possible, there should be several kinds of surfaces for outdoor play in your yard. A smooth asphalt surface, perhaps the driveway, is convenient for wheelchairs, wheel toys, and such games as hop-scotch. Grass offers the safest surface for falling, but it is slippery and difficult to run on. Hard dirt gives good traction for running, jumping, and support of crutches so long as it is free of loose, soft surface sand and pebbles.[6]

Making Things and Taking Them Apart. Many kinds of play develop around the child's interest in making things and taking them apart. Some are suggested below.

Blocks are the most versatile of all toys and have their widest use during a child's early years. Snap blocks that fit together with a click can be built into structures that are not easily knocked apart unintentionally by the child with poor control of his hands.[7] Nested blocks and tin cans of various sizes (with one end smoothly removed) encourage hand and arm control and develop the child's sense of size and space relationships.

Pots and pans with their lids, measuring cups of different sizes, cake pans, muffin tins, gelatin molds, big kitchen spoons, all offer fine combinations for one-year-olds to put together and take apart. From the store come such toys as color cones or pyramids and take-apart trains or trucks. These also develop the child's sense of order, spatial relationships, and size, form, and color. Sturdy *jig-saw puzzles* help him recognize shapes and increase his dexterity. Three- to five-piece puzzles may be enough for the child under four.

Play with a *peg-board* improves the ability to grasp and aim and to control involuntary motion. The number, size, and spacing of pegs on the board should vary according to the child's needs. A board with only half a dozen pegs, with holes spaced three inches apart so that the child doesn't knock one peg over when inserting another, may suit some children. Some children may need large pegs, an inch and a half to two inches in diameter, for easier grasp.[8]

Drawing and painting materials—finger paints, crayons, chalk, big pencils, paper, blackboards—can be fun for the child in bed or wheelchair, or in a standing table. If the child drops his pencil or crayon frequently, tie a ribbon around it and thumbtack the ribbon to his work table. If he has poor hand control, he may need pencils or crayons from half to three-quarters of an inch thick. Putting a pencil through the hole of an empty spool provides a large diameter for easy grasping.

A large work area is helpful. If you have the wall space, you may want to fasten a large piece of linoleum to the wall so that paper for painting or drawing can be thumbtacked to it. Then no harm is done if paint wanders over the edge of the paper.

Tools for pounding and banging are fun for the preschool children. They enjoy pounding pegs into their holes, or pounding nails into soft wood, and at the same time they also develop shoulder and wrist coordination.

Flannel boards let the child make a picture with little effort while he tells a story. They come with felt shapes that easily adhere to the board and can be peeled right off. You can buy figures for some familiar children's stories or you can cut felt figures to fit your child's favorite tales. Your child will want to pick out the right figures and put them on the board himself at the right point in the story. This is a happy way of telling stories to the child who cannot hear well.

Make Believe. Preschool children like to act out the real-life happenings they see and hear about, adding their own vivid details. "Let's play I'm the fire chief and you're the lady in the house that's burning up." They like to dress up for their imaginary play, either in an adult's old clothing or in a special costume, and they like to use realistic properties, such as child-size housekeeping equipment, toy telephones, dolls, doll clothing, and furniture. Almost any child with a disability can enjoy imaginary play of this type by the time he has reached the mental age of three to five years.

If your child breaks things easily because of his disability, choose sturdy "properties." There are attractive, unbreakable dolls, doll dishes and furniture; miniature village and farm sets can be found in rubber. Any play furniture that the child uses should be sturdy enough to be safe.

Hand and finger puppets are fun in imaginative play, and even the child with a hand disability can use many simple types. Peanut shells with faces drawn in ink make amusing finger puppets, or faces may be painted on the fingers of an old glove. The child can use the whole glove or cut off each finger to use separately. Paper bags used as hand puppets or masks are good for dramatic play.

Music and Rhythm. Music, rhythm, and everyday sounds give pleasure to all children. Even the deaf child can enjoy rhythmic activities such as clapping, marching, dancing, or using the instruments of a rhythm band. Ordinary neighborhood sounds help the blind child to know what the world is like; and music, whether he listens to it or makes it himself, may become a source of great pleasure to him.

Young children like to make their own sounds. A drum, bells, triangle, tambourine, and cymbals are fun and also help to develop muscular control and a sharper sense of timing and rhythm. Homemade instruments are fine; try a comb wrapped in tissue paper, or a tambourine made from a paper plate with small bells tied to holes punched around its edge. Almost any child, whether he is in bed, in a wheelchair, or on crutches can have fun with some such improvised instruments.

And young children like to sing—little songs they make up themselves, or the nursery songs you sing with them. Singing games are fun for children with disabilities. One group of cerebral-palsied children played a singing game using Robert Louis Stevenson's poem *How Do You Like to Go up in a Swing?* The children stood in a circle, partners facing one another and holding hands, swinging their arms from side to side. One child would run under the swinging arms and around the circle until the music stopped. When a child in a walker took his turn, the children adjusted their positions to make room for it to pass through.[9]

Enjoying Nature. Regardless of his handicap, the young child can find pleasure in many of the things of nature: the feel of bare feet on grass, scuffling in dry leaves, snow, rain, sand, mud, or rocks, growing plants, insects, or animals—some of them are at hand everywhere for the child's enjoyment. Pets offer companionship to many a homebound child, and seeds sown in a flower pot (choose those that come up quickly) provide a bedside garden. Full-fledged collecting usually comes later, but the preschool child may want to bring home rocks, pine cones, or other things of nature that interest him. It may be messy but the rewards are great for the child who discovers the natural world.

Stories and Pictures. Very few preschool children can read, but they usually love to look at picture books and to listen to stories. The hour when Mother or Dad tells a story to him is one of the most precious in the child's day for the companionship it brings. Even a young deaf child can enjoy the story hour if he is being taught to read lips, especially if the story is told from a well-illustrated picture book so that he can see the connection between a picture and the word shaped by the storyteller's lips.

Picture books and stories should be appropriate for a child's stage of development, his interests, and his special needs. If your child has a disability that makes it difficult for him to hold books, a book rack may overcome the problem.

REFERENCES

1. Gladys Gage Rogers and Leah Thomas. "Toys, Games and Apparatus for Children with Cerebral Palsy." *Physical Therapy Review,* Vol. 29: No. 1, January 1949.

2. *Ibid.*

3. *Alpha Chi Omega Toy Book: Self-Help Toys to Make for Handicapped Children.* Ed. by Mrs. Clark Johnson. Alpha Chi Omega Central Office, 611-619 Chamber of Commerce Bldg., Indianapolis 4, Indiana (pattern on page 16).

4. *Op. cit.,* page 8.

5. Gladys Gage Rogers and Leah Thomas, *op. cit.*

6. Valerie Hunt. *Recreation for the Handicapped.* Englewood Cliffs, New Jersey, Prentice-Hall, Inc., 1955.

7. Grace Langdon. *Your Child's Play.* Parent Series No. 2, Chicago, National Society for Crippled Children and Adults, 1957.

8. Gladys Gage Rogers and Leah Thomas, *op. cit.*

9. *Ibid.*

20

RECREATION
FOR OLDER CHILDREN

Children are designed by Nature to seek more independence the older they grow. They also become bolder. They play farther away from home, cross streets, bicycle, swim, climb into trees and onto roofs, go off to camp, drive cars. Parents gradually overcome their qualms and let their child do these increasingly risky things.

Your child's disability may limit him in some of these. But your natural apprehension about his disability may limit him even more. Many handicapped people who could have learned to travel alone are never allowed to, and they may be seriously limited in schooling, jobs, friendships, recreation. It's vitally important to let your child try his wings just as far as his doctors will permit.

A Widening Circle of Friends. Although a teenager wants independence, his disability is apt to put many obstacles in his way. He may require special transportation and not be able to fall in with spur-of-the-moment plans of his friends. Needing to have a parent take him everywhere puts quite a damper on his social life; and the question of who needs the car most usually causes conflict between members of the family. With tactful respect for his growing maturity, you can discuss such problems with him. Let him get used to going with friends or using a taxi occasionally. Teenagers are usually reluctant to take a cab, at least the first few times, because it isn't conventional at this age, but they can learn with encouragement.

Organized Games and Competitive Sports. During the school years, team games and sports become increasingly popular. Skill is prized more highly and performance judged more critically. This trend affects the disabled youngster because his companions are apt to leave him out of games if he can't contribute his share. So your child may have to learn how to be umpire or scorekeeper and how to volunteer. He can learn how to play well the games that are within his range (such as table games) so that his friends will want to play them with him.

Home as a Play Center. Home continues to be an important play center for the elementary school child and can be for the teenager if the parents create a hospitable atmosphere. Children are usually resourceful in making use of home facilities, but your child may need encouragement. The kitchen has great natural appeal. Keep it stocked with fruit, crackers, cookies. Popcorn balls, candy, banana splits, or lemonade are fun to make.

Let your teenager learn to dance at home to the music of records, radio, or piano. Later he may have enough confidence to try in a large group, even among strangers.

Perhaps there is space somewhere in your home for gymnastic equipment. Many children with varied disabilities enjoy a workout with a punching-bag, weight-lifting apparatus, or trapeze. If your yard is large enough, you might try croquet, badminton, or volleyball.

ACTIVE GAMES AND SPORTS

In looking for games or sports remember that baseball, football, and basketball are not the only interesting ones. Disabled persons have enjoyed tumbling, wrestling, jousting, bag-punching, swinging Indian clubs, rope spinning, twirling a baton, and top-spinning.[1]

Tag and running games are very popular among young school-age children. If your child runs poorly, or can't run at all, he may still join some of the running games in which some players aren't required to run. In hide and seek, for example, he may be able to hide cleverly without running and thus still enjoy the excitement of the game.

Some of the simpler team games may be suitable for the young school-age child with a disability. Back ball is one such game.[2] The children divide equally into two teams. There is one home base with one field base at about 25 feet in front of it. One player is on the field base and the other members of his team are scattered about the field. The opposing team has a player on home base. He may hit, kick, or push the ball away from him. Members of the team in the field try to get the ball and hit the player before he gets to field base and home again. The handicapped player is not at too great a disadvantage, since he may hit, kick, or push the ball when on home base, and he may have another player run for him. When playing in the field, he can do as much as he is able.

Circle games are usually simple and no one child is in the most active part for long. A child who is agile on crutches or braces can often play, and so may the child in a wheelchair if it is played on a suitable surface. "Cat and Rat" and "Hot Potato" are two old-time circle games that are possibilities. If a balloon is used instead of a bean bag in "Hot Potato," the child who moves slowly has more time to catch up with it when the other players toss it to one another. Anyone tagged while holding the balloon becomes "it."[3]

A boy who had lost his right leg selected weight-lifting as a sport, in time excelled in it, and taught other boys. A boy who was born deaf took up rowing, which he could enjoy either alone or with another boy, and he went out for the crew at college, for he could maintain the rhythm by watching the oars of the others. Bowling is an active sport in which the blind often perform as well as the sighted. The pin boy or a companion tells the player what pins remain standing. Many children with disabilities, including some with cerebral palsy, amputations or other motor disabilities, heart trouble, and blindness learn to swim. Archery is possible for many of the handicapped without adaptation beyond the choice of a light bow and a shorter distance for those with weak arms, or the use of a heavier bow for those whose shoulders are strong from crutch-walking. The archer who uses crutches may have to sit while shooting and so may need to raise his aim. The list goes on through hiking, fishing, boating, horseback riding, bicycling, and skating—all have been enjoyed by some persons with serious disabilities. There are some good handbooks (see page 365) on games. You can find many other suggestions there, some perhaps with adaptations.

A common mistake is to assume that children who are blind can't enjoy active games. In some games, sounds help them to know what is happening; in others, they can run for a goal that is easily found, or they may be part of a line, circle, or chain formation. Furthermore, the blind child can always be paired with a child who can see.

Swimming. Swimming is popular and very beneficial to many persons with disabilities, but it shouldn't be undertaken without the doctor's approval.

The physical conditions of available swimming places have to be considered. A pool is usually better than a natural outdoor swimming place for the child with a motor disability. If your child is less active than most swimmers, he may need warmer water than usual. He may need a swimming place where he can enter the water by steps, ramp, or natural incline, or where there are guards to help him in and out of the water. The presence of sturdy handrails and nonskid material around the pool edges may make a big difference.

A friendly teacher who understands a handicapped child's special problems can help the nonswimmer to feel at home in the water. The child with an orthopedic disability may have problems of body balance in the water and of controlling the direction of body movement. He may find solutions to these problems by himself, but good teaching can help him tremendously. A child who has lost one leg may find it difficult to float, because his body weight is unbalanced and he tends to roll over and sink on one side, but he can be shown how to correct the imbalance by bending the remaining leg or lowering the opposite arm.

Many swimmers who have orthopedic disabilities learn one or more of the standard strokes, but others use specially adapted strokes. In general the swimmer with one impaired arm prefers an asymmetrical stroke (side stroke, for example) whereas the person with two impaired arms uses a symmetrical stroke (such as breast stroke). When leg muscles are weak, a modified scissors kick may be preferred to a frog kick.[4]

Don't assume that a life jacket or an inner tube keeps the nonswimmer safe in deep water, because his disability may increase his hazards. If he learns to swim, he can be safe without the aid. But until then his safety should be in the hands of a teacher or a responsible buddy who can swim and who goes into the water with him. Some teachers use flotation aids effectively, but it is the teacher's presence that provides the real safety.

Many swimming pools operated by the Y's have classes

for handicapped youngsters and some children learn to swim at camp. Lacking such opportunities, you may be able to find an experienced swimming teacher who can give your child private instruction.

Some Suggestions for Adaptations. Adaptations requiring changes in equipment, procedures, or rules can be made when all the players agree. They are especially valuable when a group of youngsters with disabilities play together. Volleyball can be played with regular rules, but with a large rubber balloon for the ball. It falls slowly, giving the slow-moving player time to get to it. In some games, the play area can be reduced and lighter equipment substituted for the standard equipment. Seriously handicapped persons can play badminton, with two to four players on a side, because the rackets are light. Soccer can be played in a smaller space and can be confined to trapping and kicking the ball without dribbling. Basketball and soccer are sometimes played from wheelchairs. A volleyball court may be divided into small areas, each player being limited to a particular space. Such adaptations might not interest nonhandicapped youngsters but are very satisfying to a group of young people with limited physical abilities.[5]

Adaptations that solve the problem of retrieving a ball or other projectile are useful. Tether-ball is one such game. Tether ping pong[6] has advantages for players who need support when standing or who have poor hand coordination. A ping-pong ball may be secured to three strands of strong thread with household cement and attached to a cord. The free end of the cord is attached to a pole or to a high horizontal wire.

A shuffleboard game can be placed on a table, with pockets at each end into which the disks drop. This eliminates the retrieving problem for the person who can't easily stoop or pick up the disks from the ground. If players sit or stand at opposite ends and take turns sliding the disks, there is no problem of locomotion. Because the shoving action requires little hand coordination, persons with severe hand disabilities enjoy it.

Some games can be made easier by increasing opportunities to score. For example, in the standard game of horseshoes or ring toss, the player has only one peg or stake at which to aim. But a ring-toss target board large enough to hold nine dowel pegs can be used successfully by even severely handicapped children. Eight rope rings are used in the game. If the dowel pegs are removable, their number can be varied. When many pegs are on the board, even a child with poor coordination can expect to score. Such a ring-toss board can be placed on the floor or hung on the wall, depending on whether players can stoop to pick up the rings.[7]

QUIET GAMES

There are lots of quiet games. They are invaluable when physical activity is limited.

For some games, the child in a wheelchair needs either a wheelchair tray or a table at which he can sit comfortably. A tray can be made from plywood to be laid across the two arms. A depth of about 20 inches is usually convenient. Two small strips can be attached to the underside of the board. to fit closely against the wheelchair arms and keep the table from slipping. To prevent tipping, attach a small catch to one of the strips so that it extends under the chair arm. If a semi-circular section is cut out of the front, the tray can be brought close up to the child.[8]

Card Games. Card games are popular from about the age of six or seven. Most children enjoy the old standbys—Flinch, Authors, Old Maid, Rummy. Older children will find facility in bridge, rummy, or other games played with a standard deck of cards to be a social asset which increases in value the older they grow.

Blind persons often mark their own cards in Braille. Or they may be purchased already marked from the American Foundation for the Blind, 15 West 15th Street, New York 11, New York.

Some children with a hand disability need a card holder. A wooden or metal spice rack, which can be bought in any household supply store or in variety stores, can be used as a card holder. Or you may make your own wooden rack with a design like a Scrabble rack, but big enough to hold cards. For temporary use, take a cardboard shoebox, remove the lid, and cut away one of the long sides. The other long side becomes the floor of the holder. Make a two-inch-deep cut at each end of the bottom side; fold up the front edge of the bottom to make a one-inch fold, then fold again one inch more. Secure the front edge to the bottom, and you have a ledge against which cards can be propped, leaning against the back of the box.

To shuffle cards when only one hand is useful, the individual places the pack of cards, long edge up, in his lap. A girl can arrange the folds of her skirt to form the depression. The cards are held in the lap as if it were the second hand, and the individual shuffles them in the usual way, using his one hand. To deal with one hand, he holds the whole deck in his hand, with thumb on top and other fingers firmly clasping the bottom, then slides each card off the top with his thumb. Some one-handed players put the cards, face up, in their laps, while others lay them face down on the table and consult the cards one at a time.[9]

Word Games. There is a host of familiar ones: anagrams, crosswords, Scrabble, ghost, I-cubes, right and left spelling, and Jotto; some can be played alone, others require companions. Ghosts is typical of word games in which the child with little or no vision is not at a disadvantage, provided his experience with words and spelling has brought him to the level of the other children. These games are a lot of fun for alert, fast thinkers, but can be very frustrating to some people.

Educational games are also stimulating to many school-age children: geography, numbers, famous people, events in history can all be used in several ways.

Board Games. In dominoes, checkers, chess, crokinole, caroms, Chinese checkers, parchesi, and backgammon, if a child cannot handle the pieces, another player can move them for him as he directs. A peg-board made in the design of a checkerboard helps some children. Checkers can be made from spools with quarter-inch dowels inserted for pegs. The squares should be two inches, with a hole in the center of each for the peg.

Many board games made for blind players can be purchased from the American Foundation for the Blind. Checkerboards and chessboards are made with sunken or perforated squares. The pieces have distinctive forms so that opposing players can identify their pieces by touch. Interlocking dominoes with small brass tacks for the dots are also available for blind players. In anagrams, letter blocks are marked in Braille. A tic-tac-toe board is made with sunken squares, and round and square markers. Special bingo, parchesi, and backgammon boards are also available for blind players.

Games of Dexterity. Marbles, jacks, jackstraws, tiddly-winks, pick-up sticks, and other games of dexterity are usable by many disabled children. A child who needs foot exercises may adapt some of them to this purpose, as when the design of tic-tac-toe is drawn large on the floor and players use their feet to place jacks or marbles.

Pencil and Paper Games. These are infinite in variety. If your child has a hand disability, he may need aids to hold pencil or pen. Probably his doctor or therapist can suggest a suitable device. One type is made of two strips of aluminum, bent to form clips, and riveted together. One clip holds the pencil; the other fits over the thumb.[10]

Paper stays in place more readily in a tablet, but a clipboard will hold loose sheets.

Puzzles, Tricks, and Riddles. Puzzles, tricks, and riddles are good for hours alone as well as with friends. Metal ring twisters, maze puzzles, crossword and jigsaw puzzles are readily available. Experience with children in hospitals suggests that only the older convalescent children who do not tire easily want to undertake jigsaw puzzles with more than 50 pieces. Puzzles made of plywood with interlocking pieces that hold together firmly may be better than those of cardboard for the child with uncertain hand control.

Tricks with matchsticks or toothpicks are good for quiet fun, and string tricks and cat's cradles offer a still different type. Some string figures made by people of many lands are described in *Artists in String*, by Kathleen Haddon.[11]

Almost any public library has books of riddles that will give your child ammunition for a great deal of fun with his friends. If he is interested in card tricks or sleight of hand, there are books for that too. A toy store will supply a magician's kit.

Codes and Signaling. Toy telegraphs, battery operated, give opportunity to learn and practice the Morse code. Young children find the sputtering signals very professional sounding, and older children become quite fascinated by the code itself. The code can also be practiced with a flashlight, a whistle, or merely by tapping a glass with a pencil. If your youngster becomes really interested, he may convert you and all the family to the ham radio hobby. This activity has brought many a handicapped youngster into contact with interesting people in distant parts of the world. The American Radio Relay League, West Hartford 7, Connecticut, will send information for radio amateurs on how to obtain a federal license as a radio operator.

ARTS AND CRAFTS

Depending upon the problems created by your child's disability, he may need skilled help before he can do any arts and crafts that he would enjoy. Perhaps occupational therapy will help him find ingenious ways of using the necessary tools or materials. One person may hold a paint brush in his teeth, or attach it to the stump of his arm by a special device. Another may hold a tool between chin and shoulder; still another may use his feet.

Many devices have been invented for holding pencils, paintbrushes, knitting needles, embroidery hoops, and woodworking tools, as well as for threading needles. Some are described in *Living with a Disability*, by Rusk and Taylor.

No child should hesitate to try a new activity for fear that his product won't be any good. Tell him he isn't expected to produce a finished piece of work; the idea is to have a good time in a new experience.

When you are teaching your own child an art in which you are skilled, you should remember that a handicapped youngster usually has to take smaller steps than others in learning and that he needs more time for each step. He may need to start with the easiest process and the simplest designs. Let him start with projects that he can complete before he tires and, if necessary, follow patterns until he is skilled enough to try his own design.

Even if there is no special program of arts and crafts for the handicapped in your community, instruction is widely available through schools, community centers, private teachers, and books.

Painting, drawing, and modeling offer the person with a handicap opportunity to express deep feelings, difficult to put into words, which he may have bottled up for a long time. They turn his attention from his subjective feelings to creative activity and give him a chance to take pride in what he has made.

If disability makes one form of art difficult for your child to handle, there are many others. Finger paints, for example, may be more suitable than water colors for a youngster with hand and arm disability. Charcoal or crayon are easy to work with; pen and ink are tricky. The painter may work in oil, water color, or tempera, using a variety of techniques. Modeling can be done with asbestos clay (asbestos powder mixed with water), plasticine, modeling clay, papier maché, or plaster. There should be no trouble in finding the medium for an interested youngster.

Interest in the arts may arouse your child's desire to visit museums, take art appreciation courses or read art magazines and books even if he doesn't expect to develop his own skill in the arts.

Papercraft includes such extremes of simplicity and skill that almost any child with a disability can enjoy some phase of it. Simple examples are cutting and pasting to make a scrapbook, or folding a newspaper to make a hat. Children with greater skill can make paper flowers, kites, whistles, masks, models, or houses.

The art of Chinese and Japanese paper folding is very complex, with all the fascination of a puzzle. There is no cutting; everything is done by folding. Many books on the subject are now available, particularly on the Japanese art of Origami.

A child can enjoy puppets as a bed patient or a convalescent as well as when he is up and around. The older child may enjoy making them, or creating a story and dialogue, as well as giving a performance with the help of other children.

Boys and men in hospitals, as well as girls and women, have often been interested in one of the varied forms of sewing, such as knitting, crocheting, making stuffed toys or dolls, or doing embroidery or quilting.

Basketry, braiding, looper-clip weaving, and rug weaving are often used in occupational therapy programs and can easily be done at home. Persons with many types of disability can enjoy weaving, including those who are blind or have hand or arm disabilities.

From whittling to elaborate carpentry, woodworking is appropriate for many youngsters with varied disabilities. A youth with real skill in woodcraft and the use of power tools may be interested in the Shopsmith Home Workshop. It provides a complete set of power tools, along with special seating attachments for paraplegics and amputees.[12] Information is available from Magna Engineering Corporation, Menlo Park, California. Model kits for making boats, planes, trains, and antique automobiles are designed for people with various degrees of skill.

Many other arts and crafts (leatherwork, jewelry-making, metal enameling, shellcraft, wire twisting) are enjoyed by people with disabilities. You can help your child explore these possibilities.

THE ARTS

Reading. A book's physical characteristics are important for the child in bed or wheelchair or for any child with weak arm muscles. The child who is unable to handle large or heavy books should have a reading rack. The Read 'n Bed rack, available through Bermats Corporation, New York City, is adjustable and can be used by the bed patient who lies flat on his back. Special eyeglasses with prisms to refract an image at a ninety-degree angle allow the bed patient who is flat on his back to read while he holds the book in the normal position. One model is available through E.B. Meyrowitz, Inc., New York City. It's wise to check with your child's doctor before you invest in a pair.

If your child is homebound and you can't get to the library for books, find out whether your library has a service for homebound persons. Some libraries distribute thousands of books annually to persons confined to their homes.

Talking Books are supplied free to blind readers by the Library of Congress, along with the 16 r.p.m. play-back machine on which the records are played. A good number of books are available on the disks, some of which hold an hour's recording. Many titles, including the Bible, are also available in Braille. Many children's records of stories, poems, and songs can be had on regular long-playing records.

Perhaps you want to select books to prepare your child for going to the hospital or for some other phase of his disability. The National Society for Crippled Children and Adults publishes a list of such books, noting the school grade for which each book is suitable. It also suggests books that are helpful to the child in cooperation and adjustment, that help him cope with fear or with loneliness and homesickness, that help him feel at ease with doctors, nurses and hospitals, and those that help him adjust to new friends.[13]

Through creative writing, whether stories, essays, or plays, the disabled individual may be able to express emotions that he can't talk about readily. Some people are unable to express themselves in any other way and find writing deeply gratifying.

Dramatics. A children's theater program or a drama group in your community is worth investigating. The 1960 White House Conference on Children and Youth reported that there were about 5000 community theaters and more than 500 opera-producing groups in the country, and that children's theater programs are increasing.[14] Rehabilitation centers with recreation programs often include some form of dramatic activity. Agencies for the blind have found that dramatics helps many blind people improve in speech, facial expression, and freedom of bodily movement, as well as giving them artistic enjoyment. The blind also quite commonly enjoy the theater and movies.

Dramatic activities make use of many kinds of talents, and your child might find his niche in costuming, scenery, publicity, lighting, or some other aspect of the theater besides acting. If you think your child might be interested in any of these, inquire about dramatics in the schools or ask at your newspaper about a community theater or children's theater.

Dancing. Dancing is one of the gayest forms of recreation of many people with handicaps, just as it is for others. The dancer senses that he takes on beauty and grace to a degree. For the person who has disparaged himself because of his disability this is a wonderful feeling. Dancing has been recommended for those who are blind or deaf, who suffer from heart trouble, are mentally disturbed, have cerebral palsy or orthopedic handicaps. The amputee with an artificial leg can often learn to dance quite acceptably.

Social dancing, folk dancing, square dancing, tap dancing, ballet, and modern dance all have been done well and enthusiastically by the handicapped. A blind youngster may become proficient in tap dancing, where movement is confined to a small area. However, a youngster with cerebral palsy is more likely to enjoy social dancing, which calls for free movements and is less likely to induce spasm than the exactly coordinated movements of tap dancing.[15] The boy or girl with an orthopedic disability may enjoy square, line, or round dances more readily than folk dances with complicated step patterns. Some people in wheelchairs enjoy square dancing, especially if they can propel themselves.

If your child can participate in social dancing, he will want to learn the steps that are popular with his friends. Joining a social dancing class will give him security, and there is always the possibility that he can learn to be really good.

Music. Music from radio, television, and recordings can be part of the daily life of children who are bedfast or homebound. Even the child with severely impaired hearing may learn to respond to rhythm. Listening to music becomes particularly rewarding to the person who develops a knowledgeable appreciation of music or has specialized interests such as collecting records of a certain type.

If your child wants to play a musical instrument, he may be able to in spite of hand or arm limitations. If he is in a wheelchair, he can support a guitar or other stringed instrument on his lap. A bed patient may be able to play a wind instrument. A wide board attached to the front of the piano by L-shaped brackets gives support to the child who has weak arms but enough finger strength to strike the piano keys. One Boy Scout with no hands learned to play a guitar with his toes.[16]

There is scarcely any disability that interferes with singing. In fact, for some who have a speech disability singing is easier than speaking.

Music may fill your child's need for an emotionally satisfying interest to occupy the hours when he is alone. If he joins a glee club or listens with friends it can also be a source of friendships.

Hobbies. Some hobbies have such widespread appeal that magazines and books and clubs and societies are devoted to them. Stamp, coin, autograph collecting, photography, model railroading are popular examples, but there are hundreds more. To the youngster with a handicap a hobby can also provide social contacts.

A young boy with muscular dystrophy was interested enough in photography to solicit magazine subscriptions by telephone until he saved money to buy a Leica camera. Because of muscular weakness he could just barely snap his picture, but he studied picture composition and won a number of prizes. He joined a camera club, where he found friends. The club sometimes met in his house, and when it met elsewhere his friends helped him get there in his wheelchair.

Television and Radio. The good and the bad of radio and television are the same for children with disabilities as for those without. They enlarge any child's horizons and stimulate interests. But since it is so easy to fall back on television and radio to the exclusion of all active types of recreation, parents should place sensible limits on the time their children spend in watching and listening. This rule is as necessary for the homebound child as for others, but there is more to it than just rationing the time allowance: other activities must be available.

It's a good idea for a child to form a regular habit of looking over the program schedules in advance so that time can be allotted wisely. In addition to his regular programs the homebound child should be able to take advantage of worthwhile programs that come irregularly. This should still leave plenty of time for lessons, active recreation and hobbies, treatments and exercises.

In order to keep television and radio programs from being completely passive the child can be encouraged to turn to reference books to look up questions growing out of the programs. A dictionary, an atlas, and perhaps an encyclopedia should be handy. The parents should be ready to take the child to the public library for other books by an author he has just "discovered" on television or radio, or for books on some aspect of science, nature, music, art, history, in which the child's interest has just been aroused.

Incidentally, it is common for special programs or spot announcements to be given over to dramatic appeals for funds for organizations serving the handicapped. Some of these may be disturbing to your child, so you will want to prepare him or be ready to talk with him afterwards about questions that trouble him.

CAMPING

Camping is open to an increasing number of handicapped youngsters. *A Directory of Camps for the Handicapped* is available from the American Camping Association, Bradford Woods, Martinsville, Indiana, or from the National Society for Crippled Children and Adults, 2023 West Ogden Avenue, Chicago 12, Illinois. The National Association for Retarded Children has issued a directory of camps for the retarded. Your state association headquarters can give you information about camps in your area.

Some camps are organized specifically for the handicapped, and of these some are open only to children with a particular type of disability. Other camps make special adaptations so that they can include handicapped along with nonhandicapped children. In addition, some regular camps will accept a few children with mild or moderate disabilities who can benefit from the regular program. If resident camping is not feasible for your child, he may enjoy a day camp in your community. Family camping is another possibility.

It is hard enough for parents of an entirely capable child to decide to let him go off to camp. Parents of a handicapped child will want to be and should be even more sure that the child is ready and that the camp is right. It may have been suggested by your child's clinic or doctor. If not, you should satisfy yourself first that his doctor approves. Check on the camp through a family or a professional person who knows it first hand. Camps that are members of the American Camping Association have been visited and approved. Be sure, too, that you give the camp all the information about your child for which it has asked so that they won't accept him under any misunderstanding. Because of his disability, the camp may want information from your child's doctor in addition to the medical examination performed by the camp doctor. Follow the camp's instructions in getting the child and his belongings ready—and then let him go. It may do you as much good as it does him! Thousands of children with disabilities have a wonderful time in camp each year, come home full of tales of adventure, newly confident that they can do for themselves things that their families had been in the habit of doing for them.

As a rule, if a child's disability or lack of adjustment doesn't prevent it, it's preferable for him to go to a camp with nonhandicapped children. Camp Hidden Valley, supported by the New York *Herald Tribune*'s Fresh Air Fund, is one of these, although it is strictly limited to underprivileged children who live in New York City. About half of the children here have handicaps. They live with the nonhandicapped children in tents, six to a tent, all campers together. There are no special facilities beyond a few ramps and steps that give access to the pool. The program makes no obvious special adjustments for the disabled. All share in the same crafts, campfires, hikes, overnight trips, cookouts, and swimming activities. There are no vigourous competitive athletics; the program emphasizes outdoor living in a relaxed, leisurely atmosphere. The child with a handicap is not made to feel different.

A child may need a special camp for the handicapped for various reasons: (1) he is unable to care for himself in eating, dressing, and toileting; (2) he lacks muscular ability and coordination to take part in the usual camp activities; (3) he wears appliances or prostheses that he cannot put on or off by himself; (4) he lacks a practical understanding of his handicap and its effects; (5) he has too little understanding of social responsibilities and privileges to take part in organized group life.[17] These are questions of degree and, although your child may be unable to adjust in one camp, he may get along very well in a camp with a different program.

The physical facilities and terrain of the camp will also enter into your choice. You'll want to know whether ramps, handrails, and grab-bars are provided. Is the terrain too rocky or hilly for your child? Can he get around in wet weather? The camp director will be interested in these questions too, so that he will know how to plan for your child. Does your child need help in climbing steps or a hill, or in getting up from sitting on the ground? Must he remove braces at the waterfront, or can he take them off before going to the swimming area?

The general philosophy of the camp should be right for your child. He will probably get along very well in a leisurely program but not be able to take part in highly competitive, fast-moving activities carried out on a fixed schedule. Naturally the program should offer activities that interest him.

Some camps for handicapped children are treatment-centered and the program is determined by therapeutic goals, such as instruction in activities of daily living or speech therapy. Or the camp may emphasize medical supervision to establish the most desirable treatment program, as for the diabetic child.

SCOUTING

Scouting for the handicapped is well established in both Boy Scout and Girl Scout programs. The youngster with a disability has a chance to feel that he "belongs," not only with friends in his troop but also to a respected worldwide organization. The scouting achievements of handicapped boys and girls are proof of its effectiveness.

A boy with a handicap may become a scout in several ways. Thousands of handicapped boys have joined regular troops. Some regular troops have invited boys from a nearby hospital or special school, or a group of homebound boys, to join their membership. There are many scouting units also in hospitals, in special schools, and in special classes for the handicapped. An isolated boy far away from all groups may register as a Lone Scout, a Lone Cub Scout, or a Lone Explorer, with his father or mother as adult leader.

The Girl Scouts estimate that their present membership includes 15,000 girls who are physically disabled, mentally retarded, or socially maladjusted. The physically handicapped girl is encouraged to join the regular neighborhood troop, and troops in special schools or institutions often meet with nearby neighborhood groups.

There are scout troops for mentally retarded girls in many special schools or classes for the retarded, but the organization doesn't encourage them to join regular troops, because competition with more advanced girls might be discouraging to the retarded. The only troops for socially maladjusted or emotionally disturbed girls are in special schools or institutions.

Some scouting publications, including handbooks, are available in Braille from the American Printing House for the Blind, Louisville, Kentucky. Schools for the blind can secure the handbooks free if the superintendent requests them under the quota of government-subsidized materials allowed him from the Printing House. Blind Service Association, Inc., 127 No. Dearborn St., Chicago, Illinois 60602, has recordings of the most popular merit badge pamphlets for Boy

Scouts. They may be borrowed by scoutmasters who need them.

CHIEFLY FOR SOCIABILITY

A majority of children are good joiners. Most junior and senior high schools offer group activities in science clubs, orchestra, dramatic club, or publishing the school paper. There may be social groups in your church, or at one of the Y's, a neighborhood center, or an organization serving handicapped youth.

If there are questions as to how successfully your child might be able to participate in such a club, you should have a careful talk with the group's leader about the child's abilities and limitations. If the leader has had no experience with handicapped young people, he may want to get acquainted with your child personally. He may then decide that Johnny will do fine—or he may suggest that a friend join with him to help him over the rough spots. On the other hand, the leader may feel that he doesn't know how to carry the unusual responsibilities centering around your child's disability, or that the other group members aren't ready to accept a handicapped person. In that case, seek out another group. One rebuff shouldn't discourage either you or your child.

Letter Writing.   There is a very special pleasure in corresponding with persons in other parts of the world. Youth of All Nations, Inc., 16 St. Luke's Place, New York, N.Y. 10014, has an extensive program to encourage young people to get acquainted with others in distant lands through exchange of letters. There is a membership fee of $1.00. Letters Abroad, Inc., at 45 East 65th Street, New York, N.Y. 10021, is another volunteer organization with the same purpose.

The Telephone Line.   Considering the importance of the telephone in the social life of boys and girls nowadays, you will want to investigate devices that make the telephone usable for your child if his disability hampers him. Several commercial aids are on the market for those who have difficulty holding the phone. They are available from some hospital or rehabilitation supply houses, and have been carried by Brecks, of Boston, and Goldsmith Brothers, New York

City. If your child can't dial, the telephone company will probably be able to install equipment that requires only pushing a button to get the operator. In some cases an amplifier is used to replace the receiver. Get in touch with your local telephone company to find out what can be done.

GOING PLACES

Young people take for granted the excursions they make in their own community; but before a person with a handicap sets out there should be assurance that he won't be embarrassed or disappointed. It is worse than frustrating for the wheelchair user to go to a theater or restaurant, only to discover that there is no possible wheelchair entrance.

One young woman who, herself, uses a wheelchair has prepared *A Guide to Enjoyment for the Handicapped.*[18] The pamphlet gives important information to users of wheelchairs and crutches about public places in New York City; the number of steps, the presence of a side aisle in a theater, and the availability of assistance. This guide covers restaurants, movie houses, theaters, museums, art galleries, auditoriums, night clubs, parks, sports arenas, boat rides, temples, churches, department store shopping—and even the Marriage License Bureau.

The author suggests that the disabled person explain his situation when he buys a theater ticket. An aisle seat is most convenient for those on crutches or those who will transfer from wheelchairs. People who remain in wheelchairs will sit either in a side aisle or behind the last row of the orchestra. It is almost always necessary to sit on the orchestra level. A common difficulty is the lack of washrooms on that level.

If there is no guide for handicapped people in your community, your son or daughter might enlist the interest of other young people in preparing one. The first-hand exploration would be fun, and the project might lead to the removal of some architectural barriers that keep handicapped persons from enjoying recreational facilities.

Driving an Automobile. Driving a car adds enormously to both the pleasure and the business opportunities of many disabled people. Cars can be equipped with devices for hand operation to make driving possible for the person whose legs are paralyzed.[19] The person who has lost one leg above the knee should be able to drive any modern car with only minor adjustments in technique.[20] The car with an automatic shift greatly simplifies the problem for the driver with arm or hand disabilities. Many states permit driving by persons with disabilities, provided they can pass the standard test. Your state motor vehicle department can tell you what the regulations are in your state. If your child needs special equipment in order to drive, he should get advice from his rehabilitation center about the most suitable type for his needs.

In case of accident, the driver who is handicapped is likely to be blamed, fairly or not. This is unfortunate, but it does place an extra obligation on him to drive skillfully and cautiously at all times. Until your child has the steadiness of character and the skill to do this, he should not be permitted to drive. This restriction is for his personal welfare as well as the public's.

Travel. The stimulation of travel is good medicine for the handicapped. A travel agent can help you get information about special accommodations for the handicapped. Wheelchairs are available in many rail and air terminals, and sometimes arrangements can be made for railroad or airline employees to meet the handicapped person and help him with baggage, taxi, and so on. In making hotel reservations for a wheelchair user, it is wise to find out about steps and elevators and whether doors of rooms, bathrooms, and elevators are wide enough.

The Indoor Sports Club, a nonprofit organization of handicapped persons with 97 chapters throughout the United States, has published a guide for the handicapped individual who is planning a motor trip. It is called *Along the Wayside* and is available from Edward H. Poth, Travel Survey Chairman, Indoor Sports Club, 373 Walnut Street, Pittsburgh 38, Pennsylvania. It lists motels, restaurants, and sightseeing attractions visited by club members, giving information about the convenience of accommodations for the handicapped.

Under the auspices of the International Society for the Rehabilitation of the Disabled and the International Conference of Social Work, a project called "Wings for the Disabled" sets up tours abroad for handicapped persons, including those who use wheelchairs or crutches, although they must be able to care for themselves without assistance. Current information can be obtained from the International Society, 701 First Avenue, New York, N.Y.

An unusual service is offered by the Mary K. Houck Foundation, which maintains several motels and residences in Sarasota, Florida, providing free accommodations to blind and other handicapped persons. Meals are not served but housekeeping accommodations are available. The office of the motels is at the Adirondack Motel, 1206 Washington Blvd. (Tamiami Trail), Sarasota, Florida.

COMMUNITY RESOURCES FOR RECREATION

Your child is fortunate if the community has made special plans for including the handicapped in its recreational activities, for many have not done so.

First, ask what *public* recreational facilities there are. Your municipal offices can refer you to the correct department for this information. Inquire about play and recreation programs at schools, parks, playfields, golf courses, tennis courts, swimming pools, skating rinks, picnic grounds, camping centers, libraries, bridle paths, boating facilities, zoos, or open air theaters or concert facilities.

What recreation programs do *private* agencies provide? Look for boys' clubs, girls' clubs, Y's, Scouts, neighborhood centers, Junior Grange, 4-H Clubs, churches, fraternal organizations, unions, or organizations for the handicapped. A central group such as a Council of Social Agencies, or a family service agency, can help you.

Finally, what commercial facilities for recreation are available? If there is a neighborhood bowling alley or swimming pool, check first with the management to see whether handicapped persons are admitted and whether facilities are convenient for your child—for example, whether doors are wide enough for a wheelchair. You will want to know this about theaters, too.

If your community offers little, you and others who are interested might start the ball rolling in projects that are vitally needed. If your child is old enough, he should help. Write to the Consulting Service on Recreation for the Ill and

242 CARINGCARING FOR YOUR DISABLED CHILD

Handicapped, National Recreation Association, 8 West Eighth Street, New York City, for suggestions.

If new parks, swimming pools, bowling alleys or theaters are being built, can something be done to make sure that architectural adaptations will permit the handicapped to use them? At the request of the President's Committee on Employment of the Physically Handicapped, the American Standards Association now has a special committee to study how public buildings can be made more usable for the disabled. An inquiry addressed to the President's Committee on Employment of the Physically Handicapped, Washington, D.C., would bring information.

Is there any program of friendly visiting for the homebound children of your community? The Handicapped Children's Home Service, of New York City, trains volunteers who visit chronically ill children regularly, taking toys and hobby equipment. Since 1939, the Volunteer Film Association in St. Louis, Missouri, has taken films to homebound persons, either in institutions or in their own homes, making all arrangements for showing them. Organized efforts along the lines your community needs can bring tremendous satisfaction, not only to your child, but to others who are handicapped.

THE PLEASURE OF BEING NEEDED

It's important enough to say once more, that the satisfaction of feeling useful and needed, of being the giver rather than the receiver, shouldn't be denied to the child with a handicap. The starting place is at home. You give your child responsibilities, encourage him to do nice things for other members of the family, expect him to plan for birthday and Christmas gifts. If he's severely handicapped, it will take ingenuity on your part to think of the jobs he can do, and his "help" may mean more effort for you. But this is in a good cause. Of course, it takes more than just the assignment of jobs to make a child gracious and helpful. You have to ask for assistance in genuinely polite tones and express appreciation as you would to a respected friend; it's the spirit of kindliness you want your child to learn.

Youngsters can and do take part in a great number of service activities outside the home, too, such as clothing drives, book and magazine collections for hospitals, or reconditioning toys for needy children. A Girl Scout troop of retarded girls made hospital disposal bags, planted slips and cared for them until the plants were ready for distribution to shut-ins, made barbecue gloves for the scout camp, and decorated matchboxes for Christmas gifts. Perhaps a project requires a great deal of telephoning, which your child can do very well; or he may be good at managing the financial end, or making posters to publicize the project.

As your child grows older and has a skill to offer, he should inquire through the Community Chests and Councils, a volunteer bureau, a Council of Social Agencies, a hospital, or any of the agencies in the community that use volunteers. He may be able to do volunteer activities through one of the organizations concerned with the handicapped.

Boredom is a curse. For *real* enjoyment of life, a person needs to work toward goals. Customarily we think of such goals as being occupational. But we aren't all able to find jobs that satisfy our personal drives. The dullness of many jobs is one reason why so many people yearn for shorter working hours and longer vacations—and hate to get up in the morning.

If your child can't hold a job because of his disability, the fact that he has more leisure time on his hands than the average employed person shouldn't lead to boredom. There are many others today—particularly the retired people and the mothers whose children have grown up—who use their leisure to pursue activities they never had time for: hobbies, projects around the home, volunteer jobs.

Whether or not your child is able to hold a job, his plan of life must take account of his leisure. Help him to learn to use it as a challenge.

REFERENCES

1. Mary Eleanor Brown. "Recreational Therapy for the Orthopedically Exceptional." *Occupational Therapy and Rehabilitation,* August 1945. pp. 171-178.
2. "Games for Handicapped Children." National Recreation Association, New York. Mimeographed, 3 pp.
3. *Ibid.*
4. Valerie V. Hunt. *Recreation for the Handicapped.* Englewood Cliffs, New Jersey, Prentice-Hall, Inc., 1955. pp. 124-126.

5. *Ibid.*, pp. 114-116.

6. Paul V. Gump and Yuen-Hung Mei. "Active Games for Physically Handicapped Children." *The Physical Therapy Review,* April 1954, Vol. 34: No. 4. pp. 171-174.

7. *Ibid.*

8. Howard A. Rusk and Eugene J. Taylor. *Living with a Disability.* Garden City, N.Y., Blakiston Co., 1953. p. 105.

9. Aaron L. Danzig. *Handbook for One-Handers.* New York, Federation of the Handicapped, 1957.

10. Howard A. Rusk and Eugene J. Taylor, *op. cit.,* p. 76.

11. Kathleen Haddon. *Artists in String.* New York, E. P. Dutton, 1930.

12. Howard A. Rusk and Eugene J. Taylor, *op. cit.,* pp. 183-188, illus.

13. Vera S. Flandorf. *Books to Help Children Adjust to a Hospital Situation.* National Society for Crippled Children and Adults, Chicago. Supplements at various dates.

14. Joseph Prendergast. *New Worlds for Boys and Girls.* White House Conference on Children and Youth, 1960.

15. Valerie Hunt, *op. cit.*

16. *Scouting with Handicapped Boys.* Boy Scouts of America. New Brunswick, New Jersey, 1957. p. 32.

17. Eveline E. Jacobs. *Guide to Standards for Resident Camps for Crippled Children.* National Society for Crippled Children and Adults, Chicago.

18. Sandra Schnurr. *A Guide to Enjoyment for the Handicapped.* Privately printed, 2255 Cruger Ave., Bronx 67, N.Y.

19. Howard A. Rusk and Eugene J. Taylor, *op. cit.,* pp. 111-113, illus.

20. Donald Kerr and Signe Brunnstrom. *Training for the Lower Extremity Amputee.* Springfield, Illinois, Charles C. Thomas, 1956.

PART VI

Sexual and Social Development

There is a temptation for the parents of a seriously disabled child to think of him as if he were sexless. In some cases they wish this were so for his own sake, because they assume that a sex life and marriage are impossible for him. Even the specialists in rehabilitation have given remarkably little attention to the effect of disability on the psychosexual development of the child and his outlook for marriage.

Your child's sex is a part of him, regardless of his disability. Whether or not he marries, he needs your help in developing wholesome feelings about the opposite sex and about his own sexuality. He needs guidance in forming standards of sex behavior. Will he have a chance to know other boys and girls of his age and to learn to get along with them? This will help him to be realistic as well as romantic about the opposite sex. Is his rehabilitation program teaching him to be as physically independent as his disability allows and to become emotionally independent of his family?

John was fifteen years old when he startled his parents by saying, "I guess I'll be a C.P.A. I could support a wife and family on what a good accountant makes, and I could do it at home. I'd be good at it, too." He was confined to a wheelchair as the result of polio and always would be, and his parents had never thought seriously about his marrying. But it was clear that he was doing some careful thinking about it. Parents have to prepare themselves to deal with the question because marriage is in the front or back of a young person's mind from adolescence on.

Many, many people with disabilities do marry and have their own homes. However, there are also many for whom the effects of disability make marriage either impossible or unwise; most of these individuals sense this and rule out marriage themselves. You will probably be able to guess about the likelihood of marriage as your child develops, but he might surprise you. One cerebral-palsied youth who never could walk, and who learned to speak only at the age of twelve, nevertheless had the intelligence and initiative to get a high school and college education, to become self-supporting, and later to make a satisfying marriage. Certainly during his childhood no one would have expected these achievements.

Even if his disability is severe your child may well fall in love and wish to marry, for disability is no barrier to these longings. But the parents have to ask whether it would be wise. The first point to consider is not whether he is confined to a wheelchair, or is deaf, or blind, or uses an artificial limb. Ask first what kind of person he is. What kind of person does he propose to marry?

The couple will need the personal qualities and practical abilities that determine the success of any marriage: love that puts their mutual concerns ahead of personal and petty issues; ability to share a mutually satisfying sex life; a sharing of interests; respect for each other's attitudes on such matters as child-rearing, religion, recreational and cultural interests. Together they should be able to support and manage a home, rear children if any come. They must understand their feelings about the disability and its effect on their home life. Their love must be mature in the sense that each wants most of all to please and help the other.

You can't expect your child to score perfectly on all these points, any more than do the millions of physically sound persons who marry—often without giving much thought to such questions. But if your child's disability creates serious economic difficulties or practical problems in home management, or if it is the source of much emotional stress, he will need more than average determination and maturity to make his marriage succeed.

21

THE EARLY YEARS

A child's attitudes toward sex and love don't wait until adolescence to develop. They are forming all through childhood on the basis of his strong attachment to his parents, his desire to be worthy of them, and the growth of his own instincts. Sex and love cover a lot more ground, in early childhood as well as in adolescence, than simply the biological facts of life. They involve the sum total of his feelings toward the opposite sex (including his desire to protect, help, please, and idealize his future beloved), his eventual estimation of himself as man or woman, his attitude toward his own body, his feelings for children and his future capacity to care for them as a parent.

So all the important relationships he forms throughout childhood will contribute in one way or another to his attitude toward sex and love in this broad sense. And his total concept should be a healthy one, whether or not he is ever to marry. An individual's attitude toward his own body—whether of pride or shame—is one aspect of his sexuality, and this has particular importance for the handicapped child.

Between three and six years of age children turn very positively toward their parents. A boy develops his many ideals through his devotion to his father. He sets to work to pattern himself after his father (and other friendly males); he carefully observes his father's various occupations and how he goes about them, what he considers right and wrong, his attitudes toward women and other men, his mannerisms, which feelings he expresses freely and which he tries to conceal. The boy plays all day at manly occupations—pushing toy cars, building structures, riding horses, shooting pistols, driving cars or planes, acting the part of the father when he plays house. A girl spends a great deal of time acting out the role of wife and mother, playing at cooking, housework, and doll care.

A boy's love of his mother, which was mainly dependent before, now takes on an increasingly romantic quality. By about four he may declare he is going to marry her. But Freud pointed out the evidence that the possessive nature of his love—because he is a human being—stirs up, beneath the surface, feelings of rivalry toward his beloved father. And since he assumes, with four-year-old logic, that his father reciprocates this jealousy, and since his father is so much bigger, stronger, and smarter, the boy becomes increasingly anxious about this uneven rivalry and tries to keep it out of the conscious part of his mind. A girl, too, feeling competitive with her mother for her father's attention, imagines that her mother is resentful of this.

Tensions arise from other related sources too. By three, normal children are somewhat aware of the feelings connected with genitals and may become involved in sex play— with others or with themselves. They are interested in where babies come from. Even as early as two-and-a-half years they begin to notice intently (to the extent that they have the opportunity) the physical differences between boys and girls, men and women. They act quite surprised at first and, instead of accepting the difference, they usually show concern. A little girl who notices a boy's penis for the first time is apt to say, pointing, "What's that?" and then, after a few minutes, in a worried or resentful tone, "Why haven't I got one?" or "What happened to mine?" A boy, far from being reassured by the fact that he has more visible equipment, is apt to ask tensely, "What happened to her wee-wee?" And then he is likely to start worrying about whether some injury might happen to his penis, as he assumes it has happened to the girl's.

If parents realize that these are normal questions and normal fears at this age, they can be ready to help their children with sensible, comforting answers: "Boys are meant to be different from girls" . . . "You are made like Mommy" . . . "Girls don't have penises, but they can grow babies inside them," and so on. However, it seems that even the most reassuring answers don't altogether allay these anxieties. Strong emotions interfere with understanding. Another factor that sometimes contributes to a child's anxiety about his genitals is the parent's warning about the harm that may come from touching them.

These anxieties from various sources (the fear of the parent's rivalry, the misunderstanding about the genitals, warnings about masturbation) tend to combine to give the child the feeling that his parents are disapproving or angry about all his romantic and sexual wishes. It is believed, from the psychoanalysis of thousands of adults and children, from the dramatic play situations that children create for themselves and their dolls, and from the frightening dreams which become more frequent at this age, that this apprehension about the parents' anger is well-nigh universal at the age of five and six, although it may be mild in one individual and acute in another.

As it builds up beneath the surface, it eventually causes every normal child to strive to suppress his romantic and sexual interests at about six or seven, especially in regard to members of the family, and these feelings stay partially suppressed for the next half dozen years. From now on the boy doesn't want to be kissed by his mother (at least in public), he becomes progressively more scornful of girls and love stories, and he turns his interest toward schoolwork and other impersonal matters. A comparable process takes place in girls, but they don't usually suppress their romantic interests so deeply. It is probably a biological necessity for this suppression of sex to occur in a species which loves so intensely and jealously, and in which it is necessary for children to be dependent on their parents for fifteen to twenty years, while they learn how to get along in the world.

So in the school-age period, from six to twelve, the child turns away from his parents to outside interests and influences. Though he continues to love them deeply underneath, he usually tries to stop copying their behavior. He no longer wants to be considered their good little boy but, instead, a rough, independent man of the world; and he usually becomes sloppy and even irritating in his manners. To show that he no longer considers his parents all-wise, he argues with them about everything and quotes his teacher as a superior authority. Now his appearance, manners, and activities will be copied from his friends at school. His emotional and creative energies are turned toward more abstract matters, such as learning about the three R's, nature, science, and technology. He also becomes interested in making collections and practicing games of skill.

It is the glandular changes of early adolescence which bring an end to the comfortable middle-childhood assumption that the opposite sex can be ignored. The newly stirred up romantic feelings have a tendency to go out toward the parent again—unconsciously, as dreams often show—but the adolescent fights off any recognition of this, sometimes by being unbearably disagreeable to the parent of the opposite sex. A boy is apt to become even more intolerant of his mother's physical affection. A girl may beg her mother not to mention to her father that her menstrual periods have begun. The old rivalry with the parent of the same sex is revived—with a new intensity because the child really is approaching maturity and competition with adults. The boy, however reasonable he may be on the surface, is bound at times to feel secretly resentful of his father's authority. The girl feels that it's her turn to be the romantic woman-of-the-world, have the glamorous clothes, and go to the hairdresser; it's time for her mother to take a back seat.

This brief outline of some of the shifts in children's feelings leads to some practical questions and problems that all parents face.

The sex play that a child may become involved in with another or with himself between three and six years is not a sign of any abnormality as long as it is not intensely persistent and the child is well adjusted in other respects. A majority of parents will feel that it should be inhibited. This is best done in the matter-of-fact tone that the parent uses to stop other disapproved behavior: "Mother doesn't want you to do it," for example, or "It isn't polite." It's wise to avoid giving the child a severe sense of guilt by acting as if he had done something terrible or unnatural, and it's wise to avoid implying that the genitals will be hurt or made sick by touching. This is particularly important in the handicapped child, for the following reason. It has been discovered that most young children believe that a disease or injury comes as a punishment for being naughty. The child with a serious disability is especially apt to feel this. Then if his parents emphasize the particular sinfulness or harmfulness of touching the genitals, he guiltily blames this for his handicap.

Unusually persistent efforts, in the preschool period, to see other children undressed, and frequent handling of the genitals in a worried manner, are most often signs that a child needs more help in understanding the meaning of the physical differences between the sexes.

Young children need to be given simple answers to their questions about babies and where they come from. But some disabled children have been so limited in their experiences that they have missed the natural opportunities most young children have to learn about babies, human or animal. Observation stimulates questions, and the child who has never seen a pregnant woman can scarcely ask his mother why she looks different. The homebound child may have missed the nesting birds, or the cat about to have kittens, and in fact may never have seen a newborn baby. Whether or not he asks questions, it is worth while trying to enlarge his experiences. Perhaps you can take him to visit the home of friends where there is a new baby, or give him a pet. And there are many fine books and stories for little children that help parents tell them the exciting story of birth.

You may be tempted in the years between six and twelve to "let sleeping dogs lie" in the assumption that at this period your child isn't interested in sex. The fact is that underneath his great absorption in schoolwork and play he still has considerable curiosity about sex and some anxiety. A girl, first hearing about menstruation from a poorly informed friend, may want to ask her mother, "How do you know it will stop once it begins?" Or a youngster reading in the newspaper about the premature birth of a baby or the death of a mother in childbirth may fear that his own mother may die in childbirth; but he will be too timid to speak of his anxiety unless he has a comfortable, confidential relationship with his parents.

It's interesting to note the kinds of questions that sixth-graders in one school, on the verge of adolescence, put to their teachers each year after the showing of a film on reproduction.[1] The largest number of questions are about birth, but a high proportion indicate that the children are fearful and anxious about the illness or death of mother or baby. "Why is it a woman sometimes dies when the baby is being born?" "What happens to the mother if the baby dies inside her?" "If the woman gets sick, does the baby die?" "Labor pains make the mother sick, don't they?" "If the baby comes out after three months, what happens?" "I saw last night in the paper a baby weighed only two pounds when it was born. Do you think it can live?" Since there was nothing in the film about sickness or death, obviously these were really worrisome questions. If you use good judgment about the timing and are thoughtful about the phrasing, you can be helpful by anticipating such questions and even by voicing them for a shy child. It is far better to clear the air than to permit confused, distorted ideas to worry your child.

When a child's physical disability has made him uncomfortable about his bodily differences from other people, he will be especially apt to worry in adolescence that he will be different from others in his sexual development. Since his disability in most cases won't impair his sexual functions, he should, of course, know that. But even apart from his disability, he may have some strange ideas about the sexual development of his body. Well before the physical changes of puberty occur, many children hear about them from other children. Whether or not they have been told the facts by parents, they are apt to form some fearful and far-fetched notions about menstruation, nocturnal emissions, erections, intercourse, and the business of having a baby. Even after children have been well informed, they easily become mixed up again. Your main job is to make it easy for your child to turn to you for information, or for correction of misinformation. You should know that children ask questions readily before six, less between then and twelve, and that they are usually embarrassed to talk about sex with parents in adolescence, especially the boys.

In addition to the primary changes in the reproductive organs, a child by ten or eleven needs to understand the secondary changes: the speeding up of growth in height and weight at puberty (which occurs earlier in girls than in boys and at different ages even in the same sex), changes in body shape and proportions, the coming of new emotions, feelings, and interests in the other sex. Some good books for boys and girls of this age are listed on page 259.

Books are particularly helpful for children of shy parents and also for embarrassed adolescents. They do not entirely take the place of occasional informal talks between you and your child, but a good book may be the opening wedge for freer discussion. A book offered in a natural, easy manner implies that everyone is free to read and talk about the subject. If your child knows that you regard sex as a right and wholesome part of life, his own feelings will be more healthy and more free from fear and shame, even though there is always some of both.

In the years before adolescence your child isn't likely to be consciously concerned about whether he will marry when he grows up. If he asks you about it, you can point out that it will depend on whether he happens to meet the right person and whether he can do his part to earn money for the family or to be a homemaker.

THE EARLY ADOLESCENT YEARS

With puberty and the coming of adolescence, a girl who formerly thought boys a nuisance may long to be popular with them; a boy who scorned girls begins secretly to want their company. But it often takes several years before the young teenager feels at all comfortable in his new masculine or feminine role. In the meantime, some of his experiences may be painful. The most assured adolescent is somewhat self-conscious, and the most normal and good-looking one thinks something is wrong with him at times.

Gaining Social Ease. Even when the boy or girl with a disability has been able to go to school and mingle with other young people, the new social adjustments of adolescence may be quite hard for him. If his mobility is limited or his speech, vision, or hearing impaired, he may need help in finding boy-girl social activities that he can take part in. But whatever you do now to promote your child's social life, he should participate in the plans and should take increasing responsibility for them. Parents of a disabled child need to be particularly sensitive about this, because they have had to play such a large part in planning his activities in his earlier years.

If your child seems disturbed by what he considers his "social failure," or if he shows only negative feelings toward social activities, he may need help. Consult his teachers at school. On the other hand, he may be happily occupied with other interests—studies, hobbies, his friendships with a few pals—and it may be only a matter of time before he makes a wider social adjustment.

Their physical appearance worries most young people, even the good-looking ones. They think that no one, *no one,* could possibly like them. A young teenager may be miserably self-conscious because of slightly prominent ears, a blunt nose, a little acne, or maybe just because his eyes are green instead of blue.

At this time, the opinions of his friends become more persuasive than yours. The fact that "everybody thinks so," or "nobody thinks so," carries the greatest weight. Few youngsters are willing to expose themselves to criticism by deviating too much from the others' behavior. If your child's disability makes him physically conspicuous, or different in ways that have significance for teenagers, he may have very rough going when his friends are beginning to have dates. Companions may be friendly enough but, when it comes to dating, the disabled child is likely to be left out. The blind boy at a party may have to rely on boys who see to introduce him to the girls, or he may not be able to call for a girl or take her home from a party. Or if a boy or girl wears an artificial arm, the fact that it doesn't conform to the partner's body contours when they dance may be enough to make them uncomfortable. When boys and girls are just beginning to have dates, such obstacles may seem so important that the nondisabled are too embarrassed to have dates with the disabled. The disabled, afraid of being rebuffed, will not take the social initiative. The boy or girl who is confined to a wheelchair, or is homebound, has still greater restrictions on dating and social contacts.

It may comfort your child a little to know that, a few years from now, conventional appearance will not still be the important criterion by which his age mates judge him as a date, a "steady," or future marriage partner, as it seems to be now. Biographies of a number of persons with disabilities tell of their great unhappiness during the early adolescent years when they failed to attract the other sex. But in more mature years these persons usually gained acceptance by friends who had the sense to see beyond the physical disability and to discover the real worth.

Of course, whatever you can do to help your child develop into a likable person improves his chances for making friends. Careful grooming and good taste in dress increase his attractiveness and bolster his self-confidence. But the adolescent youngster sometimes allows his passion for good looks to interfere with wearing necessary aids such as orthopedic shoes or artificial limbs. For example, when "everyone" is wearing short-sleeved shirts or dresses, a teenager may stop using his artificial arm rather than wear a long-sleeved garment or expose the prosthesis. This tendency to stop wearing a prosthesis for cosmetic reasons appears often in teenagers and may last from a few months to two or three years, until the value of using it again outweighs considerations of good looks.[2] You'll need patience and tact to help your child find a satisfactory compromise between utility and appearance. Obviously there are some circumstances when compromise is not safe and he must use his aid.

Understanding the Body Changes of Adolescence. Young adolescents need increased understanding of physical growth and sexual development. Changes in body form, menstruation, appearance of pubertal hair, nocturnal emissions, and voice changes now take on very personal meaning. Some children go through these changes early, some late. Some girls acquire new curves and begin to menstruate well before their friends do. Some boys have a childish frame and small sex organs while others of the same age already have a manly look. Your child needs to be reassured that such differences in rate of development are quite normal and that they have nothing to do with his disability. (The average girl begins her puberty growth spurt at 11, the average boy is 13.)

A very few disabilities do affect sexual capacity. Spinal cord damage is the major cause of sexual impairment, but there are also some disorders of physical growth that interfere with normal sexual development. If this is true for your child, careful medical evaluation is needed to find out how it affects his sexual functions.

The young boy or girl who is blind has some very special problems. He doesn't have the comforting reassurance that his new physical characteristics are common to all adolescents, because he can't see the changed appearance of others. He cannot benefit by illustrated books; he isn't free to make use of his well-developed tactile sense. Anatomical models are helpful, but they must be accurate, not sexless in form. A comfortable, confidential relationship with his parent or older brother or sister, in which all kinds of intimate discussions about sex and sex differences can take place, is his best resource.

Worrisome Behavior. In the years between six and

twelve, the frequency of sex play decreases considerably, because the child is trying to suppress it. But the glandular changes of adolescence make the temptation intense, especially for those who don't have the usual outlets of dancing, dating, and free social mixing. It is believed that most children yield occasionally. All but the most brazen adolescents feel guilty about such actions—even about sexual thoughts—and particularly those youths who have unusually high moral standards. So a parent does not have to threaten. In fact he may need to reassure the guilty child that the temptation is universal and that the parent knows the child is doing his best to control it.

The truth is that in all human beings there is some guilt about sex and that it is especially strong in our own culture in carefully brought up children. This makes for the persistence of such erroneous beliefs as that masturbation causes insanity, blindness, or withering of the genitals. Of course none of this is so, but some parents tell it to their children to try to keep them from masturbation. If this threat succeeds, it may encourage distorted ideas about sex and, as a result, decrease the child's chances for a happy marriage later on. If masturbation continues, as it usually does anyway, the child will be burdened with excessive guilt and fear.

It's best if young people can understand that their awakening sexual desires are perfectly normal expressions of their glandular and emotional growth and that sex will play a normal, healthy role in their adult, married life, but that in the meantime, a certain amount of self-control has to be exercised. Probably the most important help the parent can give is to show that he can listen to a child's questions with understanding and give him answers that imply trust in his good intentions.

Another aspect of adolescent behavior that worries parents is whether a child can be trusted to behave with propriety and good sense when he is with the opposite sex. The chief difference between disabled and nondisabled children is that the disabled youngster may have much less actual experience in boy-girl social activities and so may be less assured. The best remedy is to increase his social opportunities and to make clear the expected standards of behavior. There is no reason to think that a child with a disability is less trustworthy than another.

Worry sometimes leads parents to overemphasize venereal disease or illegitimacy. Adolescents should know the facts about them and should know why promiscuous sexual relations are risky, but there is no need to dwell heavily on these. A well-adjusted person is unlikely to get into trouble merely for lack of stern warning. His good sense and moral values are the best protection.

If Your Child Talks of Marrying. Should you discourage a youngster from making plans for marriage or should you encourage him to go on dreaming? In most cases the best course is not to be emphatic in either direction. The child's maturation, in a variety of respects, will hold the answer. If he asks you can answer that it will depend on how he feels and how he is making out when he is grown up. There is no need for parents to pretend to know what in fact they don't know. It's the young adolescent's right to dream about romance. He will need to reach considerable maturity before he can analyze how his disability may affect his marriage.

As with other aspects of life, the best thing he can do is to work toward the greatest achievable competence through therapy and educational and vocational preparation. The more fully he develops his capacities, the greater his chances for managing his disability and maintaining himself as an adult who can marry. If the probability of marriage is very slight, he will in all likelihood draw this conclusion for himself in time, with less wounding of his self-esteem than if you had told him bluntly that he could never marry.

Don't overlook the fact that many entirely normal persons who are not married live happy, useful lives. Without laboring the point, you can help an adolescent for whom marriage is not likely by showing that you admire unmarried men and women in the community, that you don't think of them as "old maids" or "fussy bachelors." He may gain insight by reading the biographies of interesting unmarried men or women. You can't expect to make a child happy about not marrying, since it's normal to want to have at least the possibility, and we live in an era when the happy ending almost always means marriage. The young person should understand that loneliness is not the exclusive property of unmarried or disabled people and that inner resources are the best shield against it.

Marriage and the Mentally Retarded Child. Parents of a severely retarded teen-aged child may be worried about his or her engaging in improper sex activities. The facts, so far as they are known, suggest that the sexual development of many seriously retarded persons is quite limited, both physically and emotionally. It is entirely possible that a retarded child will be uninterested in sex and marriage. Lack of sex interest seems to be quite characteristic of those whose I.Q. rating is 35 or below.[3]

There are some retarded persons who do have normal or strong sex drives but who are not able to understand that sex behavior should be controlled. Then problems may arise which make admission to an institution the best solution. A careful medical, psychological, and social evaluation of your child will guide you in what to expect. Sound professional advice can relieve you of worry about problems that are unlikely to arise. And when you know what difficulties to expect you can be prepared to deal with them.

The retarded child who develops sexually should have such simple explanations of his body changes as he can understand. If he asks questions, he will need simple answers. A girl must be taught how to take care of herself during her menstrual periods.

Since there may be unscrupulous persons who will take advantage of retarded children, it will be necessary to take certain precautions. If a seriously retarded boy or girl can't be taught to refuse rides or other invitations from strangers, if he cannot carry out other simple rules you make, be sure that he has supervision. This doesn't mean that you must live in fear for his safety all the time or restrict his activities unnecessarily; it is only necessary to take precautions that fit the situation.

Obviously, marriage is not suitable for a child who is seriously retarded, since he will always require supervision and will be unable to support or manage a home. And probably such a child does not understand about marriage or want to marry. Misconceptions can develop, however, as shown in this story.

Lois was a retarded girl who had always been very cheerful. At seventeen she suddenly changed and became sullen and tearful. Her parents had given her a hope chest and had told her that it was just like the one given to a neighbor's daughter who was about to be married. Lois's parents had given her the chest thinking that she, too, might want to get married. But to Lois getting married meant that a girl went away from her home and parents. She was heartsick at the thought that her parents wanted her to leave them. Once they understood the reasons for her unhappiness and assured her that they wanted her to stay with them always, she was contented.[4]

For young people who are only mildly retarded and who are able to earn a living, the question of marriage is not quite so open and shut. Many of them are affectionate and industrious and want to live as others do. Under good influence and some degree of responsible guidance, this is quite possible. Some marry, and some have normal children,[5] but the risks may be considerable as shown in a study that compared the adjustments of a group of retarded young adults whose I.Q.'s were about 65 with those of a group of young adults of average intelligence. Slightly more than half of the retarded group and only one-fifth of the average group were unmarried. But the divorce rate was four times as high in the retarded group.[6] Unless medical and psychological experts advise that such a child is qualified to marry, it is advisable to discourage the retarded child from taking on this responsibility.

REFERENCES

1. Marion O. Lerrigo and Helen Southard. *Sex Facts and Attitudes.* New York, E. P. Dutton & Co., 1956.
2. John Steensma. "Problems of the Adolescent Amputee." *Journal of Rehabilitation,* Vol. XXV: No. 2. March-April 1959.
3. Marcia Morrison, *Now They Are Grown.* Dept. of Public Welfare, St. Paul, Minnesota, 1959.
4. *Ibid.*
5. Stanley Powell Davies. *The Mentally Retarded in Society.* New York, Columbia University Press, 1959.
6. "Post-School Adjustment of Educable Mentally Retarded Adults." *Exceptional Children,* Vol. 26: No. 8. April 1960.

22

ADULTHOOD AND MARRIAGE

Your teenager won't become an adult overnight. His attitude toward love and sex will continue to mature. As he leaves his early teens behind, he is apt to become more aware of his need for vocational ability, homemaking skills, knowledge about the opposite sex and marriage.

He may well want to turn to outsiders for advice—his doctor, a teacher, an occupational or marriage counselor. It's healthy for him to strike out on his own. He may profit by joining one of the discussion groups on dating, courtship, and marriage that are conducted by youth organizations and some churches. It is often particularly difficult for the youth with a serious physical disability to clarify his own set of values. Rubbing shoulders and exchanging opinions with outsiders may be very revealing to him.

It is now really urgent that he face certain realistic problems about his disability which may have a bearing upon his marrying; especially if he is already in love and his feelings crowd logic out of the picture. He will be more apt to take advice from an outsider than from parents.

Some Questions for the Doctor to Answer. A thorough medical evaluation can help clear the air about both the advisability of marriage and the adjustments the couple will have to make as the result of the disability. If the disability is in the nature of an illness—for example, tuberculosis, heart trouble, or multiple sclerosis—it is important to have a reliable medical opinion about the outlook for the individual's health in the future; also about whether his illness may bring health risks to the person he marries or to their children.

The couple should also seek medical opinion about the effects of the disability on conception, the wife's ability to bear children, or the couple's ability to rear children. Some disabilities cause sterility or otherwise make conception impossible. Some make pregnancy more hazardous.

The couple should also know whether their marriage could carry any unusual hereditary risks to their children. There is not only the question of the hereditary qualities of the disability but also whether marriage to a particular person may further increase risks to the children. For instance, there is little risk for the child of a marriage between a diabetic and a nondiabetic without a diabetic heritage; but if both parents have diabetes, there is a considerable chance that the child, too, will become diabetic.[1] If your child's doctor doesn't know the answers, he may suggest consultation at a genetics counseling center. (See page 55.)

Possibly you and your child, and even the doctor, may have shied away from talking about the effect of the disability on sexual functions, since it is such an intimate matter. It is usually more comfortable for the adolescent to talk directly and privately with the doctor or other professional rather than to his parent, and he'll probably not want his parent present. The parent can consult the doctor later.

Marriage for the Paraplegic. Spinal cord damage is the principal physical cause of impairment of sexual function, but the nature of the impairment is not at all uniform. The location and extent of the damage as well as its effects on the total health of the person determine the degree to which he is still capable of functioning sexually.

Interest in the opposite sex is usually unaffected, and secondary sex characteristics—voice changes, changes in body form, and so on—are normal. One study[2] of several hundred paraplegic and quadriplegic men patients showed that, more often than has been realized, sexual functions remain active and that in a considerable number of cases it is possible for the paraplegic to develop a reasonably satisfactory sex life. Careful individual consideration should be given to this goal in rehabilitation.

Love between men and women and the ability to respond sexually depend on many factors other than purely physical ones, whether the individual is paraplegic or not. But the paraplegic will need to understand his own particular responses, their nature, and their limitations. Many paraplegic men are able to have erections, some of them on the basis of the usual psychological factors. In others, erection occurs only as the result of local stimulation. Even when sensation has been lacking, paraplegic men have reported that intercourse was gratifying for it gave them proof of masculinity. Some paraplegic men are capable of becoming fathers, but the majority apparently are sterile. Sterility may result because loss of muscle activity makes ejaculation of sperm impossible, or because the physical condition interferes with the production of sperm. In certain cases infection of the bladder spreads from the urinary tract and obstructs the genital passages, causing sterility. A careful medical examination can throw light on all these conditions, and in a few instances can point the way to improvement.

Some parapelgic women have reported a feeling of sexual fulfillment in intercourse, even when definite physical sensation is lacking. Some have been able to conceive and to bear healthy children. The effects of spinal cord damage on the menstrual cycle and ovulation are varied; in some cases menstruation is not interrupted at all while in others it may be interrupted for some months and then resumed.

Bowel and bladder functions are impaired in paraplegia, and controlling them is a part of rehabilitation that has a bearing on marriage. If the techniques are mastered, it may be possible to hold a job, support a family, and take part in social activities of family and friends; this mastery also makes it easier to avoid esthetic problems in marital intimacies. Such problems require loyal devotion and an extraordinarily mature and cooperative partnership; the disabled person does everything he possibly can for himself while the other willingly gives what help is needed.

If a sexual relationship is not possible for your child, he need not automatically rule out the idea of marriage. There are many other rich values in marriage, and these may be sufficient for the disabled person and his spouse. But both must be ready to give more of themselves to compensate. The following remarks by wives of paraplegic men, quoted from *Paraplegic News,* should lend encouragement:

One of them wrote, "Marrying a paraplegic is no different from marrying someone else. It is only more so."[3] Another wrote, "It makes me furious when he refers to himself as 'half a man.' I consider it an insult to me, as I have chosen him as my husband and I would not have accepted anything less than the best. . . . Be sure your love is strong enough to stand many trials. . . . Once you have made your decision to marry, have faith in yourself, your love for each other, and your ability to make a go of your marriage."[4]

Talking It Over Together Before Marriage. Not everyone is able to feel as these wives did about marrying a person who has such a serious disability. Frank discussion is essential before marriage so that a chosen partner may come to realize ahead of time his inability or unwillingness to make the necessary adjustments. On the other hand, if the young couple are mature and their love is deep, such discussion helps them go ahead more confidently. Knowing where the problems lie is half the battle in solving them.

Will the wife, or the husband, regard as an imposition any special allowances that must be made? If one of the couple wears a hearing aid but frequently turns it off when half a dozen people are talking, will the other understand that he may be seeking relief from real fatigue? Will the dietary restrictions of the diabetic be a source of conflict? Will the great length of time and the labor of dressing and adjusting braces become annoying?

Or suppose a man is subject to epileptic seizures. Medically, there is no reason why an epileptic shouldn't marry when his seizures are well under control and, unless he marries a woman who also is epileptic and has seizures, the chances are small that their child will have seizures.[5] But the woman he marries has a right to know before marriage what problems may face them. In fact, concealment of the condition may be grounds for annulment. Of course, the moral obligation of the person with a disability to reveal it in advance to the one he plans to marry applies to any disability, no matter how easily it may be concealed.

Adjusting to an Unusual Role in Marriage. Disability sometimes forces either or both the husband and the wife to play unusual roles in marriage. The adjustments may cause considerable stress. The young couple should discuss those that they can foresee before they marry. Their solutions to unusual problems need not be the traditional ones, but they should give reasonable promise of success.

Financial support is certainly one problem. In some cases where the young man's disability makes it impossible for him to take a job the couple agree that the woman will work. A good many wives are glad to, but this may mean that the husband is to carry household duties and look after the children. Will he and his wife be satisfied with the arrangement year after year? Some people are. But it doesn't fit the image most of us have of the feminine and masculine roles, so it can easily result in stress and conflict.

If the wife is disabled, she may well have to limit her role as wife and mother. If she is unable to have children, she may have to bear not only her disappointment and her husband's but the critical attitude of in-laws as well. If she does have children, she may have to delegate to someone else a larger part of their care than she wants to. If she has to delegate many home-management responsibilities, there is the risk that she will begin to feel that her family no longer needs her and that she is "no good to anyone."

Fortunately, rearing children and managing a happy home do not depend on freedom from disability. The question is much more closely related to the kind of person the mother is. A recent study[6] of more than 100 handicapped mothers showed that many of the most severely disabled were quite effective in guiding the rest of the family in doing the household tasks that they themselves couldn't perform. They still took an active and responsible part in all family decisions. Since they weren't busy doing things themselves, they could give full attention to showing appreciation and maintaining good relations with their husbands and their children. In playing this special role, these mothers were noticeably happy and optimistic.

The mothers who were interviewed in this study had shown great ingenuity in managing their households. Some had made structural modifications in their homes. Many used special equipment and self-help devices. They also developed ingenious ways of caring for their children. A chief difficulty, that of carrying a young child, was solved in one of several ways: putting the baby inside the mother's blouse, pushing the child on a bathinette, or teaching the little child to hang onto his mother's neck.

Mothers who cannot physically enforce their commands are apt to anticipate problems with discipline. These women found it a great advantage to have some knowledge of child development so they could rely more fully on an understanding of their children's nature. They learned to cope with the problem of outdoor supervision—for example, by keeping a young child within a fenced area they could watch, making their back yard the neighborhood play center by providing interesting play equipment to attract other youngsters. They also succeeded in teaching very young children to do much more for themselves than is usual in such matters as washing, bathing, getting ready for bed, or straightening their rooms.

Considerable help is now being offered to disabled homemakers and mothers. The Institute of Physical Medicine and Rehabilitation of New York University-Bellevue Medical Center has for some years offered special training in the rehabilitation of homemakers. The University of Connecticut has been making a study of ways to simplify the work of caring for children when the mother has a disability, and other rehabilitation centers are beginning to give attention to such problems. Some of the publications of these and other institutions are listed in the home management section of the reading list at the back of the book.

Your Role When Your Child Marries. When you read this book your child may be much too young for you to think of the question of marriage. Even so, it is not too early for you to think about what you can do all through his growing years to help him become the kind of person who, if he does marry, will be able to make a go of it.

If your child is old enough to marry, he will need to face the kinds of questions raised in this chapter. Then he will expect to make his *own* decision to marry, just like other young adults in our society. He should do so if the chances are good that he and his spouse will be able to maintain their own home. Because of his disability you may well have been accustomed to give him more help than parents usually provide for their grown children, so it may be hard for you to feel that he is qualified to decide for himself. If you have doubts, you should talk with someone else who knows your child well, possibly his doctor or minister. Their viewpoint will be more objective than yours. Realistic answers to such questions as those given early in this chapter will help you sum up the pros and cons. If the balance seems favorable, your cue is to give your child your confidence and support. Of course, there are young people who get their hearts set on marriage who are obviously unable to carry the responsibilities. The reasons may or may not have anything to do with disability. Then parents should do their best to at least delay the marriage until the young couple have had time for second thoughts. When there is family disagreement, it is best for the couple and for the parents to talk with advisers outside the family.

If all of you still can't agree, it's not the end of the world. Lots of handicapped children marry against their parents' wishes. Some of them surprise their parents by succeeding. For the others, this may be the only way they can learn.

REFERENCES

1. Harold Brandaleone. "Rehabilitation of Patients with Diabetes Mellitus" in *The Handicapped and Their Rehabilitation,* ed. Harry A. Pattison. Springfield, Ill., Charles C. Thomas, 1957.

2. Herbert S. Talbot, "The Sexual Function in Paraplegia." *The Journal of Urology,* Vol. 73: No. 1, January 1955.

3. Judith Hover. "I Married a Paraplegic." *Paraplegia News,* November 1956.

4. Anonymous. "Have You Been Thinking About Marriage?" *Paraplegia News,* April 1956.

5. Donald J. Simons. "Epilepsy and Rehabilitation" in *The Handicapped and Their Rehabilitation,* ed. Harry A. Pattison. Springfield, Ill., Charles C. Thomas, 1957.

6. Victor A. Christopherson. "Role Modification of the Handicapped Homemaker." *Rehabilitation Literature,* Vol. 21, No. 4, April 1960.

PART VII

Tools and Techniques for Daily Living

The child with a disability is able to do more only as he masters his tools. This is how he increases his pleasures, too. His tools are his braces, crutches, wheelchair, artificial limb, hearing aid, or whatever other mechanical assistance he uses.

But not all childen—and not all parents—are able to look at it this way. The brace or crutch may be too much a symbol of disability to be able to seem a means to achievement. A few parents buy expensive braces for their child but leave them hidden in a closet—or they even object to using the word "braces." And of course there are quite a few children who balk at using braces or special shoes because they hate to look different, at least at the self-conscious ages.

Of course it's the ability, *not the* disability, *that counts. Any tools that help your child to live to the hilt of his capacities are worth using. And half the battle is won when he feels free to acknowledge his limitations openly and to use any means that help him to overcome them. This is where he'll particularly need the help of your sensible attitude.*

Separate chapters in this section offer some practical suggestions about the use of braces, crutches, wheelchairs, prosthetic devices, special equipment for the activities of daily living, and about methods of personal care for the child whose disability renders him incontinent. But first there are some household problems you must deal with: simplifying chores, getting a dependable sitter, arranging the furniture for the greatest convenience and least hazard, handling your finances.

23

SOME GENERAL PROBLEMS IN HOME MANAGEMENT

The mother's attention is always being pulled in different directions: care of the handicapped child, seeing to the needs of other members of the family, care of the home, outside activities including those that provide some fun and relaxation for herself and her husband.

A Plan for the Daily Routine. Like other children, the one with a disability thrives on a regular schedule of sleep and rest, bathing, toileting, meals, play, and work. This benefits the mother and the rest of the family too. However, the routines are likely to take *much* more time for the handicapped child, as you well know, and he often has outside appointments at the clinic or doctor's office.

Sometimes just writing down the child's schedule will help you work out a plan to meet all the other demands on your time. The schedule won't be the same for any two households. You'll have to take into consideration the very individual requirements of your own child—for help, for therapy, for tutoring, and for companionship. And compromises will have to be made from day to day.

Labor-saving Methods. The busy mother of a handicapped child should take all the short cuts and use all the help she can possibly get. Even young children can hang up their clothes and straighten their rooms. Sheets, towels, and the children's jeans, along with many other articles of clothing, can be folded without ironing. Plastic tablecloths and paper napkins save laundry. Dishes can be rinsed and left to dry in a rack. Linoleum on the dining room floor is easier to care for than a rug when children are likely to spill their food. If the handicapped child is bedfast, a plastic sheet protects the bedding when he is enjoying messy play. If his disability causes him to spill food, a square of plastic is a good protective covering. If he is confined to a wheelchair, he may be able to use a reaching device for picking up dropped objects. In fact, the best labor-saving device is to encourage the handicapped child to do *everything* for himself that he possibly can. Then he not only spares other people unnecessary effort but increases his abilities.

A household intercom system is a big help when there is a bedridden child. This small investment repays itself many times over in the time and energy and anxiety it saves.

Modifying the Physical Aspects of the Home. It is often wise to rearrange the household furnishings to make it easier for you to care for the child, make the house safer for him, help him to be more comfortable and independent.

Floor coverings are an important element in the safety of children who use crutches or a wheelchair, who have an unsteady gait, or poor vision. Scatter rugs are very dangerous. Carpeting, if it is used, should be tightly stretched from wall to wall. Hemp or cocoa matting provides a firm surface offering less resistance to a wheelchair than carpet. Rubber, asphalt tile, or plastic surfaces are easy to keep clean; they should be treated with non-skid waxes.

Railings on both sides of the stairways, in the halls, the bathroom, and on outside steps and ramps help the child who is learning to walk or who walks unsteadily.

You will want to really study the arrangement of furniture in order to provide the greatest convenience and to eliminate hazards. If your child has a problem in walking, or if he uses crutches or a wheelchair, the center of the room should be kept clear, with the furniture arranged close to the walls. There should be a minimum of small articles that can be knocked over easily. It's especially important for the blind child to know that the furniture is always placed in the same way.

Good lighting is important, particularly for the child with partial vision and the deaf child who reads lips. Lights that are hung from wall or ceiling do away with the necessity for cords along the floor, a hazard to the child on crutches. In each room there should be at least one light that can be turned on near the entrance.

Every child needs a place for personal belongings. A room of his own is desirable, but he should at least have his own drawers and shelves, placed within easy reach. The hooks in his closet should also be handy for him. A play or work table of his own, suited to his size and designed for his convenience, is very useful. (See Chapter 24 on special equipment.)

The height of a child's bed is important. If he uses a wheelchair and is able to transfer himself to it from his bed, the two should be level. If he gets about without a wheelchair, the bed should be low enough for him to lie down and get up without help. The bed of the helpless child who must always be lifted, however, should be high enough to eliminate stooping by the person who lifts him. A single bed is usually more satisfactory than a large one, especially for the child whose legs are paralyzed, because he can grasp the edges of the mattress more easily and thus use his arms in moving or turning over.

Getting Extra Help.   There are times when the mother urgently needs outside help. She may be ill, or fatigued to the point of exhaustion, or busy with a new baby—or she and her husband simply need a good vacation. Sometimes it seems impossible to get the extra help, either because of its cost or because it just isn't easy to find anyone willing to work in a household where the handicapped child creates unusual responsibilities. But sometimes there are community resources that can provide the needed relief.

You may be able to get home nursing care for a bedfast child from the Visiting Nurse Association. The visiting nurse will give baths, change dressings, care for the child's skin so as to prevent bedsores, etc. Following directions of the physical therapist, she may give the child bed exercises, heat applications, or practice in crutch-walking. In many communities, the visiting nurse service charges small fees but is available without cost to families who need free service.

Social agencies in a growing number of communities are providing "homemaker service."[1] These are family service agencies or child-welfare or public-assistance departments.

This service is not usually available on a permanent basis; it may be provided for a few weeks or months to help bridge an emergency until a more permanent plan can be made. The homemakers are not nurses, and some agencies do not allow them to do anything for the patient. Other agencies permit them to give the same kind of care to the patient that the patient's family would give under medical supervision. They are always instructed not to do what should be done only by a doctor, nurse, or therapist. Homemakers generally help with cooking, cleaning, and other household chores, and sometimes they read aloud or play games with the children, accompany them to school or clinic, or teach family members household skills. Some agencies don't charge families in financial distress, but when fees are charged, they range from less than a dollar to $1.80 an hour.

There are still other solutions to the need for outside help. Some local cerebral palsy organizations have made arrangements with a nursing home to have one or two stand-by beds available for cerebral-palsied children who need temporary care when the mother is ill or can't care for her child for other reasons.

It is sometimes possible to place the handicapped child in a foster home for a period of months; this is one of the solutions to be considered in case of a prolonged illness of the parents or other family crisis. Foster homes are carefully supervised in a number of states. In a good foster home the child has the advantages of a family atmosphere rather than that of an institution. Your state department of public welfare is one source of information about foster homes.

More and more day care centers are being established, especially for mentally retarded and cerebral-palsied children who don't qualify for any of the public school facilities. "Cerebral Palsy Development Centers" have been set up by a number of local cerebral palsy organizations, where children may attend for part of each day or two or three times weekly. The children learn about getting along with other children, and often they improve in speech, in play, and in self-care. Although the centers are primarily for the benefit of the children, they also give the mothers some much-needed freedom.

If your child is unable to walk, it's a good idea to notify your local police and fire departments. Then, in case of fire or some other emergency, they will know that there is someone in your house who needs help. In one small town, firemen canvassed the homes and mounted a small plaque on each one where there was a resident confined to a wheelchair or to bed.

Finding and Using a Sitter. Finding the right sitter may be extremely important if parents are to take time for their own recreation. This sometimes seems to be an insurmountable problem, for sitters may refuse to sit with a handicapped child. Sometimes the parents can't find anyone whom they feel they can trust with their child.

A few communities have done something to solve the problem. The local cerebral palsy organization of Phoenix, Arizona, with the cooperation of the high school authorities, arranged a special course to train students in the care of cerebral-palsied children.[2] Particular efforts were made to interest students who were planning careers in medicine, nursing, or other fields related to child care. Applicants were carefully screened.

The course, consisting of four Saturday morning sessions, covered the medical aspects of cerebral palsy, physical therapy demonstrations, the types of speech difficulties of cerebral-palsied children, techniques for communicating with children who have severe speech, hearing, or visual impairment. Before accepting full responsibility, each trainee was expected to spend two hours with a child while a parent was at home. Those who qualified were certified as "Cerebral Palsy Monitors."

The United Cerebral Palsy Association, 321 West 44th Street, New York 36, N.Y., has published a booklet, *The Cerebral Palsy Monitor Program,* which contains suggestions as to how such a program can be organized. Although the emphasis is on cerebral palsy, their program can easily be adapted to other types of handicaps.

If your efforts are confined to your personal problem, you can still find some pointers here. You might concentrate your search among students interested in medicine, nursing, or child care, as was done in the Phoenix program. The most effective approach is through school staff members.

When you find one or two young people who are interested, you will want to take some time to orient them. You can't expect to give them the equivalent of the training provided in the special courses described, but the material in the following pages will suggest what special points of information a sitter needs regardless of the nature of a child's disability. It is based on a basic child care outline prepared for the course given to the Cerebral Palsy Monitors in Phoenix.[3]

Feeding the Cerebral-Palsied Child
1. Find out from his parents whether he is to be given anything to eat or drink and whether he has any special prob-

lems or techniques. Some children are awkward and messy, others have trouble swallowing.

2. Take common-sense precautions. Give no food or drink unless the child is sitting up and you are right there with him. Give small bites or sips; use a protective towel. Odd eating patterns are just what is natural for him.

Physical Handling of the Cerebral-Palsied Child

1. Some cerebral-palsied children have night braces, worn only in bed. If the child wears one, ask his parents to show you how to put it on and take it off.

2. Ask the parents to show you how to operate his wheelchair. Be sure the brakes are on when the child is in it but not being transported. Block it with books if the brakes do not work.

3. Ask the parents to show you how the child walks and whatever techniques are to be used to assist him, whether canes, crutches, etc.

4. Be sure the child sits safely, in a chair with arms, his feet supported and restraint provided if needed.

5. Make a mental note of pitfalls such as scatter rugs, waxed floors, etc.

6. Find out what techniques are used, if any, in toileting him. Avoid hurry and distractions.

Speech

1. His speech may range from none to good. Understanding him may require much patience. Listen carefully and wait for him to finish, asking him to repeat what you have not understood. If you still have difficulty, use questions that require a simple "yes" or "no" answer. "Are you hungry? Thirsty?" Continue asking until he indicates "Yes."

2. Help him understand you. Speak slowly and clearly, repeat, using gestures and pictures if necessary.

3. If the child has no speech, find out whether he can read and write. Have paper and pencil handy. Learn what special signals or gestures he uses to communicate his wants.

Hard-of-hearing Children

1. Ask the parents to adjust the child's hearing aid before they leave.

2. If the child is wearing his aid, speak clearly and directly to him in normal tones.

3. Never pull the hearing-aid piece out of the child's ear; edge it out by making a quarter turn toward the back of the head, then toward the face, until it comes out.

General Information

1. Never talk baby talk; set a good speech example.

2. Don't move too quickly.

3. When showing pictures or books, place the child at an angle most comfortable for him.
4. Encourage the child to use speech as much as possible.

You will want to write out your own list, explaining the special problems about handling your child. The sitter will need to know how much he can do for himself and in what ways he needs help. If he is an amputee and wears a prosthesis, the sitter should be shown how the device is removed, or put on, unless the child is able to do it himself. If your child is blind, you should explain what parts of the house he is sufficiently familiar with, where he can play safely, what toys and games he enjoys, where his accustomed place of eating is, how his eating utensils are arranged, and how much he can do in feeding himself. If your child is subject to seizures, the sitter should know what to do in the way of first aid. In addition, of course, you should tell the sitter where you can be reached in an emergency, the nearest neighbor to be called if help is needed quickly, the name and telephone number of your child's doctor, and so on. Once a sitter is acquainted with your child and cares for him satisfactorily, you will want to use her repeatedly.

Don't overlook the possibilities of cooperative groups in which the parents themselves exchange babysitting or child care services. Many such cooperatives have been extremely successful, particularly within housing developments.

FINANCIAL PROBLEMS ARISING FROM YOUR CHILD'S DISABILITY

When it first becomes apparent that your child's disability will create great financial problems, you should take stock of your situation, preferably with an outside adviser. Sometimes families, overwhelmed by the crisis, have become panicky and taken steps which they later regretted, such as selling their home, withdrawing other children from college, or using savings to speculate in the stock market with disastrous results. It's wise to seek the advice of some qualified person—a financial adviser in your bank or a responsible, experienced business man—before you take any major step. Such a person can help you analyze both your assets and your obligations and can sometimes suggest solutions that you would never have thought of.

Reducing the Costs of Your Child's Disability. It is tragic when people exhaust themselves financially if there was no need to do so. Chapter 5 dealt with the type of aid offered through governmental and voluntary agencies for diagnosis, treatment, equipment, and medication. Those who are experienced in handling these problems stress the importance of applying for financial help just as early as its need can be anticipated, because these agencies, as a rule, cannot replace what you have already spent but can only help with medical care given after you have applied to them. Investigate early so that you can plan the most economical use of your own resources.

Some families require supplemental financing over and above the help provided by free and partially paid services. There are several approaches. For one thing, you should investigate what benefits are due to you under the Social Security Act. The Aid to Dependent Children program provides for payments on behalf of "dependent" children, that is to say, children who are deprived of one or both parents. Also, the disabled children of retired or disabled workers, and of insured workers who have died, can apply for social security benefits when they have reached eighteen if they have been disabled before that age. Since you would have to submit proof that your child was disabled before he reached eighteen, you should discuss your circumstances with your local office and find out well ahead of time what records and signed reports will be required. This applies in cases of mental retardation as well as physical disability. Remember that the Social Security Act also has special provisions for the blind. You should discuss your specific circumstances with their local offices.

All persons who apply for social security disability benefits are referred to the state vocational rehabilitation agency for possible vocational rehabilitation services. If your handicapped child is of working age or near it, and if he has a reasonably favorable outlook for becoming employable, the state office may provide vocational counseling, medical and surgical care required for rehabilitation, braces, crutches, training for a job, tools, licensing, and job counseling. Obviously this kind of service is a great financial advantage if it helps the disabled child to become employable.

You should also investigate allowable income tax deductions for your child's disability. Provisions for deduction of medical expenses are well established, but you may want to make sure that you are taking advantage of everything allowed. In addition to the obvious costs for doctor bills, hospitalization, and nursing care, you are permitted to include nurses' board, crutches, eye glasses, hearing aids, dentures, wheelchairs, ambulance costs, premiums for health and accident insurance policies, etc. In general, the ruling permits you to deduct amounts paid for the prevention, cure, correction, or treatment of a mental or physical defect or illness. Medical expenditures for which you were reimbursed by an insurance company may not be deducted. Consult your district office of the Bureau of Internal Revenue in order to ascertain just what allowances you can claim. If your child is retarded and is being cared for in a state institution, find out whether you can make a deduction for him as a dependent and whether you can claim payments to the state for his maintenance as medical expenses.

If You Must Borrow Money. If financial obligations pile up so that you must borrow, you will want to weigh the advantages and disadvantages of many sources: credit unions, small bank loans, borrowing on insurance policies, getting salary advances, or borrowing from a small loan company. Sometimes a member of your family is able to lend you the necessary amount on a businesslike basis.

You can expect a reliable lender to ask some questions, both for his protection and yours. He will want to know about your financial standing, your obligations, job, credit record, and plans for repayment of the loan. You, too, will have questions. How much cash will you actually receive? Is the total interest deducted in advance from the amount of the loan or is it figured each month on the unpaid balance? How much will each payment be, and how much time will be allowed for repayment? Are there extra fees? Are you signing a chattel mortgage loan on your furniture and, if so, what will happen should you default on a payment?

As a general rule, a well-managed credit union is the best loan source. Their rates are usually lower than others, and your union or the organization for which you work may have established one. Many commercial banks operate personal loan departments, specializing in small loans to wage earners. Interest rates are usually moderate because the bank makes loans only to those who are considered good risks. There are two types of loans: secured loans, backed by savings accounts, insurance policies, or other collateral; unsecured loans, made to borrowers whose character and ability to repay satisfy the bank. Co-makers are not generally required.

Before you borrow on your insurance policies, compare the advantages and costs with other plans. It is relatively easy to obtain such a loan, but if it is not paid back regularly, the cost may be very high in the long run. Furthermore, rates on policy loans are usually higher than on bank loans.

There also are many licensed small loan companies that perform a useful service and shouldn't be confused with loan sharks who charge illegal interest. Their rates may be comparatively high, but you pay only for the credit actually used.

Asking for a salary advance may be feasible for a temporary emergency, but if your emergency is likely to be of long duration, one or two advances won't solve your problem and may only involve you more deeply.

Protection Through Health Insurance. Health insurance (to cover hospitalization and perhaps also doctors' bills) is now one of the widely accepted methods of reducing the costs of medical care. Naturally, you would like a policy that will help you meet the medical expenses of your handicapped child, but some policies do not cover pre-existing conditions. Few of them cover rehabilitation services. Even if the policy you are considering does not cover pre-existing conditions, it may still give you the protection you want when other members of your family need hospitalization and medical care. Policies vary widely—in the diseases covered, the duration, the treatments, the dollar amounts. You will want to seek out the one that will best meet your problems. Be sure you understand all the limitations of the policies you are looking into. Get impartial advice if you can.

Blue Cross plans may differ substantially from one part of the country to another. Some cover pre-existing conditions, some do not. Hospital admissions primarily for the purpose of physical therapy or hydrotherapy are not usually covered. However, the costs of physical therapy may be covered when a person has entered a hospital primarily for surgery or medical treatment of a disability if that treatment *includes* physical therapy in the hospital.

A relatively recent development is "major medical" insurance, intended to give protection when illness or accident requires the expenditure of very large sums. Generally speaking, these policies give very broad coverage, whether expenses are incurred at home or in the hospital, and include private nursing charges and costs of drugs and appliances as well as hospital and doctor charges. However these policies have deductible features and the policy holder must continue to pay at least 20 per cent of the bills. They can be written on an individual or a group basis and usually cover the entire family.

Group insurance may be available to you through your job or professional associations. It costs less than individual policies and most likely provides coverage for the entire family with benefits for care of pre-existing conditions. Group policies are not tailored to individual needs, and if you are considering one, you should look for blanket coverage with few or no exceptions. (Of course, this is true as well for individual policies.) A policy that provides substantial benefits in time of real need will be more helpful than one that costs less but provides only small benefits. In view of the high cost of hospital room and board, you are making a better buy in paying a somewhat higher premium for a policy that allows $10 a day for room and board than in paying a smaller premium for $5 coverage.

Long-term Planning. If your child's disability is one that will keep him dependent, with little or no earning capacity for his lifetime, long-term provisions for the future become particularly important. Your own wishes and the welfare of the handicapped child and the rest of the family will be better protected if your will is made before the death of either spouse. Such questions as the appointment of a guardian, the inheritance of property by a minor, or the appointment of a trustee with discretionary privileges to use funds left by the parent may be vital for your child's welfare. Legal requirements for wills, trusts, and guardianships vary from state to state and must be handled by an attorney. The Legal Aid Society may be able to advise families who cannot afford to hire a lawyer.

REFERENCES

1. Wm. H. Stewart, Maryland Y. Pennell, and Lucille M. Smith. *Homemaker Services in the United States.* U.S. Dept. of Health, Education, and Welfare, Public Health Service Publication No. 644. Washington, U.S. Government Printing Office, 1958.

2. *The Cerebral Palsy Monitor Program.* United Cerebral Palsy Associations, 321 West 44th St., New York 36.

3. *Ibid.*

24

SELF-HELP AIDS

Hundreds of ingenious devices have been created to assist disabled persons in the management of almost every type of limitation. Remember, though, that the devices don't take the place of medical treatment. Their value lies in helping the child overcome limitations that medical care has not yet removed or cannot remove—they are not a substitute for therapy, which may correct or reduce the disability. The simpler the devices your child needs, the easier his life will be.

SELF-HELP CLOTHING

Clothing should be easy to put on and off, easy to wear, easy to care for, easy on the budget, and easy to look at. The last point may not have much to do with self-help, but attractive clothing is especially valuable for the handicapped person. The self-confidence that comes with looking his best will be good medicine for him and will spur him on to try for new accomplishments. Good-looking fashions to meet the special problems of disabled persons are being designed by a nonprofit organization, the Clothing Research and Development Foundation, 48 East 66th Street, New York N. Y. 10021. Their models, all labeled "Functional Fashions," were made by eight leading clothing manufacturers in 1964 and were sold in over 300 stores in 43 states.

Some of the following suggestions may help you select convenient garments for your child from ordinary sources. If you know how to sew, you may apply some of them in making his clothes.

Easy to Put On and Off.   The garment's openings should be convenient. Look for:

Easy-to-reach openings. Center-front, full-length openings are often best and are common in dresses, shirts, coats, coveralls, and snowsuits.

Over-the-head openings large enough to slip on and off easily. A front or shoulder placket is often helpful.

Expandable, rib-knit necklines in some types of clothing, such as underwear, pajamas, polo shirts, and other play or sports clothes.

If your child wears braces or is severely limited in his movements, extra openings, or extra-large openings, may be helpful. Suit trousers and slacks for men and women can be designed with full-length side-seam zippers in addition to the regulation fly front in men's trousers. Two kinds of zippers are used. A No. 5 heavy duty Gripper Zipper with two-way sliders that opens either top or bottom provides ample room for pulling on over shoes and braces. For the person who dresses in bed, a full-length separating zipper is used so that the trouser leg can be opened flat, wrapped around the leg, and then zipped up. For the girl who needs an extra large skirt opening, a placket-length zipper can be installed on each side seam. Wide facings under the zipper prevent snagging underclothes.

Fasteners should be easy to use. Zippers are fine for the child with hand or arm disabilities; the small tab can be enlarged for easier grasp by adding a ring, tassel, or decorative medallion. A dress that catches your daughter's eye need not necessarily be rejected because it opens in back— she can use a "Zipper-Upper." This device, sold in many department and notions stores, is a long chain that can be attached to the zipper tab to pull the zipper open or shut. A stick with a cup-hook screwed into one end may serve the same purpose.

Flat, smooth buttons at least the size of a nickel, and rather loose buttonholes, help solve the button problem. Buttons are easier to grasp if sewn on with a long thread shank.

The large metal hooks and bars used in men's trousers are easy to manipulate and are often useful at the waistbands of skirts, slacks, play clothes, and as fasteners on separate belts.

Large grippers, about the size of a dime, may be easier for the child with limited use of his fingers to manage than the usual small snaps. The two parts should not fit together too tightly.

Velcro, a new type of fastener, is a boon to many persons with limited use of the hands. A Velcro closure consists of two strips of nylon tape which need only to be pressed together or pulled apart. A button or hook at one end of the opening can be fastened first to make sure that the ends of the closure come out even. Stores are selling some garments with Velcro closures, and it can be bought by the yard as well.

Easy-to-Wear Styles. The choice of style may be important to comfort. For example, a short sports jacket is probably more comfortable for wheelchair wear than the conventional suit coat, or a short car coat may be more comfortable than a long top coat. Two-piece dresses are convenient for girls.

Extra fullness in the back or through the chest allows for the vigorous movement of the child who uses crutches, insuring comfort and longer wear. Full skirts are more convenient than tight skirts. A dress that opens all the way down the front is easy to put on, and a blouse-slip eliminates the problem of the blouse that hikes up out of the skirtband.

Sleeves should be wide in the armholes so that the garment goes on smoothly, but very large raglan or kimono sleeves may get in the way of a child on crutches. However, he needs room in his sleeves for well-developed arm muscles. Sleeves of coats and jackets go on more easily if the lining is made of smooth, slippery material. A cape can be a good-looking substitute if your child has difficulty putting his arms into coat sleeves.

If your child wears pants with a zipper opening down each side, an inner belt holds the garment in place at the waist when either the front or the back is dropped. The inner belt may be detachable, held in place by buttons on the inside of the pants waistband. It need be only a half-belt, reaching across the back if the child drops the back of the pants, or across the front if the front of the garment is dropped.

If your daughter is old enough to wear bras and girdles, it may be difficult to find styles that are easy to put on. A girdle that opens flat and fastens by zipper or hooks may be easier for her to get into than one that requires step-in motions. If she needs a bra that opens in front, you can cut a regular bra apart in the center front and add Velcro strips onto each side for the closure.

If your child doesn't have to wear an orthopedic shoe, find a style that is easy for him to get into. Loafers are suitable for many occasions. If an oxford is worn, elastic laces do away with the problem of tying a bow. Some shoes are made with elastic insets, and in some shoes a shoemaker can install a zipper. Shoes are now being made with Velcro closures. (Write to Gilbert Freeman, Creative Products, 151 Lincoln Street, Boston, Mass., for sources of shoes with Velcro closures.) The "Shu-Lok" shoe is convenient for some persons and is widely distributed in chain shoe stores. It has a slide fastener covered by a stiff leather tongue that snaps into place to lock the fastener.

Easy-to-Care-for Fabrics. If your child's clothing becomes quickly rumpled because his disability requires strenuous exertion in using an artificial limb or crutches, or because of erratic body movements, you will be particularly grateful for the new fabrics that are guaranteed washable, require little or no ironing, resist wrinkling, and are color fast. Garments made of these materials launder easily, making it possible for your child to change his clothing frequently and always look fresh. Simply styled clothes that open full length and are free of frills are easier to iron. As your child grows old enough to take responsibility for his clothes, he should know about easy-care features.

Easy on the Budget. If your child's disability causes more than average wear and tear on his clothing, reinforcements at the points of greatest wear may effect real economies. For a young child, you can buy many garments with padded knees or ornamental patches, or you can add such patches. For older children or teenagers, the reinforcements should be less conspicuous. Knees of trousers or slacks can be lined with strong nylon to protect the fabric from the constant rubbing of knee-locks on braces.

If you make your child's clothes, you can protect the garment against underarm wear from crutches by using a double thickness of fabric at the sides below the armholes. If the top layer of fabric wears through, turn it under and the garment is still usable. Underarm shields also protect the fabric from stains and deterioration caused by perspiration. Boys, as well as girls, may wear large underarm shields that snap into the armholes of a coat or jacket if perspiration is a problem. The shields are washable and can be changed frequently. Their color can match that of the coat lining.

Strong seams and sturdy construction are particularly helpful if your child's disability puts added strain on his clothing. A flat-fell seam is stronger when it has double stitching, and a plain seam should have a zig-zag finish so that it doesn't fray. Close, compact weaves are usually more durable than fabrics with loose or uneven weaves.

HANDY AIDS IN DRESSING

Problems in putting on socks and stockings can be solved in several ways. A supporter fastening can be sewn to each end of a long piece of tape. The fasteners are then attached to the hem of the stocking and, by pulling on the tape, the child can draw the stocking up his leg. He may need to use a long stick to hold the stocking open while he inserts his foot.

A smooth, slender stick with a cup-hook screwed into one end is a handy tool. If two loops of tape are sewn to the hem of a sock, one on each side, two of these sticks can be used to catch in the loops and draw the sock up. A smooth wire frame of a special shape, mounted on a long handle, is sold by some supply houses. The wire frame holds a rolled stocking in position and unrolls the stocking on the leg as it is pulled up.

If drop toe or flail foot makes it hard for your child to insert his foot into his shoe properly, a tape or ribbon sewn to the toe of his stocking can be held firmly to keep his toes from curling under.

A long-handled shoehorn is useful for the child who cannot stoop easily. It helps to hold the shoe open and steady while he slips his foot into it.

If your child dresses himself while he sits or lies in bed but cannot reach his feet, one good procedure is to lay out the shorts and pants at the foot of the bed. If there are loops at the waistband, he can then use cup-hook sticks to pull the garment up over his legs. When it has been worked up over his knees, he then elevates his hips to pull the pants over his buttocks.

Buttons are more easily managed with an old-fashioned button-hook. Hospital supply houses also sell especially adapted button-hooks for the disabled. Instead of the conventional hook, these devices use a loop of wire, pinched close together at its end to hold the button firmly. Handles come in different shapes to accommodate the person with a weak grasp, the one-handed person, or the one who uses a prosthetic hook.

Putting on gloves or mittens may be a problem beyond the usual age if your child has limited use of his hands. You can sew a loop to the cuff of the glove to hang over a coat button or over a convenient hook. With this aid, the child may be able to slide his hand into the glove by himself.

THE WELL-GROOMED LOOK

Good grooming is especially important for a disabled child, even though it may take extra effort. If he is at an age when he hates to wash behind the ears anyway, he may even find his handicap a splendid excuse for skipping soap and water or comb and brush. Your strategy is to match his strategy with large doses of encouragement, firmness, patience, and ingenuity. The effort is worthwhile if he learns to take pride in looking his best and managing for himself as much as he can.

Keeping Clean.   It is easier for the child sitting in a wheelchair to use the bathroom washbowl if it is hung from the wall, with no legs or pedestal to prevent the chair from approaching close to the bowl. A faucet with one-control mixing valve saves effort in regulating water temperature, and a long, lever-type faucet handle that turns readily may be easier to use than the conventional types.

Towels and washcloth should hang within easy reach. There should be a shelf or cupboard where he can conveniently place the articles he uses in the bathroom. A low mirror is a great help to the wheelchair user.

If your child has a weak grasp, a piece of sponge cut in the shape of a star may be easier for him to hold than a washcloth. Another convenience is a bath mitt made of turkish toweling with a pocket for the soap. Or the soap can hang around the child's neck in a bag of loosely woven material such as dishcloths are made of.

To get at the hard-to-reach parts of his body, he may use a

long-handled bath-brush or a washcloth or sponge attached to the end of a long, jointed handle. Supply houses offer several kinds. The "Magic Soaper Scrubber," a device that can be bought in many department stores, has a long plastic handle with a sponge-rubber head that slips off the handle and is hollowed out to hold the soap.

If your child has trouble holding his towel while he dries himself, a loop sewn to the towel can fit over his wrist so that he doesn't drop it. Or you might try cutting a hole in the middle of a large bath towel so that it drops over his head, covering the back and front of his body. He may then be able to pat and wriggle himself dry against the towel, even though he can't hold a large towel to dry himself in the usual way.

For the child's safety and ease in getting in and out of the bathtub, grab-bars should be installed on walls at the end or side of the tub or both. More than one bar is helpful for some people. A low bar helps in getting down to or up from the bottom of the tub, while a higher bar helps in stepping in or out of the tub. You can also buy an adjustable bar with a rubber suction cup on each end that fits into the tub crosswise at any convenient location. Adjustable, removable grab-bars that fit over the outside rim of the tub can also be purchased.

A rubber bath mat with suction cups should be placed in the bottom of the tub, and for additional safety one may also be used on the bathroom floor.

If your child can't lower himself to the bottom of the tub, he may use a tub seat. A wooden kitchen chair, its legs shortened to a comfortable height and fitted with rubber suction cups, can be placed in the tub. A few holes drilled through the seat permit the water to drain away. A variety of stools and benches for use in the tub are sold both in department stores and hospital supply houses. The one you select should give your child the support he needs and should stay firmly in place without tipping.

If your child has lost sensation in parts of his body, he should learn to use a bath thermometer to make sure that the temperature of the water is neither too hot nor too cold.

Using a Toothbrush. A long handle helps when your child cannot reach to brush his teeth. One that allows the toothbrush to be adjusted to different angles is sold by some supply houses, but you can make one rather easily. The toothbrush handle should be cut short and screwed or bolted firmly to a slender stick of the required length.

If your child can bring his hand to his mouth but has a weak grasp, the utensil holder described on page 291 may solve his problem. Or it may be enough to push the toothbrush handle through a small sponge for easier grasp.

Nail Care.   Most drugstores, department stores, and five and ten cent stores sell a nailbrush with curved handles that fit over the hand. If your child can't use such a brush, one with rubber suction cups can be placed on the washbowl, bathtub, or wall. It will stand firmly in place while he rubs his nails against it.

A hand disability may seem to make it impossible for your child to trim his nails himself, but there are several ingenious solutions. Running the nails regularly over a piece of fine sandpaper helps to keep them short. If the child's grasp is weak, he may still be able to use a nail clipper if its handles are extended by two pieces of wooden doweling (round sticks). A one-handed child with normal use of his legs can place an ordinary nail clipper flat on the corner of a chair and exert pressure on it with his foot while he places a finger so that the clipper can close over the nail.

You may be able to get a nail clipper for disabled persons from a hospital supply house. A battery-operated electric manicure kit is sold by Breck's of Boston. It is said to trim, shape, taper, clean and file both finger and toe nails. It is equipped with a silicone carbon speed disk, buffer, brush, and emery papers. The unit is about the size of a small flashlight.

Using Brush and Comb.   A long piece of aluminum tubing can be bent or curved to hold a rat-tailed comb, and a piece of rubber tubing can be slipped over its end for better hand grip. This device may help your child if he cannot reach up to use comb and brush. One handle that is sold by a supply house holds either a rat-tailed comb or a special brush. The brush has bristles all around a central stem and can be used by either right or left hand and can be adjusted to any angle.

Shaving.   When your son is old enough to shave, he may need a special device to hold his razor. The handle of a standard safety razor can be inserted into a piece of hollowed wooden doweling just long enough for his reach. If his problem is a weak grip, the utensil holder described on page 291 may be used. A device to hold an electric razor can be made from two strips of lightweight aluminum about an inch wide. One piece is bent to make a cuff that fits around the palm of the hand, and the other is shaped to conform to the electric razor. The two pieces are then riveted together. The Schick Company makes a special holder for its electric razor that can be attached to an artificial arm when the hook of the prosthesis is removed.

Make-up. For the girl with the use of only one hand, a lipstick with a flip top is convenient. A powder puff can be held in a snap clothespin mounted on a long handle if your daughter can't bring her hand to her face. A ready-made adjustable device is sold by some supply houses, but a pair of tongs may give the needed length. When reach is a problem, the lipstick may be mounted on a long handle.

A lightweight, adjustable around-the-neck mirror is convenient for both boys and girls for their personal grooming in overcoming hand limitations. Such a mirror can be bought in many department stores.

Blowing the Nose. This commonplace function may be awkward for the child with a hand disability. Possibly he can use a pair of ordinary kitchen tongs to hold the handkerchief or tissue up to his nose. Cover the ends of the tongs with foam rubber. They will hold the tissue more securely and will feel more comfortable.

UTILITY STICKS

Some of the many uses for long handles and utility sticks have been mentioned in connection with dressing and grooming, but these sticks have many other uses. With them, the child in a wheelchair can pick things up from the floor or reach objects that are too high. You can make some of them yourself, such as the stick with a cup hook or closet hook screwed into one end. Large kitchen tongs are often useful. Supply houses sell a number of styles. One is somewhat like the sticks used in grocery stores to reach packages on a high shelf. Another has a collapsible extension handle, which can be fixed at the desired length. An all-purpose utility stick sold by one supply house has a number of interchangeable fittings such as a shoehorn, cup hook, closet hook, sponge for bathing, and also a magnet for picking up objects made of iron and steel.

AIDS TO EATING AND DRINKING

Your child needs to share in family sociability at mealtimes and to feel at ease when eating with other people. Eating the entire meal regularly with the family may be impractical while he is still learning to feed himself and needs freedom from distraction, but even then he might eat ahead of time and sit with the family during their meal.

Before your child can feed himself he may need extensive therapy. A child with cerebral palsy must develop mouth control in biting, chewing, swallowing, or removing food from the spoon with his lips. The improvement through therapy helps him more in the long run than the use of special equipment, yet the special equipment has its place. It may take some of the struggle out of eating and help to make mealtime more pleasant for everyone while the treatment program is still going on.

Chair, Table, and Tray. A child needs a chair in which he can sit comfortably and securely while he eats. His feet should rest firmly on the floor or on a footrest. The back should give adequate support and should be higher than usual if his head needs support. Wide arms give added security but should not interfere with elbow action. Some children are more comfortable if they wear a body harness tied to the back of the chair to prevent falling forward. A young child who uses a high chair may need such a restraint. For some children, it is helpful to attach a block of wood to the center of the front edge of the high chair seat so that the child's legs straddle it.

As a rule, a table should be about elbow height. If your child's disability is severe, a table with a semicircle cut out may provide support at each side. The table should have a rim so that objects do not roll off easily. Cut-out tables are sold by some supply houses, but if you handle tools skillfully you can make one.

A tray with depressions of the right size to hold plate, cup, and bowl helps keep the dishes securely in place. If your child has uncertain control of his hands, however, he may not be able to replace the cup or glass in its holder. Some department stores sell a combined tray and dish unit which clips onto a high chair tray or a table. Or a rubber placemat on the table may serve to keep heavy dishes from sliding around.

Spoons, Knives, and Forks. Eating utensils with built-up plastic handles are now sold by a number of hospital supply houses. These handles, which are helpful to the child who has a weak grasp, may be grooved so that fingers don't slip.

You can build up a handle yourself by pushing it through a piece of sponge rubber, which can then be covered by a washable plastic fabric or oiled silk. Plaster of Paris can also be used, or a wooden file handle with a slit into which the handle of a spoon or fork can be inserted after it is cut short.

If your child can't easily pick up spoon or fork from the table, try bending the handle so that it is bowed a little more.

You can make a handy utensil holder by stitching together along their lengths two one-inch strips of leather as long as the palm is wide. Let one strip extend half an inch beyond both ends and sew on a wide elastic band to fit across the back of the hand. The handle of the eating utensil can be inserted into the pocket so that it is held with little effort. Your child can easily carry this device with him when he is going to eat away from home.

Long-handled utensils, such as an iced-tea spoon, are useful to a child who has a problem bringing his hand to his mouth. You can buy spoons and forks attached to a long, jointed handle adjustable to various angles, or you can get extra length by joining the handles of a fork and a spoon end to end.

If your child is spastic, it may be helpful for him to use a flexible rubber spoon so that he can bite down on it without bruising his lips.

Another special device is the rocker knife for one-handed cutting. It can be purchased from various hospital supply houses. Still another is the combination fork and spoon, or "spork."

Easy-to-Manage Dishes. If your child drops his dishes frequently, nonbreakable plastic dishes may make mealtime more relaxed for everyone. Such dishes are not always the answer, however, for another child may need extra heavy dishes for stability. In some cases it helps the child to have his dish anchored to the table. Large suction cups for this purpose are sold by supply houses. For a young child, a baby bowl with suction cups on the base may be satisfactory. These can be bought in department stores.

A dish with straight sides does away with the exasperation of chasing food around until it slides off the edge. Many such dishes are made for young children, but if your child thinks they are too babyish for him, try a shallow straight-sided casserole. Another device is a plate guard, a metal rim which clips onto the edge of the plate. You can make one yourself from the rim of an aluminum foil pie-tin.

A child's deep dish with a hot water compartment is especially useful when the child takes so long at his meals that food grows cold.

Easy-to-Use Drinking Utensils. If your child has difficulty holding his cup or glass, experiment with shapes and sizes to determine what is easiest for him to manage. Two-handled cups are best for some children; others may need a special holder. You can buy one that consists of an aluminum band that fits around any standard glass and an aluminum handle that fits over the hand.

There are several ways to help the child avoid spilling as he drinks. A covered plastic refrigerator dish the size of a cup can be used if a hole is punched in the cover for inserting a straw. A twin-handled covered plastic cup with a spout through which the child sucks the liquid also avoids spilling. Another covered cup with a spout is so designed that the flow of liquid stops as soon as the user stops sucking. This cup can be used by the child who must lie flat on his back, and it is helpful to any child with serious lack of hand coordination. The liquid can't spill even when the cup is dropped.

Many children drink more easily through straws than directly from cup or glass. In fact, learning to drink through a straw is often part of the therapy of a cerebral-palsied child. A glass straw should not be used because of the danger of breakage, but a cellophane or plastic straw holds up better than a paper straw. Flexible plastic tubing for drinking is sold by the yard by some hospital supply houses. Hard plastic straws that can be bent to a desired angle under hot water are sold in most stores that carry housewares.

A plastic cup with a handle that is actually a permanent drinking straw can be bought in some drug stores, five and ten cent stores, and hospital supply houses. It is popular with children and makes it easy to drink without use of the hands.

Bibs and Aprons. A large bib protects clothing and saves laundry if a child spills a great deal of food, but the older child may think a bib is too babyish. A girl may not object to an attractive apron that fits over the head. Some aprons are now made with a spring clip at the waist, eliminating ties. A small clip may be used for a neckband to make an easily managed bib. An apron of the type is sold either made up or in a kit for you to make up yourself.

Through ingenuity, you'll discover other devices to help your child help himself. An exploration of the hardware and notion stores and the gadget counters may suggest new ideas. By encouraging your child to use his imagination, you help him to develop initiative that will be a useful asset all his life.

References are suggested below and on page 368, describing large numbers of additional self-help devices.

REFERENCES*

1. Eleanor M. Boettke. *Suggestions for Physically Handicapped Mothers on Clothing for Preschool Children.* Research Center, School of Home Economics, University of Connecticut, Storrs, Conn., 1958.
2. Aaron L. Danzig. *Handbook for One-Handers.* Federation of the Handicapped, 211 West 14th St., New York 11.
3. Morton Edwards and Jacob Landau, illustrator. *Around the Clock Aids for the Child with Muscular Dystrophy.* Muscular Dystrophy Association of America, Inc., 1790 Broadway, New York 19, 1957.
4. Edward W. Lowman. *Self-Help Devices for the Arthritic.* Rehabilitation Monograph No. VI. Institute of Physical Medicine and Rehabilitation, New York University-Bellevue Medical Center, 400 East 34th St., New York 16. $1.00.
5. *Cerebral Palsy Equipment Manual.* National Society for Crippled Children and Adults, 2023 West Ogden Ave., Chicago 12, 1950.
6. Howard A. Rusk and Eugene J. Taylor. *Living with a Disability.* New York, Blakiston Company, 1953.

* In preparing this chapter, extensive use has been made of the following sources, although it was not practical to identify the source of each device, since many ideas were found in all or several sources.

25

THE CHILD WITH BRACES

Some parents and children hate the thought of braces. But braces may make it possible for a child to go to school, to play ball, to travel around with his friends, help him to develop a better looking body and a better looking walk, deliver him from jerky, futile motions and help him learn coordination—not today or tomorrow, or next week, but eventually.

Perhaps the braces will help a child to support his body weight so that he can sit or stand erect, or walk with or without crutches. They may prevent deformities by holding a part of his body in such a position as to avoid crippling contractures. They are also used to correct deformities, as in the case of a child with cerebral palsy who has a shortened heel cord and walks on his toes. In still other cases, braces prevent or control abnormal movements, as in athetoid cerebral palsy. Used for several years, they may enable a child with this type of cerebral palsy to develop a normal walk. The doctor prescribes braces only if he believes they will help the child, so the prescription is good news.

Fitting Braces to Your Child's Needs. Fitting a brace requires skilled teamwork. The physician, usually an orthopedic surgeon or a physiatrist, prescribes the kind of brace and its uses. The brace is made by a brace maker, or orthotist. The physical therapist directs the child in activity that enables him to make effective use of the braces or of braces and crutches together.

The physician takes many factors into account. The child who has never walked may face a very different problem from that of the child who has already developed some walking patterns. A child with cerebral palsy may have strong muscles and need quite a different brace from the one who has had polio and has weak, flaccid muscles. The brace may be different if the disability is likely to improve, or remain the same, or grow worse.

The doctor will consider carefully your child's age and stage of development. If a congenital disability prevents standing or walking, the doctor may prescribe braces by the time the child is a year old in order to aid his development. Bones grow more normally when the child can stand and bear his weight, and the brace may prevent deformities. A child is usually able to "ambulate" (walk) with braces and crutches by the time he has reached a mental age of three or four years.[1]

Ideally the braces should fit well, work easily, and be light in weight and as neat and inconspicuous as possible but compromises have to be made. Their durability is important too, because they are expensive. One factor to be considered is the kind of metal used. The braces should be light but they must also be safe, durable, and strong. One of the lighter alloys, such as duralumin, may suit some children, but a heavy, active child may need braces of surgical steel. If the brace is exposed to unusual corrosive conditions such as damp salt air, stainless steel is advisable. Because the brace stirrup under the shoe is exposed to heavy wear and corrosion in any climate, it is often made of stainless steel.[2]

Care of Braces and Shoes. Regular maintenance will keep the braces in working order so that your child won't be suddenly housebound on the day of final exams or his school's biggest football game. Also, braces are expensive and regular care prolongs their usefulness. As your child grows older, he can take increasing responsibility for the condition of his braces, but in the beginning these duties probably fall to you.

Any major adjustments and repairs should be made by the doctor or the brace maker. Only the expert should shorten or lengthen the brace, alter calf or thigh bands, replace rivets, correct the alignment, bend the uprights, or install or replace shoe attachments.[3] On the other hand, you or your child can prolong the usefulness of the brace and help make sure that it serves the purpose for which it was prescribed by giving it regular care and by noting needed repairs before they become serious. The following suggestions may be helpful.[4,5]

1. Examine your child's body nightly for brace pressure marks. Chafing may come from exposed metal, wrinkled

linings, poorly fitted calf or thigh bands. Take the brace promptly to the brace maker for repair or adjustment. Foam or sponge rubber can be used *temporarily* to relieve pressure.

2. Make a daily inspection, covering these points:

   Frayed shoelaces. Replace at once. A broken, knotted lace may cause irritating pressure.

   Leather parts. Dried or torn leather straps and wrinkled or worn leather linings should be replaced by the brace maker promptly. Exposed metal can be covered temporarily by moleskin, an adhesive felt sold in drug stores.

   Screws. Tighten, or replace missing screws.

   Rivets. Loose or weakened rivets must be replaced at once by the brace maker.

   Joints and locks. Loose joints and locks that work improperly should be repaired at once by the brace maker to avoid falls and accidents.

   Brace alignment. A correctly aligned brace will stand by itself. If it becomes bent or twisted, let the brace maker correct it promptly to avoid harm to your child.

   Worn heels or soles of shoes. Have the brace maker correct these at once, since worn-down shoes may throw the brace out of alignment.

3. Handle braces carefully. If they are banged around they may be bent or twisted. When taken off, they should be propped carefully against the wall or laid on the floor or table in good alignment. A brace bag will protect them from dust and lint, which clog joints, especially if the braces are kept on the floor.

4. Open all locks once a week and remove dust or lint with a hairpin or fine wire.

5. Place a drop of household machine oil in each joint once a week. Wipe away excess with a soft cloth.

6. Keep leather parts as clean and soft as possible. Saddle soap occasionally rubbed in helps preserve leather. Dry-cleaning fluids should never be used with leather because they dry it out.

7. Shoes should be maintained exactly according to prescription, even if weekly repairs are required. Regular polishing and occasional use of saddle soap help to preserve them.

8. Keep on hand a brace kit containing screws of the right sizes for replacements, a screw driver that fits the screws, new shoelaces of the correct length and thickness, foam or sponge rubber, and moleskin.

9. Have an extra set of braces, if possible, to avoid "grounding" your child in emergencies.

Braces get hard wear and can easily become shabby. It's

almost impossible to prevent leather from acquiring perspiration stains, but plastic in attractive colors is sometimes used nowadays to cover brace bands and to make the straps of children's braces. (The plastic materials can be wiped with soap and water and dried at once, an advantage over leather.) It is a job for the brace maker to put this kind of lining or straps on a brace. It may be necessary for him to perforate the plastic with small holes to permit air circulation. Some mothers have attached coverings of lighter plastic material over leather linings, but they are likely to cause sweating, may wrinkle, and sometimes irritate a child's skin.[6]

Wiping metal uprights, calipers, or stirrups with a soft, waxed cloth helps keep the metal shiny. If rust appears, remove all traces of it with fine steel wool. Some children like to have their braces painted with attractive colors. Quick-drying enamel adapted for use on metals should be used.

When leather is clean, metal is polished, and shoes are in good condition, well shined, with fresh laces, the child can take pride in his neat appearance.

Getting the Most Benefit from Braces. Your child will of course get the most benefit from his braces if he uses them in the way recommended by the doctor, at just the times prescribed, adjusted as directed. For some children the doctor prescribes the use of braces for a limited time each day, enabling the child to build up brace tolerance gradually. For example, a child with athetoid cerebral palsy may have so much tension that wearing braces for more than a short time is too exhausting at first. For others, the doctor may prescribe the use of the braces during the day but not at night; still others need to wear them both day and night.

Checking with the Doctor. Your child's doctor will expect to see him at regular intervals to make sure that the braces are properly adjusted. If your child is growing, is able to ambulate, and is reasonably active, the doctor may even wish to see him every month, since the braces of an active child may get out of adjustment quickly. If your child is not active, the interval may be longer. Corrections should be made as soon as possible, since contractures may develop rapidly in a growing child. Check with the doctor if your child complains persistently that his braces are not comfortable.

Your child may begin to outgrow his braces before the next scheduled appointment with the doctor. If the leather knee pad comes below the knee cap instead of over it, or if the knee lock is below the knee, the brace is getting too short. The thigh strap may also become too low, and then the child slumps backwards when he sits, appearing to sit on his braces.[7] When you notice such signs, arrange a prompt appointment with the doctor.

Some Aspects of Personal Care. When a child uses braces, certain aspects of personal care become particularly important. The skin should be checked nightly for pressure marks or chafing. Chafed areas should be treated with lanolin, ordinary bland ointments, or hand lotion. But the really important measure is to have the brace adjusted to obtain relief from the pressure.

A daily bath with soap and water, followed by thorough drying, is part of good skin care. A gentle alcohol rub is refreshing, especially over the hips, lower back, buttocks, and heels. It should be followed by powdering. This kind of skin care increases the child's comfort and also helps to control body odor. Because ambulation with braces and crutches is hard work, the child may perspire freely and will probably need to give special attention to cleanliness of his body and his clothing. The use of deodorants in the armpits is essential for adolescents.

The child's stockings should be long enough to give his feet ample room but not so long that they will wrinkle easily. They should be put on smoothly.

If your child is overweight, he may have to wear a heavier brace than otherwise and it may get out of adjustment more quickly. Excess weight also makes it harder for him to get around with crutches and braces. The doctor may recommend a diet.

Feeling Comfortable about Braces. Quite possibly your child's posture and his manner of walking will improve through wearing his brace. This improvement may contribute to his poise, especially if the rest of the family helps him to look on his brace as a useful tool rather than as a symbol of disability.

Even though your child appreciates what his brace does for him, he may reach a stage of development, most likely in adolescence, when he is self-conscious about it because he's so eager to be just like the rest of his crowd. You can bolster his morale by making it easy for him to wear clothing styles like his sharpest friends, and by providing him with all the aids to good grooming. The style of shoes may be an issue, especially for girls, since many high school girls wear high heels that are out of the question for the girl who wears braces. Sometimes the brace can be attached to a good-looking shoe with a cuban heel. Perhaps the brace may be enameled in a color to match the stockings she usually wears. On suitable occasions she may enjoy wearing smartly tailored slacks that cover the braces.

But your child will find his greatest protection against self-consciousness if you help him develop into a person whose company other people enjoy. Then braces, crutches, wheelchairs, and other special aids fade into the background.

REFERENCES

1. George G. Deaver and Anthony L. Brittis. *Braces, Crutches, Wheelchairs.* Institute of Physical Medicine and Rehabilitation, New York University-Bellevue Medical Center, New York, 1953.

2. *Forward Steps in Brace Design.* The Pope Foundation, Kankakee, Illinois, 1953.

3. Erbert F. Cicenia, Hyman L. Dervitz, and Morton Hoberman. "Wearer Can Add to Life of Leg Brace." *Braces Today.* The Pope Foundation, Kankakee, Illinois, June 1958 and July 1958.

4. George G. Deaver and Anthony L. Brittis, *op. cit.*

5. Erbert F. Cicenia *et al., op. cit.*

6. Reinette Lovewell Donnelly. *Getting Acquainted with Your Brace.* The National Foundation, New York, 1955.

7. Jessie Stevenson West. *Congenital Malformations and Birth Injuries, A Handbook on Nursing.* Association for the Aid of Crippled Children, New York, 1954.

26

THE CHILD ON CRUTCHES

Many children with disabled legs miraculously do learn to walk, thanks to braces and crutches. This type of locomotion, usually referred to as ambulation, requires considerable strength and skill and is accomplished only through extensive training. Learning the techniques of crutch-walking is also tedious.

Not all children with leg disabilities can depend entirely on brace-and-crutch walking. Many paraplegics, for instance, seem to keep in better health, with less danger of pressure sores, ulcers, chronic fatigue, and excessive weight loss, by combining wheelchair use with brace-and-crutch walking.[1] There are still others who simply cannot ambulate at all but who nevertheless lead a vital, active life in a wheelchair.

Encouraging Your Child's Efforts. The mastery of ambulation will cost a child a lot of hard work and aching muscles, but success is certainly worth every bit of it. Young children easily lose interest in a distant goal. Since some of them require years of effort to achieve ambulation they should be encouraged to the hilt.

A skilled therapist learns to interest the child in his goal for today. "Well, Billy, you crawled ten feet yesterday; how far can you go today? Twelve feet, you think? Very good!" Or Sally, who stood 65 seconds yesterday, may decide that she will try to stand alone for a minute and a half today. Jack, who used his crutches to mount a three-inch practice curb last week, may try a higher curb this week. Encouraged by visible success, he is ready to try the next step.

If members of the family drop critical remarks, or show impatience over crutches that clutter the floor, the child for whom crutches previously represented freedom may become ashamed of them.

Muscular Abilities Required in Crutch-walking. The use of crutches depends on particular muscular abilities. The individual must be able to use his arms to move the crutches forward. His forearms must hold his elbows at the correct angle while his hands take the weight of his body. He must be able to use thumb and fingers to grasp the handbars firmly while wrist muscles keep his hands in the correct position. And he must be able to use his shoulder muscles to support his body on the crutches.[2] The doctor considers all these factors before deciding whether a child should undertake training.

Preparing to Use Crutches. Some children require extensive preparatory programs. A child born with cerebral palsy may need special training to roll over, move his legs reciprocally, crawl, creep, draw himself up to a standing position and maintain standing balance before he is ready to make any attempt to use crutches. A child who walked before he was disabled will probably need a different program and possibly a less extensive training.

For some children, the doctor may suggest simple exercises to be done at home, such as squeezing a rubber ball to strengthen the hand grasp, flexing and extending the arms, or raising the body out of the seat of a wheelchair by gripping the arms and pushing. Other children must attend a clinic or rehabilitation center where they can be guided in preparatory exercises. Parallel bars are widely used for this purpose. The child first learns to get up from a wheelchair to a standing position within the bars and then lowers himself into the chair again. Practice with parallel bars improves his balance. He also uses them to do push-ups that develop the strength needed to lift his body off the floor in crutch-walking. He first practices crutch gaits with parallel bars. Perhaps he may be taught a jackknifing exercise (bending at the hips) so that he'll know how to recover himself if his pelvis buckles involuntarily. After the jackknife exercise has been mastered on the parallel bars it can be taught on crutches. Deliberate jackknifing is used in going up and down curbs and steps.

After the parallel bars comes practice with crutches. The child may first practice crutch-balancing against the wall, doing such exercises as sideswaying, lifting one or both crutches, or pushing up on them. Then he balances away from the wall and learns to move his crutches forward, backwards, and sideways, and to recover from a jackknifed position on crutches. After these skills have been mastered, he begins to practice crutch gaits. When he can use his crutches comfortably on level ground, he is ready to learn to get up and down from his wheelchair, a straight chair, bed, and toilet seat. Last and most difficult, he learns to climb up and down steps and to travel by car or bus, getting in and out by himself.

The program of training prescribed for your child will depend, of course, on his condition. Some children can succeed in only limited aspects of ambulation; for example, they may use crutches on level ground but may not be able to go up and down stairs. The doctor will judge whether continued therapy is worthwhile at any point when your child seems to have reached the limits of his accomplishment.

Sometimes a child's exercises are carried on at home with the parent's help. If the home program is likely to be prolonged, it may be a good idea to install some equipment. An exercise mat, parallel bars, and practice steps are the most useful. Much of the equipment can be improvised quite simply, although models for home use can be purchased from supply houses selling rehabilitation equipment.

The Right Crutches for Your Child. When a child understands how much more freely he will be able to get around by using crutches, he will look forward eagerly to the day his measurements are taken. In prescribing, the doctor will consider all the factors that contribute to comfort and efficiency. Sometimes parents, not realizing that crutches must be very carefully measured, have used their own judgment in ordering from advertisements or catalogues. By all means a doctor should do the measuring, but if in an emergency you must do it yourself, you will have to know how.

The child's length is measured from under his arm to the side of his heel as he lies flat on his back. Two inches are added to allow for the slant of the crutches. You will have to consider how the child will use them; for example, a wide-hipped child will place them farther to the side and will therefore need somewhat longer crutches than a narrow-hipped child. If crutches are too long, the child's shoulders will be pushed up and he will lose power to push his body up from the floor. If they are short, he will lean forward too far. The child's weight and the extent of his disability—whether or not his back or arms are affected—are other factors to be taken into account. Obviously this is too complex a problem for parents to handle without professional help.

There are several types of crutches, each with its particular uses. The doctor will select the most suitable type and will advise you about whether to buy extension crutches or to get a new pair when longer ones are needed. There may also be a choice between metal crutches and those made of the customary hardwoods. Metal crutches are more expensive. With the standard underarm crutch, the rubber cover of the underarm shoulder piece is important to comfort. A moisture-proof pad is now available which does not develop the perspiration odors that make the ordinary pads unpleasant after a period of use. A rubber cover for the handbar also is helpful because it reduces the danger of blisters.

For safety, the tip of each crutch should be covered with a rubber suction tip at least one and a half inches in diameter at its base. These tips hold firmly to the ground at any angle. Thin, small, round tips should never be used. Providing the right tips, and renewing them when they are worn, is the most important part of crutch maintenance.

Posture and Crutch Gaits. As your child gets used to his crutches, he should learn to stand tall and straight, head up, shoulders down in a natural position, with his body as much as possible over his feet. Since he needs a fairly large base for stability, his crutches should be placed four to eight inches forward and to the side of his toes. His elbows are bent a little as he grasps the handbars, and the underarm pieces should just clear his armpits.[3, 4]

When a child's disability prevents ideal posture, the tripod position is usually recommended. Then he places his crutches farther forward and farther apart. The two crutches form two points of a tripod, the body the third point. The body is inclined forward at its upper part with the feet well behind. Many who are paralyzed below the waist can stand in this position provided they have no contraction deformities of ankle, knee, or hip.

There are about half a dozen standard crutch gaits. In determining the best ones for your child, his doctor will consider whether he can keep his body erect, get one foot in front of the other, bear his weight and keep his balance on one or both legs, and whether he can lift his body off the floor by pushing down on the crutch handbars.

Your child ought to know at least two gaits. One should be a fast gait, the other adapted for crowded places where he must keep his balance while moving slowly. It's an advantage to know more than two gaits, for change of gait varies the muscles in use and reduces fatigue. When your child has mastered the elements of crutch-walking, he will still need lots of practice to become agile on different kinds of surfaces, as grass, dirt, and uneven sidewalks.

Using Crutches in Daily Life. There are techniques for meeting the situations that most often arise. To pass through a door that opens toward him with the knob on the right, he should stand facing it at a slight angle and to the right side so that the door can open without hitting his feet or crutches. Balancing on both feet and the right crutch, he uses his left hand to open the door. He then places his left crutch tip against the door to hold it open, takes several steps through the doorway, pauses within reach of the door, and closes it behind him with his left hand.[5]

Until your child is sure of himself, when he wants to sit down on a straight chair the chair should stand against a wall. Standing at its left side, he balances on both feet and the left crutch and leans the right crutch against the far side of the chair. Holding the chair top with his right hand for balance, he then places the left crutch on top of the right one. Next he bends down and places his left hand toward the front of the chair seat along its far side. Taking his weight on his hands, he twists his body to the right and lowers himself to the seat. He is then sitting with his legs extended to the side of the chair and can adjust his legs and unlock braces to take a comfortable sitting position. To stand, he reverses the process.[6]

When he is skillful enough to use a chair that stands away from the wall, he begins by placing his right hand on a lower rung of the chair back, or on the chair seat, instead of on the top of the chair back to avoid tipping the chair over.

To get from bed to crutches, the child sits on the edge of his bed, legs over the side with feet touching the floor, and knee locks of braces locked. Crutches should be leaning against the bed within his reach to the left. Turning his body to the left, he places his left hand behind him on the bed and his right hand on the bed just at the outside of his left knee. Putting all his weight on his hands, he lifts his body from the bed and twists around so that he faces the bed as his weight comes down on his feet. He straightens, supporting himself on both feet and his left hand while he grasps one crutch with his right hand. Taking his weight on that crutch and both feet, he picks up the other crutch and is ready to go. To get onto the bed, he reverses the procedure.[7]

Not every child can climb stairs on crutches because of the tremendous strength and skillful coordination required. If he can, he may find it easier to go up backwards, since in going up forward he must use a higher push-up and may catch his toes on the stair risers. To go upstairs backwards, the child stands with heels touching the riser of the first step, grasping the railing with one hand and holding both crutches in the other hand. Ducking his head a little, he then pushes up as straight and high as possible, jackknifing to gain more height. When his feet clear the first step, he lowers his body so that his feet rest firmly on the step, then straightens, makes sure he is in good balance, and brings his crutches up to the same step.

To go downstairs forward, he stands well balanced with one hand on the railing, both crutches grasped under his other arm. He leans forward slightly over the first step, then pushes up on the railing and the crutch handbars so that his feet clear the floor, and lowers his body to the step below by bending his elbows. When he is in good balance, he brings his crutches to the same step and slides his right hand down the railing.[8]

Until your child has good control of his body and his crutches, and until the doctor considers him ready, he should not attempt stair climbing without having had expert instruction. Clinic practice usually begins with a very low step, perhaps only one inch high. As skill increases, the practice steps get higher. Most stair risers in homes are eight inches high, whereas bus steps are about twelve. If he must learn at home without expert instruction, he should begin with one or two low steps with a sturdy railing and not attempt more until he is proficient.

The technique for going up and down curbs is harder than for stairs, because there is no hand railing. If the child can move one leg at a time, he may use this method to go up a curb: Standing with his back to the curb, he unlocks the hip locks of his braces. He supports himself on the right leg and both crutches, bends forward a little and swings his left leg back and up so that his heel lands on the curb. Taking his weight on both crutches and the left leg, he then swings the right leg up and back onto the curb. Straightening his body and making sure of his balance, he moves his feet back from the edge of the curb, then moves his crutches nearer to the curb and lifts them one at a time up onto the curbing.[9] To go down, he reverses the procedure.

Whether your child finds it easier to get into the front or the back seat of a car depends partly on its construction. In a four-door sedan, the back seat may be easier to approach; on other models the front seat may be easier.

To begin, he stands close to the car but out of the way of the door he wishes to open. Supporting himself on both feet and holding to the car for balance, he opens the door wide and rolls down the window so that he can grasp the frame. Then he turns around with his back to the seat, holds onto the window frame for balance, and leans both crutches against the car. This is the time to open the hip locks. To enter the right front seat, he places his right hand on the back of the seat, holds the window frame of the open door with his left hand, and lowers his body to the seat. Then he places his crutches in the car, lifts his legs into position in the car, unlocks knee locks of the braces, and settles into the seat.[10] To get out, he reverses the procedure.

The ability to use a public bus—the school bus, for example —is an obvious advantage to any child. If he can move his legs alternately, he can enter the bus forward. Standing facing the door of the bus, he holds onto the door while he places both crutches on the step inside the bus. Hip locks should then be unlocked. Holding on with each hand to a pole inside the bus, he bends forward at the waist and swings his left leg up onto the step. He then pulls his body weight up and forward so that the right leg follows onto the step. With both feet on the step, he straightens up and grasps both crutches with one hand while he holds to a rail with the other. Hip locks should then be locked.

To get off, he stands on the bus step with his back to the bus. Holding to the bar inside the bus with his right hand, he places both crutches outside on the street to his left. Placing his left hand on top of the crutches and pushing, he pulls with his right hand at the same time so that he lifts his body clear of the step and lowers it to the ground.

If he can't move his legs separately, he gets into the bus backwards. With his back to the bus steps, he leans against them while with his right hand he grasps a bar inside the bus and places his crutches to the left of the door. Pushing on the tops of his crutches with his left hand and pulling with his right arm, he hoists his body to the bus step. Then he turns around, places both crutches under one arm, and holds onto a bar or railing with the other hand. In getting off, he reverses the process.[11]

Crutches at School. A crutch bag, which straps to the crutches at the handbars and fastens at its lower part to the crutch upright, provides an easy way to carry books or a school lunch. These bags can be made of sturdy material or bought from supply houses that sell rehabilitation aids.

You may wish to discuss several points with your child's teacher. Should your child go up and down stairs with his class, or should he go ahead of the other children—or after them—to avoid being pushed in a crowd? Arrangements must be made for taking care of his crutches in the classroom. They should always be within his reach but should not be placed so that they trip other children or get banged around. The type of clip holder used for brooms may solve the problem if the clip can be attached to your child's desk or to the wall within his reach.

Your child's teacher should know something about his use of braces and crutches if he will need her help at times. She can also be helpful by explaining to the other children that unusually well-developed shoulders and upper arms, as well as hand callouses, are caused by the hard work of crutch-walking and by suggesting courtesies that your child will appreciate, such as carrying a cafeteria tray or books for him. Her understanding and thoughtful cooperation can make your child's school adjustment much more satisfactory.

REFERENCES

1. Dana M. Street. *Paraplegic Bracing.* American Academy of Orthopedic Surgeons, Instructional Course Lectures, Vol. XIV, 1957. J. Y. Edwards, Pub., Ann Arbor, Michigan.

2. George D. Deaver and Anthony L. Brittis. *Braces, Crutches, Wheelchairs.* Rehabilitation Monograph Series, Institute of Physical Medicine and Rehabilitation, New York University-Bellevue Medical Center, New York, 1953.

3. Edith Buchwald. *Physical Rehabilitation for Daily Living.*
New York, McGraw-Hill, 1952.
4. Deaver and Brittis, *op. cit.*
5. Edith Buchwald, *op. cit.*
6. *Idem.*
7. *Idem.*
8. *Idem.*
9. *Idem.*
10. *Idem.*
11. *Idem.*

27

USING A WHEELCHAIR

Mike was a six-year-old whose only transportation was a go-cart, and he often had to sit there helplessly, waiting for his mother to find time to move him from one place to another. At the clinic, he envied the children he saw propelling themselves in wheelchairs. The wheelchairs seemed as magical as space ships to Mike. But his body and arms were so weak that no one thought he could use one. One day the therapist gave him a chance to try. That was the beginning. With practice, he learned to propel a wheelchair, slowly but with increasing sureness as weak muscles became stronger. The day his own wheelchair arrived was to Mike the most wonderful day of his life. It opened the road to freedom.

The wheelchair conquers distance for children. Some of them wear braces and can use crutches for limited ambulation; for others, the wheelchair is the only means of locomotion. If a wheelchair is to play an important role in your child's life, his doctor will take pains to prescribe one that is just right for him.

Types of Wheelchairs. The modern wheelchair has a light-weight, chromium-plated metal frame with leather or fabric seat and back. It has two large wheels and two smaller ones, with hand-rims on the large wheels. In adult-size chairs, the large wheels are usually 24 inches in diameter, although 20-inch wheels are available. The small wheels, or casters, are usually five inches in diameter, but there is an eight-inch size too. The small wheels swivel. Most standard wheelchairs are collapsible, folding to a width of about ten inches, and can readily be carried in cars.

Every wheelchair should be equipped with brakes, but the list price of some models does not include them. A device called a "squeezer" allows the user to reduce the width of the wheelchair by as much as five inches while he is sitting in it.

Although there are many variations in accessories, there are only a few main types of chair.[1] The type with the large wheels in the rear is probably most generally convenient, indoors and out, and can easily be tilted to go up curbs and steps. A chair with large wheels in front can make a complete pivot in a smaller space than one with large back wheels and so is convenient for indoor use when space is limited. A third type is intended for persons who have lost both legs. The rear wheels are set farther back to avoid tipping backwards as a result of the loss of the weight of the legs in front. Still a fourth type is designed for persons who can use only one arm. Two handrims are attached to the wheel on the side of the good arm. When the user grasps both rims with his hand, the chair goes in a straight line. By grasping only one rim, he can turn it to the right or left. There are also motorized wheelchairs, but these are very much more expensive.

In general, wheelchairs are made in adult, junior, and child or "tiny tot" sizes. The smallest ones are suitable for children of preschool age. One manufacturer makes a chair designed to "grow" with the child who uses it, from six to sixteen years, by adjusting or changing footrests and upholstery to the junior size when the child is about ten years old.

A wheelchair should be ordered according to prescription, because a child's doctor and his physical therapist together usually draw up specifications so that the chair will be just right for him.

Both the area in which your child will most frequently use his wheelchair and the nature of his disability must be considered. Though a chair with the large wheels in front may be more convenient indoors when space is limited, the doctor may recommend one with the large wheels in the rear if your child has weak trunk muscles, since the child must naturally lean back a little to propel it. If the large wheels were in front he might lean forward, with the risk of falling forward on his knees. If the child can't grasp a handrim easily, the prescription might call for a handrim with projection knobs. The paraplegic or quadriplegic finds it helpful to be able to slide out of the chair backwards onto bed or toilet seat. In that case, the chair back can have a zipper or an opening that fastens with small slide-buckles.

A wide number of adaptations can suit the child's special needs for good posture, comfort, and convenience. Removable armrests make it easier for him to use a table or desk or to transfer sideways from wheelchair to other furniture. There are desk arms so designed that they slide under a desk or table without having to be removed. Standard footrests are adjustable to the child's height. They can be raised out of the way but they can also be ordered to swivel, to be detached, or to be fitted with toe loops and heel straps to keep the foot in place.

A tray that fastens to the wheelchair arms is a necessity for some children. It can be made at home of plywood or ordered from a supply house. If your child spends much time in his wheelchair, he will need a foam rubber cushion or an air cushion both for comfort and to help avoid pressure sores. There are crutch holders, pockets, small trays that clamp to the armrest to hold a snack or a drink, and many other special gadgets.

Care of a Wheelchair. A little regular attention helps prolong the life of the wheelchair. Although you should follow the manufacturer's directions for maintenance, here are some general instructions:

Chrome parts should be wiped weekly with a damp cloth and then be coated with wax or chrome polish or wiped with a cloth lightly oiled with household machine oil. Leather should be sponged and waxed weekly. Occasional use of saddle soap is good for leather. Some washable upholstery materials are now used. Chrome and leather should be wiped dry whenever they become wet. Hubs and folding crossbars need cleaning weekly. Lint and dust should be removed, and if the parts are dirty they should be oiled lightly.

Air pressure should be checked weekly in pneumatic tires, and a hand pump should be used to reinflate them. A few drops of oil may be needed on the center bolt of the crossbars and in oil holes in the underframe, if there are any, at monthly intervals. A little vaseline will lubricate the axles. The telescoping parts (removable armrests, hinges, etc.) should not be oiled or greased. A light application of paraffin wax will correct sticking.

Chairs should be checked once a year by the dealer, at which time the wheel bearings can be repacked. Repairs, unless they are very minor, should be made by the dealer; do-it-yourself repairs may leave the chair insecure and cause accidents.

Wheelchair Convenience in Your Home. Arrange your furniture so that the child has a clear path from room to room, and make adjustments that will enable him to manage independently. He should be able to reach light switches from his chair, and electrical outlets will be accessible to him if they are placed one or two feet from the floor. Easy handling of a regulation-size wheelchair requires a doorway 36 inches wide. If your doorways are too narrow, you can obtain greater usable width by removing the doors. You may even want to widen certain doorways structurally. In general, it helps if you remove as many inside doors as you can, retaining only those needed for privacy or temperature control.

The child's bed should be the same height as the seat of his wheelchair for easy transfer from one to the other. It is best to remove small rugs and to secure even the larger ones to the floor to avoid entangling the small wheels of the chair in wrinkles. And you may consider installing a washbasin that hangs from the wall so that the wheelchair can be brought right up to it.

If there are steps leading to the outside entrances to your home, at least one entrance should be equipped with a ramp, constructed at an angle of eight to ten degrees for easy wheelchair ascent. The maximum approved angle is 18 degrees, but this may be too steep for your child.[2]

An elevator is an ideal solution to the problem of stairs, but because it is so expensive it is hardly worth while unless you anticipate the need for it over many years. If you do plan to install one, make sure that it conforms to your state and municipal building regulations. A less elaborate but still expensive device is an electrically operated seat, installed on the stairway.

Houses are rarely built for the convenience of the individual with a disability, but if you are fortunate enough to be able to build your own home, you can plan many accommodating features. A one-story house, built close to the ground on a level or nearly level piece of ground, does away with inside stairways and outside steps and saves hours of effort for the child with an orthopedic disability, whether he is on crutches, wearing braces, or in a wheelchair. (It also saves time and effort for those who might otherwise have to carry him up and down.) Gently sloping ramps or walks outside, and outside doors with minimum-size sills, save additional exertion. A compact house designed to eliminate hallways is more comfortable for a wheelchair user and saves distance for those who walk with difficulty, but if halls are necessary they should be at least 54 inches wide. Steps should not be more than seven or eight inches high and should be at least ten inches deep. Closet space is more accessible if closets are wide rather than deep, and if doors are in the center. Sliding closet doors are the most convenient. The garage should be accessible from inside the house. Information about plans for houses suited to handicapped persons is available from the Institute of Physical Medicine and Rehabilitation.

The Child's Use of the Chair. Your child will have more satisfaction from his wheelchair if he learns to manage it himself, and it will be to his advantage to have instruction by a physical therapist. To the extent that his age and his disability allow, he will need to learn to open and close it, propel it, use the brakes, raise and lower the footrests, and adjust any other accessories.

If your child's hand, arm, and trunk muscles are usable, he will probably learn quickly to propel the chair forward and backwards and to turn it. But if weak muscles make this hard for him, his doctor and therapist may teach him methods adapted to his condition. For example, if power is lacking in the triceps muscles of his arms, he will be unable to propel the chair by pushing on the handrims, but if he has power in the biceps muscles he may be able to propel it by pulling on the handrims. Practice usually increases the strength and skill of weak muscles.[3]

If the small wheels of the chair are in front, they should be turned straight forward when your child gets in or out so that the chair is less likely to tip. The wheel should *always* be braked when he is getting in or out.

TRANSFERRING TO AND FROM THE WHEELCHAIR

Many people find it convenient to move from the wheel-

chair to another seat by using a strong, smooth board as a
bridge and sliding along it. A bridge board is usually from
eight to twelve inches wide, and about ½-inch thick, tapered
to ⅛-inch thickness at each end. Length varies from two to
three feet. Sometimes the board is padded with foam rubber
and covered with a smooth plastic fabric, though it may be
sanded and varnished. These are easy enough to make, but
they can be bought from a rehabilitation supply house.[4]

From Bed to Wheelchair.   There are a number of ways to
move between bed and wheelchair. (Keep in mind that the
bed must be the same height as the chair.) In one method,
the wheelchair faces the side of the bed, as close to it as possible, with the footrests under the bed. The child sits up
straight on the bed with his back to the chair, legs extended
across the bed. He grasps one of the chair's armrests and,
with his other hand on the bed close to his hip, he pushes on
both hands to lift his body a little and slides back into the
chair. He then unlocks the brakes, moves the chair back
slowly until only his heels rest on the bed, and locks the
brakes again. He can then use his hands to lift his legs down
one at a time so that his feet are in position on the footrests.
Unlocking the brakes, he is ready to go. To get from wheelchair to bed, he reverses the procedure.[5]

Using a bridge board, he can slide from bed to wheelchair.
If the wheelchair armrests are detachable, he can slide into
the chair from the side. If armrests are not detachable, the
chair is brought close to the bed at a slight angle, the child
sits with his legs over the side of the bed, and he slides into
the wheelchair seat from the front.

A very common method is to place the wheelchair beside
the bed at a slight angle, facing forward. The child sits with
his legs over the edge of the bed, close to the chair. When the
chair is on his right, he places his right hand on the right
armrest and his left hand on the bed behind his left hip.
Pushing on both hands, he raises his body a little and lifts
himself across and down into the wheelchair seat.[6]

If armrests are removable, the wheelchair can be placed
with one side close to the bed and the child can slide sideways into the seat. If possible, one or both feet should rest on
the floor as he makes the transfer. To prevent tipping, he
should put no weight on the footrests while he transfers.

It is also possible to use a straight chair in making the
transfer. The chair is placed with one side against the bed,

facing the foot. The wheelchair, facing the bed, is placed close against the other side of the straight chair. The child sits with his legs over the edge of the bed, facing the foot of the bed. If the straight chair is to his right, he places his right hand on the seat of the chair toward its far edge and his left hand on the bed near his hip, then pushes himself up with both hands and slides over to the straight chair. He can then grasp the right armrest of the wheelchair with his right hand and, placing his left hand on the seat of the straight chair, push up with both hands and slide or lift himself into the seat of the wheelchair, turning his body to the right as he does so. He is then sitting squarely in the wheelchair.

From Wheelchair to Straight Chair. If wheelchair armrests are removable, the child can slide sideways from the wheelchair to the seat of the straight chair. If they are not removable, he may sit in his wheelchair facing the front of the straight chair. He raises the left footrest and then places both feet on the floor as far to the left as possible. He then rolls the wheelchair closer to the straight chair so that, if possible, the right footrest slides between the front legs of the straight chair. Wheelchair brakes are then locked. He places his right hand over the back edge of the straight chair seat and grasps the left wheelchair armrest with his left hand. Pushing down on both hands, he lifts his body, turning to the right and shifting himself to the seat of the straight chair. He is then sitting somewhat sideways in the chair and will have to unlock the wheelchair brakes and push it away a little before he can adjust his legs and braces and turn to sit squarely in the chair.

He may sometimes transfer to a straight chair and from it to another piece of furniture when the wheelchair cannot come close enough. If your bathroom is too small for the wheelchair, for example, he might transfer from it to a straight chair and, if necessary, to several straight chairs to reach the toilet seat.[7]

From Wheelchair to Toilet Seat. The best method depends on the child's physical abilities and the position in which the wheelchair can approach the seat. If the wheelchair can be moved close to the side of the seat, he may be able to place one hand on the far rim of the toilet seat while he grasps an arm of the wheelchair with the other hand and then lifts himself from wheelchair to seat. If wheelchair arms are removable and the wheelchair can come close beside the seat, he can slide sideways from chair to seat. Sometimes the most convenient method is for the wheelchair to have a back opening so that the child can slide backwards from wheelchair to toilet seat, then forward again to the wheelchair. Some children may prefer to slide forward from the wheelchair into a straddling position on the seat.

If the wheelchair cannot come close to the seat, the child may be able to transfer from it to a sturdy bench, then slide along the bench and transfer from it to the seat.[8]

In many cases, the toilet seat needs to be raised somewhat to be on the same level as the wheelchair. (See Chapter 29 for ways of doing this and for toilet seats that give special support.)

From Wheelchair to Bathtub or Shower. Here again, the method depends on the child's abilities and the available space. Unless he is very sure of his movements, he will probably need the help of an adult who can grasp him around the waist for support when he makes the transfer.

In one method, the child wheels his chair toward the side of the tub but stops while there is room to lift each leg over the edge of the tub without hitting his feet against it. The chair is braked while he does this. Unlocking the brakes, he then wheels as close as possible to the tub and locks the brakes again. Sliding forward in the wheelchair, he uses one hand to grasp the far rim of the tub or a grab bar, if one is attached to the wall. With the other hand, he grasps either an armrest of the wheelchair or the near rim of the tub. Pushing hard on both hands, he lowers himself into the tub slowly, with support from an adult who grasps him firmly around the waist.

It's helpful to use a stool or seat of some kind in the bathtub so that the child needs to lower himself only partway into the tub. (See page 287.) If a stool is used, it should have rubber suction tips on all legs. There should also be a rubber mat with suction cups in the bottom of the tub.

If the wheelchair has detachable armrests, he may find it easier to transfer to the tub from the side of the wheelchair. If the chair can't be brought close to the tub, he may be able to transfer from it to a straight chair or bench and then to the tub.

The child may be able to use a stall shower if a bench is placed against the shower wall. Possibly he can transfer directly from the wheelchair to this bench. Sometimes it is easier to use two benches, one outside the shower and one inside, with their ends adjoining. Then he transfers first to the outside bench and slides along it to the inside bench. Or he may prefer a kitchen chair inside the shower. In that case, rubber suction tips should be placed on each chair leg. There should also be a rubber mat with suction cups on the shower floor.[9]

From Wheelchair to Crutches. After a child has learned to walk fairly well on crutches, he may learn to get in and out of his wheelchair with crutches. Until he has developed some skill, the wheelchair should be placed with its back against the wall for security. Brakes should always be locked while he gets in and out of the chair.

To get into the wheelchair, he stands facing it. Balancing himself on both feet and one crutch, he uses the other crutch to raise the footrests, then moves closer to the chair. Taking his weight on his feet and the left crutch, he places the right crutch against the wall to the right of the chair and at once grasps the right armrest for balance, keeping as much weight as possible on his feet. Then he places the left crutch against the wall on the left and at once grasps the left armrest with his left hand. Supporting himself with both hands, he bends at the waist and buckles at the pelvis so that weight is distributed between hands and feet. First making sure that he is in good balance, he adjusts his feet forward or backwards, if necessary. Then leaning on both hands, he transfers all weight to his hands as he twists and turns his body and lowers himself into the seat by bending his elbows. He then adjusts his position so that he is sitting straight in the wheelchair, unlocks his braces, and adjusts his legs on the footrests. He can then place crutches in the crutch holders on his wheelchair, unlock the chair brakes, and start on his way.

To get out of the wheelchair, it is safer to back it against the wall. Brakes, of course, are locked. Leg braces are locked. Crutches are placed one on each side of the chair. After footrests are raised, the child places his right foot in front of and to the outside of the left foot, keeping both feet on the floor in this position. Reaching behind his body with his left hand, he grasps the right armrest. Placing his right hand across the front of his body, he grasps the left armrest. Then he shifts all his weight to his hands as he lifts his body from the seat, then transfers weight to his feet as he twists and turns so that he faces the wheelchair. Still grasping the arms of the chair, he buckles at the pelvis so that he can distribute weight between hands and feet and moves his feet nearer to the wheelchair if necessary. Then he straightens, tilts his pelvis forward for erect posture, and keeps his right hand on the right armrest for balance while he picks up the left crutch. With his weight on the left crutch and his feet, he picks up the right crutch. A few steps sideward or backwards put him in a position to walk away from his wheelchair.[10]

Lifting and Carrying the Helpless Child. Some children are so handicapped that they are quite unable to manage the transfers to and from their wheelchairs. Such a child must be lifted and carried about. This is apt to cause great fatigue in those who care for him. The child should be encouraged to give as much assistance as possible. If he is to be lifted from his bed, he may be able to move himself over to the edge, or he may be able to assist by putting his arm around the neck of the person carrying him. Sometimes a child will help the therapist quite readily but may have such ingrained habits of dependence on his parents that he fails to help himself unless they insist on it.

The fatigue of lifting and carrying can be lightened by observing certain general principles of body mechanics. These principles have been stated in detail in two booklets dealing with the cerebral-palsied child, *Lifting and Carrying in the Home* and *Lifting and Carrying Outside the Home,* published by the United Cerebral Palsy Association. The following pointers are elaborated in these booklets.[11, 12]

Planning ahead makes the job easier. There must be ample room for good footing, and furniture or other obstacles should be cleared away before you start. Face the child squarely so that you won't have to twist as you lift and keep your feet close to him, spaced apart about the width of your hips. In preparing to lift the child, lower your body to the child's level by bending your knees, but not beyond a right angle. (Leg muscles are stronger than back muscles, and less likely to be strained.) Keep your back straight, not arched. When you have slid your arms under him, make a preliminary heft to be sure you have a firm grasp. (If his weight is more than one-fourth of your weight, or if you must work from an awkward position, you should get someone to help you.) Lift the child by straightening your legs with a steady thrust, keeping your back straight as you resume an upright position. Hold him close to you as you carry, with his weight over your feet. If you must change direction at any time, step around and turn your entire body—don't twist.

Remember to make use of whatever supports there are—to rest yourself, to shift your grasp, and to take part of the child's weight.

When you lower the child, make sure you have enough room for good footing. Spread your legs to hip width and lower him slowly by bending your knees, keeping your back straight. Extend your arms straight downward, keeping him close to your body.

There are many detailed applications of these principles. Should you be faced with any special problems, ask advice from a physical therapist or public health nurse.

Find a way to handle the child when he must be transported outside the home so that your fatigue will be kept to a minimum. If you must do your marketing and other errands when there is no one with whom you can leave your handicapped child, perhaps you can take him the entire distance in a wheelchair. If you take him in your car, the wheelchair can be folded and placed either in the trunk or the back seat. In lifting even a lightweight wheelchair, use the basic principles of lifting that have just been described.

Instead of a wheelchair, a specially constructed chair, made to measurements, may serve the particular needs for relaxation and support of the cerebral-palsied child. Such a chair, often called a relaxation chair, is mounted by stout hooks to a low platform on casters so that it can be wheeled from room to room. The chair may be mounted on another platform with large, swiveling wheels, five to six inches in diameter, for outdoors. Relaxation chairs can be purchased from rehabilitation or hospital supply houses.

A large wagon works well for young children. You can buy or make a long wagon with built-up, detachable sides and with four wheels on the rear axle for additional stability. A severely handicapped cerebral-palsied child can enjoy riding in such a wagon if he is seated in his own special chair inside it. If the young child is able to ride in an automobile, it may be possible to place his special chair on the seat and attach it securely to the back. He may even be able to use a jump seat that hooks over the back of the car seat. It should provide firm back support and may need restraining bands to help him remain upright.

When you are helping with the child's physical therapy at

home, you will tire less quickly if you place him on a low, steady table, wide enough so that he is not afraid of falling. You can then sit beside the table at the same level as the child, and thus eliminate the need for bending and stooping. You can also sit on a stool with casters when you are helping the young child learn to balance and take his first walking steps. This places you on the child's level and still permits you to move with him.

A mechanical lift will enable members of the family to move the very large or quite helpless child without risk of his falling and without danger of strain to themselves. This consists of a sturdy, movable hoist which, by a block and tackle arrangement, permits the lifting of heavy weights with a relatively light pulling effort. From its frame a canvas seat is suspended. The seat is made of two detachable canvas slings, which form the bottom and the back of the seat. They are put into position by having the child lie on his side in bed and roll over onto the two partially unrolled strips, one centered beneath his back and the other beneath his hips. The slings are then hooked onto the chains of the lift. The hoist raises the child and lowers him into his wheelchair, and the canvas slings are then unhooked from the chains. The sling under the child's buttocks can be left in place.

REFERENCES

1. George D. Deaver and Anthony Brittis. *Braces, Crutches, Wheelchairs.* Rehabilitation Monograph Series. Institute of Physical Medicine and Rehabilitation, New York University–Bellevue Medical Center, New York, 1953.

2. Howard A. Rusk and Eugene J. Taylor. *Living with a Disability.* New York (Garden City), Blakiston Co., 1955.

3. Alice B. Morrissey. *Rehabilitation Nursing.* New York, G. P. Putnam's Sons, 1951.

4. Howard A. Rusk and Eugene J. Taylor, *op. cit.*

5. Edith Buchwald. *Physical Rehabilitation for Daily Living.* New York, McGraw-Hill Book Company, 1952.

6. *Idem.*

7. *Idem.*

8. *Idem.*

9. *Idem.*

10. *Idem.*

11. John M. Cooper and Laurence E. Morehouse. *Assisting the Cerebral Palsied Child: Lifting and Carrying.* Booklet I, *In the Home.* United Cerebral Palsy Associations, 321 West 44th St., New York 36.

12. John M. Cooper and Laurence E. Morehouse. *Assisting the Cerebral Palsied Child: Lifting and Carrying.* Booklet II, *Outside the Home.* United Cerebral Palsy Assoications, 321 West 44th St., New York 36.

28

USING AN ARTIFICIAL LIMB

Children learn to use their prostheses with remarkable skill. Even a very young child, early in his training, can take the paper off a lollipop with the hook of his arm prosthesis. In time he can feed and dress himself, write and carry on his school activities, do household tasks.

Many youngsters with artificial limbs can swim, play ball, rollerskate, enjoy archery, ride a bicycle, and even compete in these sports on an equal basis with others of their age. The youth who has lost a leg may learn to dance, and some persons with an arm prosthesis play the piano well. Of course not every child with a missing limb uses a prosthesis so successfully. Parents can do a great deal to help their child succeed.

Growing Up with the Prosthesis. Some parents feel that they should wait until the child is old enough to make his own decision about using a prosthesis. This point of view usually means that the parents themselves are reluctant, which is natural. But in general, the earlier the child is fitted with a prosthesis the better he will use it. It becomes part of him while he is growing up. Without a prosthesis, he forms habits that he must unlearn if he later uses one. He also runs the risk that disability and deformity will grow worse because of contractures, and the weakening of muscles from disuse.[1]

By using a prosthesis early, a child begins to enjoy at the proper time all the activities that normally nourish growth. If a baby is born without an arm, the use of a prosthesis with a plastic mitt from the age of five or six months stimulates his development. With two arms of equal length, he is better able to balance himself as he learns to sit up, crawl, and stand. When he normally begins to use his hands purposefully, the mitt helps him. One mother reported that at eight and a half months her son used his mitt to bat balls and to squeak his toy kitten. Just past one year he tried to pack sand and mud into the palm of the mitt, and at twenty-one months he used it as an aid in eating.[2]

In the period between two and four years, when a child's manual skill normally increases a great deal, he can probably learn to use a prosthesis with a voluntary-opening hook. Then he can grasp objects with his prosthesis, and as he grows older he can develop many manual skills that would not be possible with one hand. The principle of operation does not change greatly from then on. When the youngster reaches his teens, however, his emerging interest in social life and personal appearance may make a mechanical hand and cosmetic glove desirable.

Similarly, if a child is missing a leg, the early use of the prosthesis enables him to learn to crawl and creep, stand, walk and run, and join other children in their play. The first leg prosthesis for a young child may be simple, without a knee joint or foot. Children between fourteen and eighteen months usually can learn to stand and walk with a prosthesis.[3]

Getting the Prosthesis. There is more to getting a prosthesis than ordering it and paying the bill. First the doctor evaluates the child's needs and prepares a prescription for a prosthesis exactly suited to him. Possibly your family doctor will refer you to a clinic for children with similar problems. There are now a number of child amputee centers where the physician, limb-maker or prosthetist, physical and occupational therapists, and other specialists work together.

In writing the prescription, the specialists consider the child's age and stage of development along with other facts about his amputation. If a leg is missing, is the amputation above or below the knee? In the case of an arm, is it missing above or below the elbow? How long is the stump? Is it in healthy condition? Are there any contractures that make it hard for the child to use a prosthesis?

The experience of child amputee centers suggests that a child will probably accept and use his prosthesis successfully:

if the prosthesis fits comfortably and is practical for his stage of development;

if physical therapy is available when needed to improve

the condition of the stump, the nearby muscles, and the nearest joint;

if the child has training in learning to use it;

if follow-up services are available to keep the prosthesis adjusted to the child's physical growth and to keep it in good mechanical condition; *and*

if the family understands the prosthesis and encourages the child to use it.

Many clinics consider the last point so important that they take pains to instruct the parents, as well as the child, in the use of the prosthesis. If the parents or the child are uncomfortable about its use, a chance to talk it over with someone at the clinic may help them understand their reasons and change their attitude.

After the doctor has prescribed the prosthesis, it may take the limb-maker about six weeks to prepare it for the first fitting.[4] Sometimes this period is used for the physical therapy conditioning program. Training in the use of the prosthesis must, of course, follow.

It's important to try to find the rehabilitation or amputee center or clinic that includes the five types of services mentioned above. A bit of history provides an interesting illustration. Shortly after World War II, the Michigan Crippled Children Commission, pioneering in service to child amputees, made a survey of children in the state who were missing arms and found that *seven out of eight* were not wearing their prosthesis. A service program was then established, and at the end of ten years there was almost universal acceptance of the prosthesis among the young amputees and their families.[5, 6]

Possibly your state's program for handicapped children includes services to child amputees. If not, arrangements might be made through the state to send your child to the clinic of the Michigan Crippled Children Commission in Grand Rapids.

Becoming Acquainted with the Prosthesis. Although there are many variations in materials used and in mechanical details, the following descriptions give an idea of the major parts of typical arm and leg prostheses.

Arm Prostheses. If the child has lost his arm below the elbow, his prosthesis usually consists of a hook to replace the hand, a forearm socket which encases the stump, elbow hinges which allow the child's natural elbow to move freely, and a cuff or pad around the upper arm to stabilize it. A webbed harness attached to the cuff by a forked strap crosses the child's back and loops over and under the other shoulder and arm, making a figure 8 in shape. A fine cable connects this harness to the hook.

The child's shoulder and stump muscles operate the prosthesis. He sets his shoulder forward on the normal side and then moves his stump forward. This action widens his back and, through the harness, puts tension on the cable so that it opens the hook. To close it, the child relaxes his shoulder and brings his stump back so that tension is relieved and the hook closes.

If the arm is missing above the elbow, the prosthesis includes the hook and forearm, a mechanical elbow joint, and an upper arm socket, which encloses the stump. The figure 8 harness again provides tension for the cable operating the hook, but there is a second cable system to operate the mechanical elbow. It, too, is connected to the harness. A typical elbow can be locked in eleven positions, permitting the arm to be held straight or bent at varying angles.[7]

For a substitute hand (called "terminal device"), infants use the plastic mitt already mentioned or a hook that does not open and close. Children from about two years on use a voluntary-opening hook. Young people in their teens usually want a mechanical hand with a cosmetic glove for social activities, although they continue to use the hook for practical tasks.

Leg Prostheses. If the leg is missing below the knee, a typical prosthesis includes an artificial foot, a socket which encases the stump and replaces the missing shin, a hinged knee joint, and a cuff which fastens around the thigh. A forked strap is attached to the socket and to a belt around the waist or pelvis. In young children, it may be supplemented by a shoulder harness. A checkstrap from the cuff to the socket behind the knee helps to control knee action.

If the leg is missing above the knee, the prosthesis includes a mechanical knee and the thigh socket to enclose the stump in addition to the artificial foot and shin. Some above-the-knee prostheses are held in place by a pelvic belt, some by a shoulder harness. Still others use a suction socket and don't require a belt or harness.

If the amputation is above the hip joint, the prosthesis has a large pelvic socket conforming to the body contours and a mechanical hip joint which locks and unlocks.[8]

Some artificial feet are made entirely of rubber; others are made of wood or metal with felt and rubber parts. The limb-maker adjusts the angle of the foot to the shin when he makes the prosthesis, taking into account the height of the shoe heel the child will wear. All his shoe heels should be of the same height. Otherwise the prosthesis is thrown out of alignment. A broad, low heel gives most stability.

Cineplasty. A cineplastic arm amputation calls for a prosthesis that operates on a different principle and is usually performed only on adults or children over fourteen. By surgery, a tunnel is formed in the muscles of the upper arm or shoulder and a metal, plastic, or ivory peg is placed in the tunnel. The peg is used to transmit power from the muscles to the prosthesis by cables or cords. The figure 8 harness is not needed.

Time for Training. The length of the training period depends both on how quickly the child learns and on the type of prosthesis. Usually a child learns more quickly if he has a long stump and, in general, children learn to use artificial legs more easily than artificial hands and arms. A below-elbow or below-knee prosthesis is more easily mastered than an above-elbow or above-knee limb. It usually takes about sixteen days at the Michigan center to train an infant or toddler to use a below-elbow prosthesis with a mitt. When the mitt is replaced with a voluntary-opening hook, the training usually takes fifteen to twenty-one days.[9]

Checking with the Doctor. A child is likely to need at least four or five regularly scheduled return visits to his doctor or clinic each year. Visits are also necessary whenever adjustments for growth must be made, even between scheduled appointments. Changes in the length of an artificial leg may be required every three months. Sockets also must be made larger to allow for the increasing size of the stump muscles, and the figure 8 harness may become too tight because of the child's growth. Mechanical failures may also require a return to the clinic.[10, 11]

A number of adjustments can be made to allow for growth, but eventually the prosthesis must be replaced. A child wearing a below-elbow prosthesis may require two or three completely new arms between the ages of four and twelve. The youth who uses a hand and cosmetic glove for all occasions may need a new glove every three to five months but will need fewer gloves if he depends mainly on a hook.[12] A child needs a new foot when it becomes too small for the shoe size of his natural foot.[13] The doctor supervises all such replacements.

When a child complains of pain, or if his stump becomes irritated, he should see his doctor promptly so that the cause of irritation can be corrected. Occasionally a growing child suffers swelling and pain in the stump because the growth of the bone outruns the growth of the soft tissues. This is called overgrowth and unless it is treated the bone will eventually protrude. The overgrown bone is shortened by surgery. Overgrowth rarely occurs when the child was born without the limb.[14]

ENCOURAGING YOUR CHILD TO USE HIS PROSTHESIS

Your interest in helping your child learn to use his prosthesis shows him that you value it as a tool and that you are not embarrassed by his amputation. But you also help in practical ways.

Practice Makes Perfect.   Even after training at the clinic, your child needs supervised practice until the advantages to him outweigh his self-consciousness, so that he would rather wear the prosthesis than go without it. The supervision will be up to you. You'll need patience and ingenuity to supervise without nagging, so that your child himself feels that the practice is worthwhile. One way is to encourage him to use his prosthesis in doing something he likes to do; riding a tricycle is more fun than just walking around the room. And it will be more fun for a little girl to hang up the clothes, using her arm prosthesis, if her mother is there to work with her companionably.

Your child needs to do things for himself if he is to gain skill. Yet this rule doesn't need to be carried so far that the child is deprived of a helping hand when he gets into a tight spot.

Watching Your Child's Gait.   Most children with a missing leg are so eager to do away with crutches that they need little urging to try to use their artificial leg. If it fits well, and if the child has had the necessary training, he can usually learn to walk with a nearly normal rhythmic gait. However, some children develop poor walking habits because they favor one leg or develop an unnatural body sway. If you notice such faults in your child's gait, consult his doctor right away. He may have grown so that the normal leg is longer than the prosthesis, or a defect in the socket may be irritating the stump. The difficulty should be corrected promptly so that a faulty habit doesn't become fixed.

Using Two Hands. If your child has become accustomed to using only one hand, you may need to look for opportunities to encourage two-handed activities using the prosthesis. Many toys and play activities require two hands: riding a bicycle, jumping rope, playing with tinker toys, model planes, etc. And it is just as easy to offer your child his coat, or a toy, or a piece of candy, so that he will take it with his prosthesis instead of his natural hand. Give him things to do that he enjoys.

Time Out. There are times, of course, when a child doesn't have to wear his prosthesis. At first he may be able to wear it for only part of the day while he becomes used to it. He doesn't wear it at night, and he may want to remove it for his nap. It may need to be removed in strenuous games in which it might endanger his playmates, and he doesn't wear it when he is swimming or bathing. If he says that it hurts, he shouldn't wear it until it has been checked by the doctor, especially if the stump is irritated.

Care of the Stump. The stump should be examined each night and if there are bruises, red marks, or chafing, the doctor should be consulted. It's important to keep the stump clean. The child with a missing limb perspires a great deal, partly because the stump is encased in a socket. The stump should be washed at least twice a day with warm water and a rich lather of good quality soap. Possibly the doctor will recommend a soap that contains a disinfectant. After washing, the stump should be carefully dried.

With some types of prosthesis, the child wears a stump sock. Whether or not he wears a sock with an arm prosthesis, he should wear an undershirt with sleeves, such as a T-shirt, as protection against chafing by the harness. He should have a clean stump sock and undershirt each day, and oftener in hot weather or when he is very active.

The figure 8 harness should be kept clean. It is usually

made of a quick-drying synthetic material which readily dries overnight, but it is convenient to have at least two harnesses. Gentle scrubbing with a handbrush is good.

If your child uses a stump sock, the doctor or clinic will advise you about what kind, how many he needs, and where to buy them. They come in various shapes, sizes, and materials, including cotton, wool, and the synthetics. Wash them in luke-warm water and mild soap and rinse them without wringing, twisting, or stretching. Dry them away from heat. In this way they keep their shape and softness longer.[15]

A warning is in order against sunburned shoulders. Sunburn is aggravated by pressure or rubbing, and this means that the child won't be able to wear his arm prosthesis for as long as it is painful.

Care of the Prosthesis. If your child's prosthesis fits comfortably and he uses it well, he'll be playing actively with other children. Naturally, vigorous activity takes a toll in breakage: cables will fray faster, hooks or hands get bent, feet and ankles break down. Wear and tear really shows that the prosthesis is helping the child lead a normally active life. In fact, lack of wear is a sign that it is failing its purpose.

Although you should accept the inevitability of wear and tear, you can help your child realize that he has a responsibility for taking reasonable care of such a valuable tool and for using it as it was intended. The prosthesis will stand up under the ordinary demands of work and play, but its life will be short if he uses it as a hammer, a spading fork, or a crow bar.

The following general instructions will help you care for the prosthesis.

1. Run your fingers along the cable daily. If spots feel rough or frayed, it is time to have it replaced.
2. Keep the joints of the prosthesis clean, removing dirt, lint, and dust regularly with cotton and a toothpick or a small, soft brush.
3. Cleanse the socket daily if necessary. Use mild soap and water, rinse with a cloth wet in warm water, and dry thoroughly. If there is a valve in the socket, unscrew and remove it at night to allow air to circulate through the socket.
4. Clean the leather parts with saddle soap weekly. If leather becomes stained and smells unpleasant, the limbmaker will have to replace it in time.

5. If your child uses powder when he puts on his prosthesis, he should take care not to let it accumulate in the valve. It may be removed with a soft brush from both the valve and the valve-threading in the socket. If the valve leaks or doesn't seat properly, the limb-maker should repair it.

6. The ball-bearing joint on the terminal device should be oiled lightly with household machine oil every two or three weeks, unless you are given directions to the contrary. Some new synthetic materials should not be oiled.

7. Both shoes should be kept in good repair. If heels or soles are worn or run over, your child's gait and posture may become faulty.

8. If shoe and artificial foot get wet, the shoe should be removed until both are dry. Any sand and dirt should be removed while the shoe is off, and the foot should be cleaned. Sand or dirt in the ankle joint should be removed by the prosthetist.

9. Amateur repairs may be costly. Don't try to remove screws or take the prosthesis apart unless you know what you are doing.[16, 17]

Going to School. There is no reason why the child who wears a prosthesis shouldn't go to a regular school. If he has been fitted with it a year or so before entering kindergarten he should be able to take care of himself by then.

It may make school entrance easier if you can explain to his teacher what he can do with his prosthesis. She may want to explain it to the other children, and she may arrange for your child to show them how it works. With curiosity satisfied, young children usually accept the amputee child quite readily. This doesn't mean that they may not tease him— "Captain Hook" is a natural—but if he has confidence in himself he can ride it out.

Return to school may be harder for the older child who has just lost a limb and must now adjust to his prosthesis and to a somewhat different way of doing things. If social life has just become important, a thoughtless rebuff or teasing may seem disastrous to him. But again, if the child's family has confidence in him and in his future, he will probably learn to surmount his concern over being different.

REFERENCES

1. Carleton Dean. *Upper Extremity Prosthetic Devices for Children.* Michigan Crippled Children Commission, Lansing, Michigan, 1957.

2. *Idem.*

3. Charles H. Frantz. "The Child with an Amputation," in *The Child with a Handicap,* ed. Edgar E. Martmer. Springfield, Illinois, Charles C. Thomas, 1959.

4. *Idem.*

5. Carleton Dean, *op. cit.*

6. Charles H. Frantz, *op. cit.*

7. *Idem.*

8. Donald Kerr and Signe Brunnstrom. *Training of the Lower Extremity Amputee.* Springfield, Ill., Charles C. Thomas, 1956.

9. Carleton Dean, *op. cit.*

10. John Steensma. *A Guide for Parents of Child Amputees.* Michigan Crippled Children's Commission, Lansing, Michigan, 1956.

11. Charles H. Frantz, *op. cit.*

12. Carleton Dean, *op. cit.*

13. John Steensma, *op. cit.*

14. Charles H. Frantz, *op. cit.*

15. Donald Kerr and Signe Brunnstrom, *op. cit.*

16. *The Child with a Missing Arm or Leg.* Children's Bureau Folder No. 49. U.S. Dept. of Health, Education, and Welfare. Washington, U.S. Government Printing Office, 1959.

17. Charles A. Hennessy. *Maintenance and Care of the Prosthesis.* Prosthetic Education Dept., University of California, Los Angeles.

29

MANAGING BOWELS AND BLADDER IN SPINAL CORD DAMAGE

The most serious complication of spinal cord injury is lack of bowel and bladder control, medically called "incontinence." Learning how to keep clean and dry so that incontinence is no longer a barrier to social life, school, and job is a vital part of rehabilitation.

Dr. Guttmann's work in rehabilitation of paraplegics at the Stoke Mandeville Hospital in England during World War II (see Introduction) led to the rehabilitation of children with spinal cord damage. They too, it was found, responded well to a complete program of care. One girl of sixteen had been helpless for eight years after an automobile accident injured her spinal cord. She had made no attempt to use a bedpan or the toilet, was wet all the time, and required daily enemas. She could not ambulate. After eight months of treatment she was nearly always dry, had regular bowel movements without enemas, and could walk on braces and crutches.[1]

Another girl, fourteen years old, was born with spina bifida. She had never stood and could get around only by crawling. She was always wet. After eleven months of rehabilitation she could walk on braces and crutches, she kept dry with few accidents, and was independent in all toilet functions. Best of all, with incontinence under control, she was able to go to school and to use the school bus.[2]

Many children with spinal cord damage have been treated at the Institute of Physical Medicine and Rehabilitation in New York with similar results. The greatest obstacle has been that many of the children have gone so long without adequate medical care and rehabilitation because their parents didn't realize that they might be helped.[3]

Planning for rehabilitation should begin early—at birth

in cases of spina bifida and as soon as medical treatment permits in cases of illness or accident. Then greater physical recovery is possible, and the child can take a more positive attitude toward himself instead of vegetating in hopelessness.

We are mainly concerned here with the control of toilet functions, but this is only one aspect of total rehabilitation. The child with spinal cord damage may need several kinds of specialized medical care. Urological study is essential to understand the condition of his urinary tract. Surgery may be necessary. Physical therapy, with instruction in ambulation, may be required. To use braces and crutches, the child needs a healthy skin, free from pressure sores or ulcers. If he can ambulate, he can take himself to the bathroom and keep clean and dry, and this accomplishment in turn helps to avoid skin ulcers and urinary infection. Moreover, it frees the child from social embarrassment and eliminates the principal obstacle to school attendance. These measures are all closely related and all have direct bearing on the child's rehabilitation.

The child with spinal cord damage will need medical supervision throughout his life and he will need repeated urological examinations at intervals of about six months. Keeping these appointments faithfully may save his life because, even though he learns to keep clean and dry, this is not a guarantee against disease of the urinary tract. His condition must be watched so that changes in the treatment can be made as called for. The doctor may want to see the child between appointments if he has cloudy urine, fever, or any setback in toilet control.

Substitutes for Normal Bladder and Bowel Control. A healthy baby eventually develops the ability to control urination and bowel movements. In the process, he learns to recognize the physical sensations that are signals to him, and he learns to hold back until he goes to the toilet. Parents naturally expect their child to develop these abilities. In fact, this expectation is so strong that the parents of a paraplegic child sometimes catch themselves feeling that he could control his bladder and bowels if only he wanted to, even when they know that his injury makes this impossible.

When a child's spinal cord has been damaged, he may lose both the sensations that serve as signals and also the ability to control the muscles involved. The loss may be partial or complete, depending on the extent and location of the injury. Substitute methods help the child keep clean and dry, but they do not restore the lost sensations or muscular control. It will be easier to discuss these methods after a brief description of the urinary system and the intestinal tract.

The urinary tract consists of two kidneys, one on each side of the abdomen, each connected to the bladder by a narrow tube called a ureter. The urethra is different. This is a third tube which leads from the bladder to the outside. The kidneys' vital work is to filter waste substances and excess water from the blood, forming urine. The urine passes from the kidneys through the ureters to the bladder, where it accumulates. At the mouth of the bladder there is a muscular valve, or "sphincter," which normally is subject to voluntary control. When it opens, the urine flows from the bladder into the urethra and out of the body. The bladder is emptied by the contraction of its own muscles assisted by deliberate contraction of the abdominal muscles.

The rectum is the lower end of the large bowel. When the waste materials from digestion accumulate in the rectum, their pressure on the inner sphincter of the anus signals the brain that there is need for evacuation and, if the individual responds, a bowel movement follows. The anus has two valves, an internal sphincter and an external sphincter, about an inch apart. The external sphincter is partially under voluntary control, but the internal sphincter is not.

There are two types of control of the bladder and bowels. The nerves for voluntary control (deliberate, conscious control) run all the way up and down the spinal cord. The sense of fullness is carried up to the brain. The impulse to relax the sphincter (valve) and squeeze the abdomen travels down from the brain. If there is damage to the cord, this control may be lacking or partially lacking. However, there is also what's called a reflex control, which we can see in a young baby: when the bladder or bowel becomes sufficiently full, the muscles in it contract and the muscles in the sphincter (valve) relax. The brain receives no message and sends out none. This reflex control will not meet the requirements of the older child, of course.

TRAINING AND CARE

A special type of bladder training (to be described below) helps some children with spinal cord damage to develop what is called an "automatic bladder" so that instead of emptying very frequently, or at any time, it empties itself only when it is full, or at certain regular times. The child with an automatic bladder usually can remain dry by going to the toilet at those times and by regulating fluid intake.

Not every child can develop an automatic bladder. In some cases the bladder is spastic. It tightens up and expels urine frequently in small amounts as the result of any mild stimulation or the presence of a small amount of urine. In other cases the bladder muscles are weak and are unable to overcome the resistance of the sphincter sufficiently to expel the urine. The bladder then stretches and fills to more than its normal capacity, causing urine to back up into the ureters and kidneys. In still other cases, the sphincter is weak, permitting a constant leakage of urine that is increased by any bodily movements or by laughing.[4]

When the doctor has studied your child's urinary condition, he can plan a program to suit his particular needs. If it seems unlikely that he can develop an automatic bladder, he may still improve his condition by a regular routine of drinking and voiding. He will also need to use special clothing or equipment to stay dry externally in spite of leakage.

Using a Catheter. Some children must use a catheter, a small rubber tube that is inserted into the urethra to drain the urine. The doctor prescribes the type and size to be used. Sometimes a catheter is worn continuously for a while at the beginning of bladder training. It may be needed for years, perhaps permanently. In some cases, it is used only occasionally when other methods fail to empty the bladder completely. If a catheter is needed but for some reason can't be inserted into the urethra, an operation to make a small extra opening into the bladder may be recommended so that the catheter can drain the bladder completely.

If your child is to use a catheter after coming home from the hospital, the doctor will give you instructions. If you don't fully understand them be sure to ask questions until you do.

Your child's health is more important than any worry about bothering the doctor. Be sure that you understand his instructions on these points:

When should the catheter be clamped shut and when should it be open? It may be open all the time for constant drainage or it can be clamped shut, to be opened at regular intervals. In the latter case, it *must* be opened on schedule. Failure to open the clamp, or a clogged catheter, may cause urine to back up into the ureters or kidneys, which may result in infection with high fever. You should report to the doctor any leakage around the closed catheter—it may mean that intervals between opening it should be shorter.

An automatic bladder is brought about—in some cases, not all—by a period of training of weeks or months in which the child follows a regular schedule of opening and closing the catheter. At least this training may improve the bladder's functioning and reduce wetting.

If the catheter is worn by a bedfast child, its outer end is attached to a large container in which the urine is collected. If he is getting around in a wheelchair or on crutches, he wears a rubber reservoir bag strapped to his leg. The bag must be emptied before it is full.

When should the catheter be changed? The doctor will change the catheter periodically; you will be responsible for taking your child to the doctor at the time he has set. A month is the usual interval between visits, but it may be longer or shorter.[5] Unless your doctor gives very explicit instructions, you should not remove the catheter.

What should be done if the catheter gets clogged? The doctor will give you instructions about irrigating or washing out the catheter and will probably advise you to call him promptly if it cannot be cleared readily.

How often should bladder irrigation be done and what methods should be used? The doctor will tell you how often to do an irrigation. It may be necessary twice a day to keep the catheter free of mucus, to maintain normal bladder capacity, and to insure proper drainage of urine.

A bulb syringe is commonly used for irrigation. The syringe and the container for the solution should be sterilized by boiling them completely submerged in water for five minutes. After they have cooled, the syringe should be touched only on the bulb and the container for the solution only on the outside.

To prepare a salt solution for the irrigation, add two teaspoons of table salt to three glasses of water and boil for five minutes. After the solution has cooled, it can be poured into the sterile container. Fill the syringe and inject the amount specified by the doctor into the end of the open catheter, then allow the fluid to run out into a separate container. Repeat as many times as the doctor has instructed you to. You may be told, for example, to fill the syringe with one ounce of solution and repeat ten times.[6]

Some doctors prescribe the use of a special antiseptic or medicinal solution. The bladder is filled with the solution and then the catheter is clamped shut to allow the solution to exert its effect. Your doctor may prefer some other method of irrigation for your child. The important thing is to make certain that you understand his instructions for each step.

Keeping a Record.   At the beginning of bladder training, the doctor may ask you to keep a record of the child's voiding and drinking habits for a while. He may want to know when the child goes to the toilet, about how much he voids, times when diapers or absorbent pads are changed, and whether they are soaked, moderately wet, or just damp. He may ask whether the child has any bodily reactions that signal the need to void. Some paraplegic persons sweat profusely, or have shivers, chills, flushes, or goose pimples, even though they do not feel the usual sensations.

An equally important part of the record shows the fluids the child takes—what he drinks, how much, and at what times. The record will indicate whether he has formed a pattern of voiding automatically at certain times, whether voiding usually follows drinking within a certain time period, and other facts that help the doctor plan the bladder training program.

Daily Intake of Fluids.   Bladder control depends a great deal upon the amount and regularity of fluid intake. Milk, water, soups, fruit juices, soft drinks, hot drinks, Jello, custards, and ice cream all count as fluids. Carbonated drinks overstimulate the bladder and are not recommended.

Logically you might think that the fluids should be cut down in order to decrease urination, and some paraplegic persons try to keep dry by drinking as little as possible. Actually, everyone needs a generous amount of fluids. From two and a half to three quarts daily for older children and adults, and at least a quart and a half for younger children, are advisable. Lots of fluids keep the urine pale and dilute and prevent formation of the strong, dark urine that may hasten urinary infection, kidney stones, and skin irritation.

Emptying the Bladder. If your child lacks the sensations that normally signal a need to void, be on the lookout for any of the other body reactions mentioned earlier. By going to the toilet promptly on such a signal, he may be able to keep dry. Not every paraplegic experiences them; apparently many young children do not.[7]

A child needs a comfortable, relaxed position when he tries to empty his bladder. The most satisfactory method, of course, is to use the regular toilet. An added advantage is that the activity of getting to the bathroom sometimes helps to initiate voiding.

If your child must use a bedpan, voiding is probably easier in a sitting position than lying down. As he sits in bed, there should be pillows behind his back for support, and his knees should be bent and supported by pillows too. It's still better if he can sit with his legs dangling over the side of the bed. For additional support, let him lean on the back of a straight chair placed close to the bed. The physical therapist will have taught him how to get on and off the bedpan without spilling. The child should manage this himself if he can.

The child who can't get to the bathroom may be able to use a commode placed near the bed, or even a bedpan on a straight chair.

To overcome difficulty in starting the flow of urine, it may help to drink a few swallows of water, to bend forward while sitting, and even to massage the abdomen lightly. Sometimes stroking or tickling certain trigger points is helpful—the navel, hips, outer or inner surfaces of the thighs, or the area around the sacrum or coccyx.[8] By emptying his bladder as completely as possible every time he voids, he is more likely to remain dry between trips to the bathroom.

A child should not feel hurried, but don't let him become discouraged by remaining too long on the toilet without success. Twenty minutes should be enough.

Timing of Drinking and Voiding. At the start of the bladder training program, the doctor will suggest a trial schedule of drinking and voiding. If the child is usually wet at certain times, he should go to the toilet a little ahead of those times. Voiding usually follows drinking within fifteen or twenty minutes, although the interval may be longer. If your child has a certain natural interval, the doctor will consider it in making the schedule.

A common schedule of drinking calls for two glasses of fluid with each meal, two glasses between meals, and one glass after the evening meal. The schedule for voiding may call for going to the bathroom before breakfast, after each meal, after each drink between meals, before going to bed, and once or twice during the night.

Your child may try several changes in schedule before the doctor finds the most satisfactory one. Perhaps he may need to cut down more on fluids after the evening meal, or to go to the bathroom more frequently in the morning than during the rest of the day. If he voids involuntarily whenever he takes active exercise, he may need to go to the bathroom first.

Once a schedule of drinking and voiding has been established, your child should follow it regularly, with but few exceptions. Naturally, there may be times when an exception is wise. If your child is going to a ball game or any place where bathroom facilities are not accessible, he may need to omit liquids for three or four hours beforehand and to make an effort to void completely before starting out.

Bowel Management. Establishing a regular time for the bowel movement is the soundest basis for its control, but regularity in meals and fluid intake, with a well-balanced diet and daily exercise, all contribute to it. If your child has bodily reactions that signal the readiness of the bowel to empty, he can time his trips to the bathroom accordingly. If possible, he should go to the bathroom and use the toilet seat. If not, he can use the positions for voiding already described.

Doing push-ups, or just bending forward while sitting, sometimes encourages the bowels to move. Stroking the abdomen lightly from right to left may help, or touching or circling the external sphincter with a finger covered with a finger cot. Prune juice taken regularly is preferred to cathartics. The doctor may suggest taking half an ounce of mineral oil with the prune juice until a regular bowel habit is formed.

Glycerin suppositories are often helpful. The suppository must be inserted well above the internal sphincter, about the length of an adult's forefinger. Sometimes two or three are necessary. When a child is old enough, he may insert it himself. After it is in place, there is a waiting period varying from about twenty minutes to an hour before the bowels are ready to move. Then the child goes to the toilet, although he may have to sit there for another few minutes. When his usual waiting period is better known, the suppository can be inserted long enough ahead so that he can have the bowel movement at a convenient time.

Enemas are not recommended as regular practice, although they may be needed in emergencies. If used frequently, they tend to reduce the ability of the sphincter to contract spontaneously. They are usually ineffective anyway, because most paraplegic children can't retain the water or give it to themselves. Furthermore, regular enemas decrease the child's independence in self-care.

In some cases, the doctor finds it necessary to recommend removal of feces with a finger covered with a finger cot or rubber glove coated with vaseline.

In working out the bowel schedule, the doctor takes into account any former habits of the child and whether his bowels now empty involuntarily at certain times. He also considers the question of convenience if your child expects to go to school or work. There may be more time at night, but the child may feel more secure against risk of involuntary bowel movements if he goes to the toilet before leaving home in the morning.

PROTECTIVE DEVICES AND CLOTHING

The child who has developed automatic bladder and bowel control may not need special protection, but he may feel more relaxed and secure if he has it. Protection is necessary, of course, for the child who cannot establish effective control.

Protection for Boys. Preschool youngsters past infancy wear absorbent pads and waterproof underpants. They are more acceptable than diapers, which make the child feel like a baby. Older boys also may need to wear pads and waterproof underpants in early stages of bladder training or until wearing a urinal is advised.

The waterproof underpants should have a front opening so that they can be worn under braces and so that absorbent pads can be changed without removing the braces. One convenient pattern has a front panel with fastenings across the top and down each side so that the entire panel can be dropped. Elastic bands at the waistline and thighs give a snug fit. To avoid catching the skin, snap fasteners are used instead of zippers. Plastic or waterproofed nylon materials are preferred to rubber because they allow air to circulate. Underpants of this type are available from supply houses, but a mother who sews can make them.

Rubber urinals in child's sizes are available from supply houses, and some boys as young as six or seven years have learned to wear them; but a boy of that age needs help in its use and care. Here are some points of personal care:[9]

The genital area should be checked for a rash every morning and night. The urinal should not be worn when a rash is present.

There should be a daily check for skin irritations caused by the urinal's waist or thigh straps. Apply powder to the skin and place padding under the strap where irritation appears or threatens.

If there are breaks in the skin, the genitals should be bathed with soap and water, dried and powdered three times daily; the urinal should not be worn.

The urinal should not be worn at night.

After taking the urinal off for the night, the body parts should be bathed with soap and water and dried carefully.

A small child may need to be reminded that the urinal should always be adjusted in private.

Care of the urinal is important for your child's cleanliness and also to prolong the usefulness of this fairly expensive equipment. These points are important:

Powder should be applied to the urinal before it is put on. The urinal and the retaining bag should be rinsed with cold water at once whenever they are removed.

Once or twice a day the urinal should be taken apart and washed with luke-warm water and soap and scrubbed gently with a hand-brush to remove all hard crusts. After thorough rinsing, parts should be connected and the entire urinal soaked for 15 minutes in an antiseptic solution. Your doctor may approve one of these or suggest another (only one of these methods should be used):

1. Mix three parts of household bleach with one part of vinegar and add one ounce of the mixture to a basin of water.
2. Dissolve one tablespoon of baking soda in one quart of tepid water.
3. Mix one teaspoon of Sanovan into a basin of water.

After soaking, the entire urinal should be thoroughly rinsed with plain water and hung to dry, with the urinal turned inside out.

The urinal should never be kept near radiators or in sunlight. Oil or ointments should not be used on the penis when the urinal is worn.

The child will need two urinals, one for use while the other is being washed.

Night protection can be provided in several ways. Some boys sleep face down, using a beret-type shower cap placed under the genitals. A piece of cellucotton about a yard long and half an inch thick is rolled, then tucked all around inside the cap with only a thin layer in the center. A piece of fine gauze is placed loosely over the cellucotton so that it does not stick to the penis. The cellucotton absorbs the urine and can be changed during the night. Boys who aren't comfortable sleeping face down may prefer to cover the genitals with a loosely fitting plastic bag with cellucotton inside to absorb urine.

Protection for Girls. Girls and women usually wear absorbent pads with a sanitary belt and waterproof underpants for additional protection. If your child wears braces, a style like that described for boys is convenient. If not, the conventional style with elastic at the waist and thigh bands are satisfactory. Some department stores as well as supply houses carry waterproof panties. Female urinals are available, but they don't give thorough protection.

The waterproof underpants and elastic sanitary belt should not be worn at night as their continuous use tends to irritate the skin. The child may be able to use an absorbent pad at night without attaching it to an elastic belt.

Underpants should be changed just as often as necessary. Waterproofed nylon is convenient because it dries quickly. Absorbent pads should be changed frequently when wet. If wet or soiled undergarments are washed soon after they have been taken off, stains and odors can be removed.

Keeping the Bed Dry. A wet or soiled bed should be changed promptly. A wide sheet of plastic material under the sheet protects the mattress. A piece of old sheeting—just two or three feet long but wide enough to tuck in on both sides of the mattress—can be placed under the buttocks. This serves as a hospital-style drawsheet that can be changed quickly without disturbing the entire bed. Squares of plastic cloth or quilted material can be placed under the buttocks to keep the drawsheet dry. They can easily be washed and re-used. Disposable pads of thick, soft cellucotton covered with paper are available from supply houses but are more expensive in the long run than cloth pads that can be re-used.

An older child who is usually wet once or twice during the night may train himself to wake and use the bedpan. Some children use an alarm clock for this purpose. If this isn't practical, the child who wakes and finds himself wet may be able to change wet bed-pads or sanitary pads for dry ones.

MAKING THINGS EASY AT HOME

When your child comes home from the hospital, the change in surroundings and routines may cause a setback in bladder or bowel control. This isn't surprising, for many things affect his success in this complex matter. In the hospital, doctors and nurses accepted your child's lapses without embarrassment or annoyance. Understanding his problems, they concentrated on helping him with his training. It may be harder for you to take this calm approach and to create an atmosphere of calm understanding about accidents. If you can, the freedom from tension will help your child carry out his recommended daily program more readily.

On the other hand, it is a mistake to let a child gain the impression that you don't care whether he becomes dry. You can show that you care, that you know he cares, that you know he is trying hard. Your encouragement will help him. Becoming clean and dry are not merely social conventions; they are important for the health of the child with spinal cord damage.

Helpful Household Arrangements. Your youngster may make a number of week-end visits home while he is in the hospital. The doctor or nurse should tell you what equipment and supplies he will need for home use. The list will include such items as these:

> waterproof underpants, absorbent pads, sanitary belt
> two urinals
> plastic shower cap with cellucotton and gauze for night use
> bedpan
> suppositories
> enema equipment, if doctor advises it
> basin, syringe, and irrigation solution
> commode chair, if needed
> wheelchair
> household deodorizers

The items your child uses in caring for himself while he is in bed—bedpan, change of absorbent pads, cellucotton, bedpads—should be within easy reach.

Bathroom Convenience. The bathroom should be arranged so that your child can conveniently use the toilet seat. He may need grab bars. They require a heavier type of installation than towel racks, and usually have to be installed by a plumber. Safety arms, or sturdy safety frames with arms on each side for support, are available from supply houses in portable styles or for permanent installation.

Some children need a higher seat than that of a regulation toilet. These can be purchased in kit form with seat and metal brackets that can be assembled to give four, five, or six inches of additional height. The brackets are shaped to fit in and rest on the china bowl and are covered with rubber tubing to keep them from slipping. The raised seat makes transfer from the wheelchair easier.

Another method is to make a wooden bench of the right height, wide enough to fit over the toilet seat, with an opening cut out over the toilet bowl. Still another, taking no extra space, is to have the entire toilet bowl placed on a small raised platform.

Foam rubber toilet seats are available. They provide extra comfort for the child whose skin is sensitive or subject to pressure sores.

For small children, special toilet seats can be bought in department stores. But the paraplegic child may need higher and firmer support at back and sides than these seats provide. In selecting a toilet seat for a small child with a disability, these points are helpful:[10]

> The size of the seat should be such that the child can sit with hips and knees bent to at least a right angle. A comfortably secure position aids the child who has difficulty in voiding or moving his bowels.
>
> There should be support for his feet; dangling legs cause strain and prevent relaxation.
>
> The seat should be sturdy and secure, with stout back and arms, and should not tip.
>
> The child with weak trunk muscles may need straps, ties, or a cut-out tray to keep him securely in the seat.
>
> The seat should be easily cleaned, attractive, and easily placed on or removed from the regular toilet seat.

A sturdy wooden seat for young disabled children can be bought from the Bruce Company, 413 Vley Road, Scotia, N.Y. It comes with a foot support, cut-out tray, and attachments for safety straps, and it folds into a compact unit of eight pounds.

There should be a convenient place in the bathroom for whatever equipment the child needs.

Fluids and Food. If your child doesn't drink enough, try tempting his appetite with a variety of appealing tastes and colors. But be firm—it's very important. As he grows older he ought to understand the reasons why fluids are important and to take increasing responsibility for drinking enough. You can think up many ways to help your child remember to drink his fluids. Perhaps an attractive alarm clock, or a watch of his own, may help him keep track. A convenient thermos, filled with a drink he likes, may serve as a reminder.

Regular, well-balanced meals help to maintain regularity in toilet functions. The diet the doctor recommends probably is planned to prevent constipation and overweight as well as to provide the required fluids. Avoiding overweight makes it easier for your child to ambulate and to enjoy active exercise.

Encouraging Physical Activity. Probably your child's doctor and therapist have recommended certain physical activities for him. If he is confined to bed or wheelchair, he may be expected to roll over or change position in bed, or shift his position and do push-ups in the wheelchair at intervals. If he can't walk but can stand, he may be instructed to stand for short, regular periods. The upright position and physical activity help prevent needed minerals from leaving the bones and forming stones in the bladder or kidneys. In general, the greater his mobility the greater his success will be in controlling toilet functions.

Keeping His Morale Up. Reasonable success in managing his bladder and bowels can be a great boost to your child's spirit. With assurance that he can keep dry and clean, he will feel more confidence about going to school, playing with other children, and carrying on social activities. As he grows older, he can look forward to having a job and sharing the interests of adult life. Occasional lapses and social embarrassments need not be viewed as impassable barriers to a normal life.

REFERENCES

1. Edith Buchwald, Margaret McCormack, and Emilie Raby. *A Bladder and Bowel Training Program for Patients with Spinal Cord Damage.* Rehabilitation Monograph III. The Institute of Physical Medicine and Rehabilitation, New York University-Bellevue Medical Center, New York, 1952.

2. Mary Eleanor Brown and Moira M. Ward. "Toilet Problems of Seven Children with Spina Bifida." *The Physical Therapy Review,* Vol. 33: No. 12, December 1953.

3. Seymour S. Bluestone and George G. Deaver. "Rehabilitation of the Child with Spina Bifida and Myelomeningocele," *Journal of the American Medical Association,* Vol. 161: No. 13, July 21, 1956.

4. Pablo A. Morales, George G. Deaver, and Robert S. Hotchkiss. "Urological Complications of Spina Bifida in Children." *Journal of Urology,* Vol. 75: No. 3. March 1956.

5. *Idem.*

6. *Primer for Paraplegics and Quadriplegics.* Patient Publication No. 1, Institute of Physical Medicine and Rehabilitation, New York University-Bellevue Medical Center, 1957.

7. Bluestone and Deaver, *op. cit.*

8. Buchwald, McCormack, and Raby, *op. cit.*

9. *Idem.*

10. Moira M. Ward. "Toilet Seats for Disabled Children." *The Crippled Child,* June 1957.

WHERE TO LOOK FOR HELP

FOR INFORMATION ABOUT SPECIALIZED MEDICAL
CARE AND REHABILITATION FOR DISABLED
CHILDREN

Start with your family doctor or pediatrician if you have one.
If not, try these sources:

Ask your local medical society, or your local health department what diagnostic clinics, treatment centers, or rehabilitation centers for handicapped children are available to you.

If you need the names of specialists in private practice, ask
your local medical society.

Your local or state health department can give you the address of the Federal-State crippled children's services headquarters in your state or area. The address of the state
department of health is probably in your state's capital. Or
write to the Children's Bureau, Washington, D.C., for the
address of the nearest clinic operating under the Federal-
State crippled children's services.

A local family service agency may have a social worker on
its staff who can help you locate the medical care your child
needs.

A great many national health organizations for serving the
handicapped have local chapters. A local family service
agency, or a council of social agencies, or your local department of health can help you find out what organizations in
your community provide services that would be useful to
your child.

The Federal-State services for crippled children include some facilities serving areas larger than one state: rehabilitation centers for children who have lost an arm or leg, and centers where heart surgery is performed by specialists. Remember these if your child needs either type of care.

FOR INFORMATION ABOUT EDUCATION
OF EXCEPTIONAL CHILDREN

Ask your local Board of Education what the public schools provide for disabled children in your community. Your State Board of Education (usually in the state capital) can tell you about state facilities for education of handicapped children, if the local Board of Education does not have the information. Forty-seven states have diagnostic clinics for mentally retarded children; in many cases these are operated by the State Department of Health.

A local family service agency or Council of Social Agencies can tell you what the public schools and the private schools of your area provide for handicapped children, and what residential schools are available in your area. Possibly some nongovernmental organization interested in the handicapped, such as the United Cerebral Palsy chapter, may have established special classes in cooperation with the schools. A family service agency should be able to help you discover any such special services that will help your child in his education.

Porter Sargent's *Directory for Exceptional Children*, 1962 edition, lists 2,000 programs for training and education of exceptional children, including 1,100 clinics.

Facilities are listed alphabetically by state and city. If you live where there is no agency, or social worker to advise you, this directory is excellent. Of course no directory takes the place of personal counseling by a person who knows your child and your family, as well as the institutions suited to your child's needs. This volume is published by Porter Sargent, 11 Beacon St., Boston 8, Mass., 618 pages. $6.00.

The Council for Exceptional Children, a Department of the National Education Association, 1201 16th Street N.W.,

Washington, D.C., is a source of publications and information about handicapped children's education. Write for publications list and price schedule.

FOR INFORMATION ABOUT VOCATIONAL
REHABILITATION

Find out about your local school system's program of guidance, testing, and counseling as it applies to children with disabilities. Inquire early enough so that your child can take full advantage of it at as early an age as possible.

If your public schools do not have a program of vocational counseling or rehabilitation for handicapped children, find out whether there is a rehabilitation center near you that offers a vocational rehabilitation program that would help your child. If not, inquire whether a nearby college or university offers vocational counseling services.

Get in touch with your nearest State Office of Vocational Rehabilitation. Every state has such an office, and most states have several local offices. Get the address of the nearest office from the telephone directory, or from the local, county or state health department, from a family service agency, or a council of social agencies, or from your local or state department of education. Or write to the Vocational Rehabilitation Administration, U.S. Department of Health, Education and Welfare, Washington 25, D.C., for the address of the office nearest you.

If your child is blind, mention it in making your inquiries, as there are separate vocational rehabilitation offices for the blind in many states.

Make such inquiries before your child is of working age but near enough to it so that he is eligible for vocational rehabilitation.

After vocational rehabilitation, when your child is ready to look for a job, he should remember to apply at the State Employment Service. Most states have a special program for selective placement of the handicapped. The state offices make vocational counseling available to applicants who have problems in choosing, finding or holding a job.

A family service agency, or a council of social agencies, will provide information about vocational rehabilitation opportunities, such as sheltered workshops, offered by private organizations. Some local or state affiliates of national organizations (for example, the National Society for Crippled Children and Adults, the United Cerebral Palsy Associations, the American Heart Association, the National Association for Retarded Children, or organizations concerned with tuberculosis, arthritis, or diabetes) provide medical services or physical aids to improve the individual's vocational abilities. Others sponsor sheltered workshops or provide vocational counseling or job placement.

FOR INFORMATION ABOUT RECREATION FACILITIES

Some recreation facilities can be used by both disabled and non-disabled persons. Public parks and gardens, for example, can be enjoyed by anyone who is able to get to them. If your child is able to go camping with you, he can enjoy the state camp sites or state parks. But it may be worth your while to ask at your municipal recreation office whether any public recreation facilities are especially equipped so that persons with your child's disability may use them.

Ask at a council of social agencies or a family service agency what special recreation activities for the handicapped are offered by rehabilitation centers or private organizations concerned with the welfare of disabled persons. Local chapters of the United Cerebral Palsy Associations, or the National Association for Retarded Children, may have special recreational programs. Ask also about commercial facilities, such as bowling alleys or swimming pools, that are open to use by disabled persons.

You may have to investigate yourself to find out what theaters are accessible to persons in a wheelchair.

If your local rehabilitation counselor, doctor, social worker, school or family service agency cannot recommend a good camp suitable for your child, write to the American Camping Association, Bradford Woods, Martinsville, Indiana, or to the National Society for Crippled Children and Adults, 2023 West Ogden Avenue, Chicago 12, Illinois, for a Directory of Camps for the Handicapped.

Write to the National Recreation Association, 8 West 8th St., New York, N.Y., for information about what can be done, and is being done in some communities, to improve recreational opportunities for the handicapped.

FOR INFORMATION ABOUT SPECIAL EQUIPMENT
AND SELF-HELP DEVICES

Your child's doctor, his specialist at the rehabilitation center, his therapist, or rehabilitation counselor will probably tell you where to obtain special equipment, such as braces, crutches, wheelchairs, artificial limbs, and so on. All such equipment should be prescribed by the medical personnel caring for your child.

Many other self-help devices, such as special reading racks or drinking glasses, equipment for using the telephone or for eating, are available from hospital supply houses or specialty companies. If your doctor or therapist does not have recommendations about sources of needed equipment, get one or both of the following publications. Then consult with your doctor or therapist before ordering the equipment or device that may help your child:

Self-Help Devices for the Arthritic, by Edward W. Lowman, M.D. Rehabilitation Monograph VI, Institute of Physical Medicine and Rehabilitation, New York University-Bellevue Medical Center, 400 East 34th Street, New York, N.Y. 1959. $1.00. Lists nearly 300 special self-help devices, giving the manufacturer, where the device can be bought, and approximate cost. Also lists a number of responsible hospital supply companies, specialty companies, mail-order houses, and department stores that handle certain special devices. Also lists chain stores carrying 'SHU-LOK' fastened shoes, manufacturers of 'lifters,' hand and foot controls for automobiles.
Resources for the Orthopedically Disabled, issued by the Federation of the Handicapped, 211 West 14th Street, New York

N.Y. $1.65. A mine of useful information. Lists medical and dental services, sources of special equipment for disabled persons, transportation facilities for the handicapped, agencies which serve the orthopedically handicapped, schools, vocational services, housing facilities, recreation and vacation programs, and information about insurance for the disabled. Lists certain free and low-cost publications. Although written especially for New York, this book is useful for persons in other areas, for in reading it, parents would discover types of resources to investigate in their own communities.

Another publication, more expensive, is *Self-Help Devices for Rehabilitation,* which was developed at the Institute of Physical Medicine and Rehabilitation. Sold by J. A. Preston and Company, 71 Fifth Avenue, New York, at $5.20 for mail orders, $4.90 when picked up in person. Contains photographs and information about some hundreds of self-help devices. Should be used in consultation with your child's physician.

Remember that Sears, Roebuck and Montgomery Ward carry such equipment as crutches, wheelchairs, some types of grab bars, and bathroom safety devices, as well as some other aids for the handicapped.

Consult your local telephone company for information about devices that make it possible for the handicapped individual to use the telephone.

Books for the blind are available from certain specialized libraries and some public libraries in every state and territory. In addition to books in Braille and other embossed printing, talking books, which are long-playing recordings of classical and contemporary literature, may be borrowed. Machines for playing talking books are distributed through fifty-five agencies on a free loan basis. Get in touch with the American Foundation for the Blind, 15 West 16th Street, New York, N.Y., for details.

SUGGESTED READING

FOR CHILDREN AND YOUNG PEOPLE

Flandorf, Vera S. *Books to Help Children Adjust to a Hospital Situation.* National Society for Crippled Children and Adults, 2023 W. Ogden Ave., Chicago 12, Illinois.

Lists of children's books that have been used successfully with younger and older children in a children's hospital. Grade level given for each book. Issued periodically.

Sever, Josephine Abbott. *Johnny Goes to the Hospital.* Published for the Children's Hospital, Boston. Houghton, Mifflin Company, Boston, Mass. 32 pp. 1953.

Compiled by the Staff of the Children's Medical Center of Boston in the hope of allaying the anxiety of children faced with hospitalization. It is the story of Johnny, whose stomach hurt, and who went to the hospital to have something done about it. For preschool or primary school children.

Sever, Josephine Abbott. *Johnny Visits His Doctor.* A Medical Information and Education Service of The Children's Medical Center, Department of Public Relations, 300 Longwood Avenue, Boston, Mass. 32 pp. 1955.

Written for parents to read to their young preschool children before a visit to the doctor's office.

Sever, Josephine Abbott. *Johnny's First Visit to His Dentist.* A Medical Information and Education Service of The Children's Medical Center. Dept. of Public Relations, 300 Longwood Avenue, Boston. 32 pp. 1957.

For parents to read to the young preschool child before his first visit to the dentist.

MEDICAL CARE AND REHABILITATION

Linck, Lawrence J. *"You are not alone"—Help for Your*

Crippled Child. National Society for Crippled Children and Adults, 2023 West Ogden Avenue, Chicago 12, Illinois. 28 pp. 1959. Parents' Series No. 4.

Emphasizes the help available to parents in caring for their handicapped child, and discusses the kinds of medical specialists and institutions that may be needed.

Robertson, James. *Young Children in Hospitals*. Basic Books, New York, 1958.

A physician who has studied widely the experiences of young children in hospitals analyzes the causes of their emotional problems, and methods of minimizing their anxiety and distress.

Rusk, Howard A. *Rehabilitation Medicine*. The C. V. Mosby Company, New York, 1958.

A textbook intended for physicians, nurses, therapists, and others who work professionally with the handicapped, but contains much that is of interest to the well-informed parent.

Shriner, Mildred. *Foundations for Walking*. A Practical Guide for Therapists, Teachers and Parents of Cerebral Palsied Children. National Society for Crippled Children and Adults, 2023 W. Ogden Ave., Chicago 12, Illinois. 1951.

Equipment needed, and methods of helping the child to reach goals of locomotion; chairs and other equipment needed to aid sitting balance; sitting and getting around on wheels; being lifted and carried; standing and walking.

HANDICAP IN GENERAL

Gould, Joan. *Will My Baby Be Born Normal?* Public Affairs Pamphlet No. 272. 1958. Public Affairs Pamphlets, 22 East 38th Street, New York, N.Y.

Brief presentation of the causes of birth defects and what is known about their genetic origins.

Bowley, Agatha H. *The Young Handicapped Child*. Educational Guidance for the Young Blind, Cerebral Palsied, and Deaf Child. Williams & Wilkins Co., Baltimore, Md. 1957. 127 pp.

Written especially for parents, this short book is easily read and contains many practical suggestions as well as helpful discussion of the psychological needs of parents and their handicapped children.

Children's Bureau. *Services for Crippled Children*. Children's

Bureau Folder No. 38, Revised 1955. U. S. Dept. of Health, Education and Welfare, Social Security Administration, Washington, D.C.

   Gives the general outline and plan of services to crippled children that are offered by the federal government in cooperation with the states.

Kennedy, Millicent V., and H. C. D. Somerset. *Bringing Up Crippled Children.* New Zealand Council for Educational Research and New Zealand Crippled Children Society. Whitcomb & Tombs Ltd., Christchurch, New Zealand. 1951. 94 pp.

   Suggestions for parents, teachers and nurses about the emotional needs of handicapped children, about problems of daily living, going to school, enjoying play and social life. Chapters on the adolescent and the adult handicapped person.

Kershaw, John D. *Handicapped Children.* William Heinemann, London. 1961. 228 pp.

   Written for social workers, nurses and teachers, but also for doctors. A serious examination of public attitudes, the relationship of parent and child, education, recreation, and work for the handicapped, with about a dozen chapters on specific handicaps.

Kessler, Henry H. *Rehabilitation of the Physically Handicapped.* Columbia University Press, New York. 1958. 275 pp.

   The point of view of an internationally known authority about rehabilitation, vocational guidance, what can be done to help the crippled children, the injured worker, the chronic disabled.

Martmer, Edgar E., editor. *The Child with a Handicap.* A Team Approach to His Care and Guidance. Charles C Thomas, Springfield, Illinois. 1959. 409 pp.

   Chapters on the role of physician, parent, psychiatrist, social worker, and teacher are followed by a chapter on adoption agencies, one on counseling in medical genetics, and then a series of chapters dealing with specific disabilities. Not too technical for the informed parent.

Michal-Smith, H., editor. *Management of the Handicapped Child.* Grune & Stratton, New York. 1957. 276 pp.

   Chapters by different specialists on behavior disorders, nervous habits, the mentally gifted, the child with speech and

language disorders, impaired hearing, visual handicap, cleft
lip and palate, disorders of physical growth, and chapters on
the child with neuro-muscular disease, cystic fibrosis, celiac
disease, and nephritis. Fairly technical.

Pattison, Harry A., editor. *The Handicapped and their Rehabilitation*. Charles C. Thomas, Springfield, Illinois. 1957.
944 pp.
   A technical volume with chapters on many major disabilities, also on methods of rehabilitation, and the functions of
various specialists in rehabilitation. For the worker in rehabilitation.

Stern, E. M., with E. Castendyck. *The Handicapped Child, A
Guide for Parents*. Wyn, New York. 1950.
   Treatment and rehabilitation for children suffering from
some common disabilities, such as cerebral palsy, epilepsy.

Taylor, Edith Meyer. *Psychological Appraisal of Children
with Cerebral Defects*. Published for the Commonwealth
Fund by Harvard University Press. Cambridge, Mass.
1959. 499 pp.
   Technical discussion of methods of psychological appraisal
which have been found to give useful results when used with
children who have cerebral defects. Intended for specialists,
but a well-informed parent would find some parts helpful.

Wishik, Samuel M. *How to Help Your Handicapped Child*.
Public Affairs Pamphlet No. 219. 28 pp. 1955.
   A clear, brief discussion of questions any parent must face
in helping his handicapped child: What is the handicap? What
caused it? How severe is it? What should parents do? What
will it cost? How will it affect the child's personality? How do
parents and family feel about it? How can community services
be improved?

SPECIFIC DISABILITIES

Arthritis and Rheumatism Foundation. *Home Care in Arthritis. A Handbook for Patients*. Arthritis and Rheumatism
Foundation, 10 Columbus Circle, New York, N.Y. 1958.
24 pp.
   Exercises which can be done at home by the arthritic
patient, under the supervision of physician and therapist, to
prevent unnecessary crippling.

Bice, Harry C. *Let's Think It Through*. United Cerebral Palsy

Associations, 321 West 44th Street, New York, 36, N.Y. 52 pp.

A booklet for parents which considers what cerebral palsy is, the medical and psychological questions involved, and the relationship of the cerebral-palsied child to his family.

British Council for the Welfare of Spastics. *Parents' Handbook*. British Council for the Welfare of Spastics, 13 Suffolk Street, Haymarket, London, S.W.1. 24 pp.

Notes for parents on the home care of children handicapped by cerebral palsy. Illustrations of special equipment. Discussion of the characteristics of the athetoid child and the spastic child, with suggestions applicable to both.

Cardwell, Viola E. *Cerebral Palsy, Advances in Understanding and Care*. Association for the Aid of Crippled Children, New York. 1956. 625 pp.

A technical book, covering the medical background and diagnosis of cerebral palsy, the characteristics of the individual with cerebral palsy, his total rehabilitation, and the community aspects of cerebral palsy.

Children's Bureau. *The Preschool Child who is Blind*. Children's Bureau Folder No. 39. U. S. Dept. of Health, Education and Welfare. 22 pp. 1953. 10 cents from Supt. of Documents, Govt. Printing Office, Washington 25, D.C.

Brief discussion of how to help the child who is born blind, or becomes blind early during his preschool years.

Children's Bureau. *The Child with a Missing Arm or Leg*. U. S. Department of Health, Education and Welfare, Social Security Administration, Washington, D.C. 25 pp. 1959.

Attitudes of parents, child and family about the missing limb and use of the prosthesis; where to find clinics to help the amputee child, and information about getting the prosthesis, fitting it, and training the child in its use.

Crothers, Bronson, and Richmond S. Paine. *The Natural History of Cerebral Palsy*. Harvard University Press, Cambridge, Mass. 1959. 299 pp.

Written for parents as well as for the professional expert, this book is based on extensive experience in treating cerebral-palsied children at Children's Hospital in Boston. Valuable insights into the psychology of parent-child relationships and methods of guiding the development of the cerebral-palsied child as he grows up.

Danzig, Aaron L. *Handbook for One-Handers*. Federation of the Handicapped. 211 West 14th Street, New York, N.Y. 55 pp.
    A practical guide for those who have lost the functional use of an arm or a hand. Contains suggestions on dressing, personal care, preparing and eating meals, looking after the house, taking part in sports, business activities, and social life, with a final chapter on love and marriage.

Davis, Hallowell, and Richard S. Silverman, eds. *Hearing and Deafness*. Holt, Rinehart & Winston, New York. 1960.

Denhoff, Eric, and Isabel Robinault. *Cerebral Palsy and Related Disorders*. McGraw Hill. New York. 1960. 386 pp.
    Technical, for physicians and specialists in rehabilitation, but parents would be interested in material on aspects of rehabilitation which prepare children and youth to join in the life of the community.

Dinsmore, Annette B. *Methods of Communication with Deaf-Blind People*. American Foundation for the Blind, 15 West 16th Street, New York 11, N.Y. 48 pp. 1959.
    Careful description of manual alphabets, the use of the International Morse Code and other codes, Braille Hand Speech, such methods of communication as printing in the palm, and special devices such as the alphabet glove or plate, the Braille alphabet card, cut-out letters, and so on.

Facts on Mental Health and Mental Illness. Public Health Service Publication No. 543. 11 pp. 10 cents from Supt. of Documents, U. S. Govt. Printing Office, Washington 25, D.C.
    Discusses hopes for the rehabilitation of the mentally ill, what is being done and needs to be done further.

Fischer, Alfred E., M.D., and Dorothea L. Horstmann. *Handbook for Diabetic Children*. Intercontinental Medical Book Corp., New York. 1954. 64 pp.
    Dr. Fischer, Chief of the Children's Diabetic Clinic of Mount Sinai Hospital, and Miss Horstmann, Instructor in the School of Nursing there, prepared this handbook for the young people themselves, since there was little material directed to children. The contents cover planning meals, using

insulin, exercising each day, keeping healthy. Sample diets are included.

Johnson, Wendell. *Children with Speech and Hearing Impairment.* Bulletin 1959, No. 5. U. S. Dept. of Health, Education and Welfare. U. S. Govt. Printing Office, Washington 25, D.C. 32 pp.

Primarily for teachers, this bulletin contains definitions of types of impaired speech and hearing which are also informative for parents.

Jones, Morris Val. *Speech Correction at Home.* Charles C. Thomas, Springfield, Ill. 1957. 66 pp.

Written for parents to help them understand the speech problems of children, and what parents and family can do to help the child who has speech problems.

Phelps, W. M., T. W. Hopkins, and R. Cousins. *The Cerebral Palsied Child.* Simon and Schuster, New York. 1958. 237 pp.

Written for parents, from the background of very extensive experience in treating cerebral-palsied children, this book deals with medical care, therapy, education, parent and child relationships, and other significant problems.

Primer for Paraplegics and Quadriplegics. Patient Publication No. 1. Institute of Physical Medicine and Rehabilitation. New York University-Bellevue Medical Center. 38 pp. 1957.

Describes the nature of paraplegia, points out how the activities of daily living can aid in rehabilitation. Gives practical pointers about wheelchair, braces, care of the skin to avoid pressure sores. Suggests important aspects of diet, and methods of managing the kidneys, bladder, and bowels.

Public Health Service. *Mongolism: Hope Through Research.* Public Health Service Publication No. 720. U. S. Dept. of Health Education and Welfare. 6 pp. 5 cents from Supt. of Documents, U. S. Govt. Printing Office, Washington 25, D.C.

Brief discussion of the signs and diagnosis of mongolism, and the hopes held out by recent research for greater understanding of this problem.

Richardson, N. K. *Type with One Hand.* South-Western Publishing Co., 5101 Madison Road, Cincinnati 27, Ohio. 15 pp. 1946.

Information for the person with only one useful hand for whom typing is helpful.

Steensma, John. *A Guide for Parents of Child Amputees*. Area Amputee Program, Michigan Crippled Children Commission, Lansing, Michigan. 1958. 30 pp.

Practical suggestions to parents about supervising their child's use of a prosthesis (below elbow, above elbow, below knee, above knee), about what their child should do to achieve a normal, desirable gait, and about care of the stump and care of the prosthesis.

Strokes. American Heart Association, 44 East 23rd St., New York, N.Y. 18 pp. 1958.

Explains simply the causes, prevention and treatment of strokes, discusses the essentials of rehabilitation, suggests ways of helping the patient with a speech difficulty, and helping the patient to help himself in daily activities.

Taylor, Martha L. *Understanding Aphasia*. Patient Publication No. 2. The Institute of Physical Medicine and Rehabilitation. New York University-Bellevue Medical Center, New York. 1958. 48 pp.

A practical guide written for the family and friends of a person who has aphasia (a disturbance in ability to speak fluently), to help them understand the patient's problems and to know how to help him.

EDUCATION

Cruickshank, William M., ed. *Education of Exceptional Children and Youth*. Prentice-Hall, Englewood Cliffs, New Jersey. 723 pp. 1958.

Standard text covering all phases of education for exceptional children, such as mental testing, school environment, curriculum planning. For educators, but is a comprehensive source for the parent who wishes to understand education for the handicapped child.

Cruickshank, William M., ed. *Psychology of Exceptional Children and Youth*. Prentice-Hall, Englewood Cliffs, New Jersey. 594 pp. 1955.

Psychology of exceptional children as it relates to their education. For educators, but parents familiar with psychology will find much of interest.

National Catholic Education Association. *Directory of Catholic Facilities for Exceptional Children in the. United States*. Washington, D.C. The Association. 1958. 248 pp.
    A useful source of information about Catholic schools and institutions serving the handicapped.

Sargent, Porter. *The Directory for Exceptional Children; Educational and Training Facilities*. Porter Sargent, Publisher, 11 Beacon St., Boston 8, Mass. 1962. 618 pp.
    Lists 2,000 programs for training and education of exceptional children, including 1,100 clinics. Facilities listed alphabetically, by state and city. Auxiliary sections give information on associations, societies, foundations, federal and state agencies and their personnel, which are concerned with exceptional children. Financial data include Congressional appropriations and average monthly rates of some leading private residential facilities.

What is Special about Special Education? Reprinted from Exceptional Children, issues of 1952-53. The Council for Exceptional Children, Dept. of Natl. Education Assn., 1201 16th St. N.W., Washington 6, D.C.
    A series of short articles discussing the programs of special education that are needed by children with various disabilities: Blindness, mental handicap, deafness; the child who is hard-of-hearing, the crippled child, the partially seeing child, the speech defective child, and the gifted child.

HOME MANAGEMENT

The Cerebral Palsy Monitor Program. A Service for Parents of Cerebral Palsied Children. United Cerebral Palsy Associations, 321 West 44th St., New York, N.Y. Program Bulletin No. 13, 1959. 16 pp.
    How to organize the Monitor program to provide a supply of young people who are educated to act as "sitters" with cerebral-palsied children. Parents can use the basic child care outline to guide them in instructing their own sitters if there is no group training program in their community.

Cooper, John M., and Laurence E. Morehouse. *Assisting the Cerebral Palsied Child. Lifting and Carrying*. Booklet I, In the Home. Booklet II, Outside the Home. United Cerebral Palsy Associations, 321 West 44th Street, New York 36, N.Y., 1959. Booklet I, 40 pp; Booklet II, 38 pp.
    Detailed instructions for lifting and carrying the child from

many positions, such as into and out of bed, up and down stairs, helping him to and from the toilet seat. In Booklet II, instructions for helping the child into and out of automobiles, buses, and in other away-from-home situations.

The Functional Home for Easier Living. Designed Specifically for the Physically Disabled, the Elderly, and those with Cardiac Handicaps. The Institute of Physical Medicine and Rehabilitation, New York University-Bellevue Medical Center, 400 East 34th Street, New York 16, N.Y. Free upon request.

A floor plan, and many photographs with information about special modifications of windows, closets, stove, furnishings, bathroom equipment, and so on.

The Handicapped Homemaker Research Center, University of Connecticut. Storrs, Connecticut. Bulletins available include:

#2. *Suggestions for Physically Handicapped Mothers on Clothing for Pre-school Children.* 32 pp. 1960. Designs and fabrics to encourage the child to dress himself.

#5. *Child Care Equipment for Physically Handicapped Mothers.* 38 pp. 1961. Selection and adaptation of equipment to enable mothers to be independent in caring for their children.

#6. *Play Experiences Handicapped Mothers May Share with Young Children.* 34 pp. Ideas for nature study, crafts, music, story telling and equipment for outdoor and indoor play.

#s 2, 5 and 6 of interest to disabled teen-aged or young adult women planning to marry.

Lasser, J. K., and Sylvia F. Porter. *Managing Your Money.* Henry Holt and Company. New York, 1958. 430 pp.

Basic suggestions for budgeting and managing the family's money; information about the best methods of borrowing, buying life insurance, planning for illness and accidents.

Rusk, Howard A., *et al. A Manual for Training the Disabled Homemaker.* Monograph VIII. Institute of Physical Medicine and Rehabilitation. New York University-Bellevue Medical Center, 400 East 34th Street, New York 16, New York. 1955. 167 pp.

Written primarily for those who are planning a program of training for disabled housewives, but the chapters, "Saving Energy in Housework," "Retraining the Homemaker with

Hand Difficulties," and "Retraining the Homemaker with Lower Extremity Disabilities" contain scores of practical suggestions of interest to the young person who wishes to manage a home in spite of disability.

Rx for the Disabled Housewife. Institute of Physical Medicine and Rehabilitation. New York University-Bellevue Medical Center, 400 East 34th Street, New York, N.Y.

Photographs of labor-saving and work simplification devices for the disabled home-maker.

Waggoner, Neva R., Eleanor Boettke, and Clari Bare. *Self-Help Clothing for Handicapped Children,* National Society for Crippled Children and Adults. 2023 West Ogden Ave., Chicago 12. 84 pp. 1962.

RETARDED CHILDREN

Dittman, Laura L. *The Mentally Retarded Child at Home.* A Manual for Parents. Children's Bureau Publication No. 374, 1959. 99 pp. 35 cents from Supt. of Documents, Government Printing Office, Washington, D.C. 20402.

Discusses the development of the retarded child in his early years, practical methods of developing independence in toilet training, dressing, cleanliness and manners, as well as discipline, speech, play, and psychological tests for the retarded. Chapters on school, school-age development, and adolescence.

Ecob, Katharine G. *The Retarded Child in the Community.* Practical Suggestions for Community Care. The New York State Assn. for Mental Health, 105 East 22nd St., New York, N.Y. 22 pp. 1956.

Brief, practical discussion of the nature of retardation, its diagnosis, problems about schooling, home care, employment, and procedures to follow in seeking to place the child in an institution.

Ecob, Katharine G. *Deciding What's Best for Your Retarded Child.* New York State Assn. for Mental Health. 105 East 22nd St., New York, N.Y. 14 pp. 1955.

Goes right to the point in considering the questions that must be answered in deciding whether to keep a retarded child at home or to place him in an institution.

Kirk, S. A., M. D. Karnes, and W. D. Kirk. *You and Your*

Retarded Child. Macmillan, New York. 1957. 184 pp.
A practical guide for parents. Discusses what retardation is, and has chapters on education, the question of a residential school versus keeping the child at home, and also on helping the child to become more competent in self-care, play, speech, and social relationships.

Morrison, Marcia. *Now They Are Grown*. Minnesota State Department of Public Welfare, St. Paul, Minnesota. 60 pp.
A helpful pamphlet for parents of teen-aged and young adult trainable retarded children. It discusses emotional and behavior problems, the development of suitable interests, family and community acceptance, and questions of sexual development, marriage, and employment.

BIOGRAPHIES

Buck, Pearl S. *The Child Who Never Grew*. John Day, New York. 1950.
The story of the mentally retarded child whom Pearl Buck and her husband adopted.

Carlson, E. R. *Born that Way*. John Day, New York. 1941.
Born with cerebral palsy, Carlson became an eminent physician known for his work with the handicapped. He relates that in his adolescence he felt different from other youths, but by his mid-twenties had won the affection of a girl for the first time in his life, and no longer felt cut off from the community.

Fraser, Sir Ian, ed. *Conquest of Disability*. St. Martin's Press, New York. 1956.
Each chapter contains a biographical sketch of an individual who has surmounted a serious disability to live a useful, often a distinguished life. Stories are about adults.

Hathaway, K. B. *The Little Locksmith*. Coward-McCann, New York. 1943.
Well-written autobiography of a young woman who suffered from a tubercular infection of the spine and was bedridden through her middle childhood.

Henrich, Edith, ed., and Leonard Kriegel. Commentary. *Experiments in Survival*. Association for the Aid of Crippled Children. 345 East 46th St., New York, N.Y. 1961.
Ordinary people tell in honest, first-hand accounts what it is like to live with a physical handicap.

Killilea, Marie. *Karen*. Prentice-Hall, Englewood Cliffs, New Jersey. 1952.

A mother tells the story of her cerebral-palsied daughter, and the struggle to secure satisfactory treatment, to provide education, and to gain acceptance for Karen, at a time when much less was known about rehabilitation for cerebral-palsied children than today.

Tucker, Charlotte D. *Betty Lee*. Macmillan, New York. 1954.

A mother's story of unrealistic hopes and tender love which finally accepted the truth about her daughter's handicap of mental retardation.

Viscardi, Henry, Jr. *A Man's Stature*. John Day, New York. 1952.

Biography of a man born without legs who has become famous for what he has done to improve educational and vocational opportunities for the handicapped. He is the founder of Abilities, Inc., a Long Island concern which employs only disabled persons.

RECREATION

American Camping Association. *Directory of Camps for the Handicapped*. American Academy of Pediatrics, American Camping Association, and National Society for Crippled Children and Adults. Issued by American Camping Association, Bradford Woods, Martinsville, Indiana. 50 pp., 1963. Available from American Camping Association or from National Society for Crippled Children and Adults, 2023 West Ogden Ave., Chicago 12, Illinois.

Of value to parents who have no local sources of information about camps suitable for a disabled child, but chiefly useful for persons or organizations working with handicapped children.

Boy Scouts of America. *Scouting with Handicapped Boys*. Boy Scouts of America, New Brunswick, New Jersey. 64 pp. 1957.

Primarily for Scout leaders, but of interest to parents who would like to know what possibilities scouting holds for their handicapped child. Activities for the blind, crippled, cerebral-palsied, deaf, mentally retarded, and other handicapped boys are described.

Buell, Charles E. *Recreation for the Blind*. American Founda-

tion for the Blind, 15 West 16th St., New York, N.Y. 1951. 39 pp.
    Describes hobbies, social and quiet games, and sports and active games which blind persons may enjoy.

Camp Fire Girls. *Services With and for Handicapped Children*. Camp Fire Girls, Inc., 16 East 48th St., New York N.Y.
    Describes the Camp Fire Girls' program for the handicapped.

Cardozo, Peter. *A Wonderful World for Children*. Bantam Books, New York. 1958. 246 pp. paperback.
    This inexpensive book lists thousands of items, such as travel posters, information about pets, gardening aids, children's hobbies, Boy Scout equipment, which children can obtain free.

Carter, Joan L. *Working with the Handicapped*. A Leader's Guide. Girl Scouts of the United States of America, 840 Third Ave., New York. 1954.

Children's Bureau. *Handbook for Recreation*. U. S. Department of Health, Education and Welfare. Children's Bureau Publication No. 231. 148 pp. 1960. 75 cents from Superintendent of Documents, Govt. Printing Office, Washington, D.C. 20402.
    Specific directions for a large number of games and recreational activities. Parents who have to think up games and entertainment for their child, handicapped or not, can make good use of it.

Children's Bureau. *Home Play and Equipment for the Preschool Child*. Children's Bureau Publication No. 238. Supt. of Documents, Government Printing Office, Washington, D.C. 20402.
    Instructions for making play equipment such as swings, climbing bars, ladders, see-saws, sandboxes.

Frantzen, June. *Toys, the Tools of Children*. National Society for Crippled Children and Adults, 2023 West Ogden Ave., Chicago, 12, Illinois. 16 pp. 1957.
    A study of hand and arm development of young children, and toys suited to developmental stages and the child's maturing interests. Toys for handicapped children should be

selected according to the stage of hand and arm development, and also interest level. Illustrated charts show the sequence of stages of development.

Hartley, Ruth E., and Robert M. Goldenson. *The Complete Book of Children's Play*. Thomas Y. Crowell, New York. 1957.

The child's development in relation to his play and recreation, from infancy to adolescence. Written for parents, it gives useful insights into the child's play needs, though it does not deal specifically with handicapped children.

Hunt, Valerie V. *Recreation for the Handicapped*. Prentice-Hall, Inc., Englewood Cliffs, N.J. 340 pp. 1955.

For recreation leaders. Part I presents a philosophy of recreation with applications for the handicapped. Part II discusses recreation for persons with specific handicaps—the deaf, blind, diabetic, orthopedically handicapped, and so on.

Johnson, Mrs. Clark, ed. *Alpha Chi Omega Toy Book: Self-Help Toys to Make for Handicapped Children*. Alpha Chi Omega Central Office, 611-619 Chamber of Commerce Building, Indianapolis 4, Indiana.

Diagrams and instructions for making toys for the handicapped.

Langdon, Grace. *Your Child's Play*. National Society for Crippled Children and Adults, 2023 West Ogden Ave., Chicago 12, Ill. 1957. 26 pp.

Against a background discussion of the individual nature of the play provisions needed by each child, many practical suggestions are made concerning play materials and facilities, and ways of encouraging friendships for the handicapped child.

McMullin, Marjory D. *How to Help the Shut-In Child*. 313 Hints for Homebound Children. E. P. Dutton, New York. 1954.

Highly useful in helping parents find interesting activities for their homebound child.

Rathbone, Josephine L., and Carol Lucas. *Recreation in Total Rehabilitation*. Charles C. Thomas, Springfield, Ill. 398 pp. 1959.

Primarily for recreation leaders, but Part III would be

helpful to parents about media used in rehabilitation: music, the graphic and plastic arts, handicrafts, hobbies, aids to reading and enjoyment of literature and the theater, as well as games, sports, dancing, and parties.

Rogers, Gladys Gage, and Leah Thomas. *Toys, Games and Apparatus for Children with Cerebral Palsy*. Reprint from Physical Therapy Review, vol. 29, No. 1, January, 1949. Available from National Society for Crippled Children and Adults, 2023 West Ogden Ave., Chicago 12, Ill.
    Practical description of toys, games and apparatus which can be used by children with cerebral palsy.

Smith, Anne Marie. *Play for Convalescent Children in Hospitals and at Home*. A. S. Barnes and Co., New York. 1960. 176 pp.
    Written from experience in directing play programs for children in hospitals, this book discusses the value of play in the child's recovery, and makes many practical suggestions about play activities suitable for convalescent children.

SOURCES OF SELF-HELP AIDS AND OTHER HELP

"Cerebral Palsy Equipment." National Society for Crippled Children and Adults, 2023 W. Ogden Avenue, Chicago 12, Illinois. 268 pp. 1950. Looseleaf.
    Available for physicians and professional personnel; for use only under medical supervision.

Deaver, George G., and Anthony L. Brittis. "Braces, Crutches, Wheelchairs, Mode of Management." *Rehabilitation Monograph V*. Institute of Physical Medicine and Rehabilitation, New York University-Bellevue Medical Center, 400 East 34th St., New York 16, N.Y. 1953. 61 pp.
    Technical, for doctors, nurses, therapists, rather than parents.

Lowman, Edward W. "Self-Help Devices for the Arthritic." *Rehabilitation Monograph VI*. Institute of Physical Medicine and Rehabilitation. New York University-Bellevue Medical Center, 400 East 34th St., New York 16, N.Y. 1959. 149 pp.
    Many of the devices described are useful in many disabilities, not only arthritis. Information about self-help devices for dressing, bathing, grooming, eating and other daily

activities; information on using crutches, wheelchairs, driving an automobile with special controls; energy-saving home-making devices, devices to make communication easier, and so on. Lists firms where many of the devices can be purchased.

Oates, Wayne E. *Where to Go for Help*. Westminster Press, Philadelphia, Pa. 1957.

Brief guide to the most fruitful channels to explore in searching for help in various kinds of need: medical, family problems, educational, vocational problems.

Rusk, Howard A., and Eugene J. Taylor. *Living with a Disability*. The Blakiston Company, Garden City, New York. 1953. 207 pp.

Full of practical suggestions, well illustrated by photographs, or drawings, for self-help aids to daily living: eating, dressing, sleeping, using the kitchen, bathroom, wheelchair, crutches, and getting around indoors and out.

PSYCHOLOGY AND PHILOSOPHY

Garrett, James F., ed. *Psychological Aspects of Physical Disability*. Rehabilitation Service Series Number 210. Office of Vocational Rehabilitation. For sale by Supt. of Documents, U. S. Govt. Printing Office, Washington, D.C. 20402. 195 pp. 60 cents.

Written primarily for workers in vocational rehabilitation, this pamphlet may provide insight and information for the parent accustomed to scientific material. Authors include Dr. Howard A. Rusk, Dr. Karl A. Menninger, Dr. Berthold Lowenfeld, and Dr. Beatrice A. Wright among a long list of experts.

Miers, Earl Schenck. *Why Did This Have to Happen?* National Society for Crippled Children and Adults, 2023 West Ogden Ave., Chicago 12, Ill. 28 pp.

An inspirational "open letter," with insight rooted in personal experience of the problems faced by the handicapped.

Palmer, Charles E. *The Church and the Exceptional Person*. Abingdon Press, 201 Eighth Ave., Nashville 2, Tenn. 1961. 174 pp.

For ministers, teachers, and lay members of the church. Traces changing attitudes toward exceptional persons, suggests responsibilities the church should recognize, and gives general pointers to be remembered in work with the handicapped. It defines the problems of persons with a wide variety of handicapping conditions, and makes specific suggestions on ways of helping them, and organizing the services of the church in their behalf.

Wolf, Anna W. M. *Helping Your Child to Understand Death*. Child Study Association of America. 9 East 89th St., New York, N.Y. 63 pp.

If there is a death in the family, or if the disabled person suffers from an incurable disorder which brings death near, this pamphlet may help parents to assist their children to understand it.

Wright, Beatrice A. *Physical Disability—A Psychological Approach*. Harper & Brothers, New York. 1960. 408 pp.

A comprehensive treatment of the psychological reactions both of disabled persons and of society toward the disabled. Contains chapters of particular interest to parents: The Parent as a Key Participant, Motivating Children in the Rehabilitation Program, and The Adolescent with a Physical Disability. An illuminating book for the serious reader.

VOCATION

Better Business Bureau, Educational Division. *Facts You Should Know about Earn-Money-at-Home Schemes*. The National Better Business Bureau, Inc., 230 Park Avenue, New York, N.Y.

Describes about a dozen common types of scheme used to extract money from elderly, homebound, or handicapped persons.

Help for Handicapped Women. U. S. Dept. of Labor and U. S. Dept. of Health, Education and Welfare. Women's Bureau Pamphlet Five: 1958. 52 pp. 40 cents from Supt. of Documents, U. S. Govt. Printing Office, Washington, D.C. 20402.

Information about vocational rehabilitation for women; occupations of women after rehabilitation, easing the financial burden, community resources, and careers in rehabilitation. Of interest to the older teen-aged or young adult woman with a handicap.

Jobs for Young Workers. Bureau of Employment Security, U. S. Employment Service, U. S. Dept. of Labor.

This guide is prepared for young workers to help them decide what type of work they will aim for. New editions are issued from time to time to give current information. Information is given for almost 100 types of job. The usual duties, characteristics of the job, qualifications, employment prospects, advancement opportunities, and where the job is found are listed for each type of job.

Not written especially for the handicapped, but may help any youth to have a realistic approach in selecting the kind of job he can do as a young worker.

FAMILY LIFE AND SEX EDUCATION

Your public library can suggest many publications in this field. Though not written especially for the disabled, they can help meet the needs which disabled children and youth share with other children for guidance about sex and family life.

The following series was written under the sponsorship of the Joint Committee on Health Problems in Education of the National Education Association and the American Medical Association, and are available in paper from the American Medical Association, 535 North Dearborn St., Chicago 10, Illinois:

Lerrigo, Marion O., Ph.D., and Helen Southard, M.A. Medical consultant, Milton J. E. Senn, M.D.

Parents' Responsibility. 1962. For parents of young children of preschool and early school age.

A Story about You. 1962. For children in grades 4, 5, and 6.

Finding Yourself. 1962. For boys and girls of approximately junior high school age.

Approaching Adulthood. 1962. For young people of both sexes, about 16 to 20 years.

Facts Aren't Enough. 1962. For adults who have any responsibility for the sex education of children.

The books in this series are also available in hard covers from E. P. Dutton & Co., New York, N.Y., under slightly different titles: *Parents' Privilege; A Story about You; What's Happening to Me? Learning about Love; Sex Facts and Attitudes.*

INDEX

A

achievement tests, 123

activities of daily living, 39
training in, 107-11
(*see also* self-help)

A.D.L. (*see* activities of daily living)

adolescent (*see* teenager)

Aid to Dependent Children program, 276

ambulation, 295, 300
with spinal cord damage, 333

American Association of Marriage Counselors, 54

American Medical Directory, 62

American Red Cross, 68

American Speech and Hearing Association, 111

amputee centers, 67, 323-24

amputees, federal aid for, 67
(*see also* orthopedically handicapped child; prosthesis)

anesthetic, administration of, 93

aphasia, 111-12

apron, 205, 293

aptitude tests, 123, 177

archery, 223

arm prosthesis, 324-25, 326-27, 328-30

arthritis, medication for, 76

Arthritis and Rheumatism Foundation, 43

artificial limb (*see* prosthesis)

arts and crafts, 109, 197, 229-33
(*see also* hobbies)

attitudes
of child, 25-42, 167
of nonhandicapped people, 38, 41, 206-07, 208-09
of parents, 17-23, 26-27, 36-37
toward discipline, 30-32
toward each other, 51-53
toward education, 115-19

audiologist, 60, 72

audiology centers, 140

automobile
carrying child in, 319
driving, 239-40
entering, with crutches, 306

B

backrest, 204

balloons, 215, 223, 225

balls, 214-15, 225

Baltimore Hearing Society, 208-09

bathroom
self-help aids in, 286-88

ABOUT THE AUTHORS

DR. BENJAMIN SPOCK, who requires no introduction to the reader, has been hailed as "the second most important man in a woman's life between 18 and 34." As Professor of Child Development at Western Reserve University School of Medicine, and through his research and writings, Dr. Spock has dedicated his life to improving the quality of child care at all levels.

MARION O. LERRIGO in 1926 was the first person to receive a Ph.D. in Health Education. Ever since, she has worked as a researcher, and is the author or editor of 19 books and numerous articles in the field of health education.